Dying to Get Married

DYING
TO GET
MARRIED

The Courtship and Murder of
Julie Miller Bulloch

By Ellen Francis Harris

A Birch Lane Press Book
Published by Carol Publishing Group

A Birch Lane Press Book
Published by Carol Publishing Group
Birch Lane Press is a registered trademark of Carol Communications, Inc.

Editorial Offices: 600 Madison Avenue, New York, N.Y. 10022
Sales & Distribution Offices: 120 Enterprise Avenue, Secaucus, N.J. 07094
In Canada: Musson Book Company, a division of General Publishing Company, Ltd.,
    Don Mills, Ontario M3B 2T6

Queries regarding rights and permissions should be addressed to Carol
Publishing Group, 600 Madison Avenue, New York, N.Y. 10022.

Carol Publishing Group books are available at special discounts for bulk
purchases, for sales promotions, fund raising, or educational purposes.
Special editions can be created to specifications. For details contact:
Special Sales Department, Carol Publishing Group, 120 Enterprise Avenue,
Secaucus, N.J. 07094

Manufactured in the United States of America

10 9 8 7 6 5 4 3 2 1

Library of Congress Cataloging-in-Publication Data

Harris, Ellen Francis.
    Dying to get married : the courtship and murder of Julie Bulloch /
by Ellen Francis Harris.
        p. cm.
    "A Birch Lane Press book."
    ISBN 1-55972-091-3 (cloth)
    1. Homicide—Missouri—Saint Louis Metropolitan Area—Case
studies.   2. Bondage (Sexual behavior)—Missouri—Saint Louis
Metropolitan Area—Case studies.   3. Trials (Murder)—Missouri—
Saint Louis County.   4. Bulloch, Julie, 1954–1986.   5. Bulloch,
Dennis.   I. Title.
HV6534.S19H37   1991
364.1'523'0977865—dc20   91-26564
                                                              CIP

To Shirley Francis Harris

who always said to stand up
and be counted when it mattered;

who always encouraged me
to do whatever I wanted
even when that differed
so much from her values that
she must have felt
she was raising a changling;

who always was generous
even when she must have felt
as though she were wearing
a necklace of serpents' teeth;

and who never complained,
Well, not very often.

CONTENTS

Introduction

The Bulloch case is not one of those modern morality tales called a murder mystery or true crime story in which evil is so satisfyingly punished and good rewarded. The story of Dennis Bulloch is the reverse. It is the story of Prince Charming turning into the frog.

But in this sad story there is one atavistic folktale or moral: Don't judge by appearances. Judging by the jury verdict in the first trial, we have not progressed much from ancient prejudices in which people who were beautiful were believed good and the misshapen evil.

There are three reasons why Dennis Bulloch is not on death row today: He is exceptionally good-looking, especially for a criminal defendant. His criminal defense attorney succeeded at an impossible task. And the jurors chose to believe the unbelievable.

Their verdict was doubly ironic. An essential part of St. Louis is its inherent Midwestern values. That terminal status anxiety one finds on the East Coast where one's real worth seems to be one's net worth does not operate here. The people with real class here are those who treat everyone the same. They may have several sets of silver, but they use only one set of manners. They do not have to run an acquaintance through a "power" computer to determine if the person is worth consideration.

But to Dennis Bulloch, to be decent to the "unimportant" was like overpaying his taxes. To Dennis, to be decent was to be ordinary and to be ordinary was failure.

Dennis acheived his goals. He is not ordinary.

The jury verdict in 1987 so outraged me I began this book a month later. It was a why-done-it and an examination of legal issues. Then key issues and themes emerged. Why was there no sympathy for the victim? Why is such violence against women condoned? If Americans become more aware that domestic violence can lead to murder, will the verdicts become more just? Had there been a shelter for abused women near her home and had she gone to one for sanctuary and counseling, would Julie Bulloch's life have been saved? How bad were the scars left on the families and friends by this crime? What good qualities were there in a man who had no conscience? Was there anyone who could always count on Dennis's loyalty?

With one exception, Ed Schollmeyer, a high school chum, Dennis's friends and former friends and teachers who were interviewed asked that they not be identified. They are afraid Dennis will violently revenge himself on their children or them-selves. Julie Bulloch's friends and brother who were interviewed asked for the same protections. Consequently, not only have the names of these people been changed, so have physical appear-ances and occupations.

To make this book read more easily, three conversations were reconstructed, based on interviews: the one between Lt. Niere and the firefighters and police officers at the crime scene May 6, 1986, in Chapter One; the scene with Julie and her father in Chapter Five; the conversations with her brother and mother in Chapter Six. Other dialogue, including that in Dennis's amatory exercise in assault and his beating of his first wife the night she left him, follows police reports, pre-trial depositions, trial testi-mony, and conversations repeated to me during interviews.

Quotations from Dennis's letters and diary have been para-phrased, except when used as evidence in the three trials. Then, the citations are a matter of public record. Similiarly, most quotations from Julie's diaries and audiotape have been para-phrased.

Acknowledgments

This book would have been at best a magazine piece without the generosity, decency, and unflagging help of Tom DePriest and Lt. Dennie Niere. The linchpin was DePriest. There is no way to write about a crime, especially a complicated one, without the help of the prosecution. I also wish to thank the former St. Louis County Prosecuting Attorney Buzz Westfall, his former Chief Assistant Larry Mooney, his former Chief Trial Assistant John Ross, former Assistant Prosecutor Tom Mehan, and DePriest's once and future investigator, Jack Patty. The current St. Louis County Prosecuting Attorney, Bob McCullough, helped in the last stages.

And what may be equally remarkable about all the prosecutors and defense attorneys and the police lieutenant is that on and off the record they only had good things to say about each other. In such a sordid murder case, it was enlightening and a releif to work with such professionals as the men mentioned above and the defense team led by Art Margulis. The defense is traditionally reticent compared to the state in criminal matters, but in this case the defense attorneys, Margulis and Bill Grant, were very helpful. And patient in explaining legal matters.

My editor Hillel Black helped pare this manuscript by saying those words every writer dreads, "Just cut the first half in half." It has been a pleasure learning from him what it is to tell a story, not a journalistic recounting, but a story in the traditional sense. But then Black is a traditional, hands-on, working-with-every-word editor. I thank my agent Harvey Klinger for believing there was a book in this all along and patiently helping me with the proposal. And Ben Petrone for his enthusiasm and boundless energy. And Mel Wulf for keeping me legal.

Without the constant ecouragement, advice, and humor of Meg Crane, Byron and Ellen Kinder, and Mary Scarpinato this story would have wilted. Sometimes, the four must have felt as though they were giving mouth-to-mouth resuscitation to the book. It was Crane who helped rewrite the endless drafts of the proposal. The Kinders and Scarpinato read the early drafts of the book which not even my mother would have loved. Judge Kinder and Scarpinato helped immensley with the second half of the book, as did Judge Theodore McMillian, who spent two hours helping me understand the thirty-nine exceptions to the hearsay rule, which is more difficult than memorizing the poems of Rudyard Kipling. My loyal friend David Rosen explained more legal concepts.

Three friends generously proofread the galleys: Charlene Bry, publisher of *The Ladue News*, and Larry Katzenstein, my attorney, who both made vital suggestions. Bry kindly offered research from her unpublished book-to-be, *Ladue: A History*. Larry Katzenstein provided his ethical, legal advice along with other suggestions. Mary Scarpinato read it in its last and final stage.

Others, not quoted in the text, provided information: Charles Brown of the St. Louis Mercantile Library, Charles Lowenhaupt, Eric Thomas, Bill Lhotka, Bob Mohme, Lenny Frankel, Carol Harris Wall, Mitch Wall, Sharon Tettenhorst, Stephanie Krause, "The Observer," Prof. Jules Girard, Ed Fisher, and the anonymous psychiatric expert.

Sally Barker, Paul Schoomer, Al Wiman, Andrew Davis, Pat Rich, Zelda Harris, Jeff Rainford, Carol Bolt, Kirsten Hart-Zell, George Johnson, and Sandra Johnson helped along the way.

Without violating the child labor laws, Circe Wall and Tommy Wall read portions of the manuscript to see if it was understandable to those with less than an eighth grade education.

The General Manager of KMOV-TV Allan Cohen, the News Director Al Holzer, Assistant News Director Michael Castengera, and Assignment Manager Pete Barrett juggled my schedule so that I could continue to work there and research and write this book.

I would like to thank all those generous people who knew Dennis Bulloch and Julie Miller Bulloch and provided background on them. Their names have been changed at their request.

So many generous, decent people helped, that if my memory has slipped, they have my apologies and thanks.

Part One

The Bride's Homicide and the Bridegroom's Suicide

May 6–May 11, 1986

One

The Fire

May 6, 1986

A police dispatcher had called Lt. Dennis Niere at home at five forty-five that morning. "Lt. Niere, there's a suicide in a fire on White Tree Lane," she had blurted.

"Have the officers at the scene process it," Niere had told her. With that response, he had gone back to sleep. He was on vacation, and he did not need to check out someone who had overdosed.

At six, the dispatcher had called back.

"Lieutenant, I'm sorry to bother you again," her voice was tense. "Now we have two bodies. One's real bad."

That message jarred Niere out of bed and caused him to fumble for his glasses.

A double suicide? he thought. How often do you have two people willing to die at the same time?

As he sped along in his car over quiet country roads, Lt. Niere found it ironic that on such a clear, cool morning in May he was hurrying to a crime scene in Ballwin, Missouri. A pleasant suburb in far west St. Louis County, Ballwin had not had a murder case in eleven years, not since 1975. Ballwin was an All-American suburb of old frame farmhouses and newer colonial-

3

style homes flanked by large graceful trees. Niere had been raised around there on his family's farm. The area remained semi-rural.

The police lieutenant swung his long, thin body out of the car and walked past the fire trucks to 251 White Tree Lane, trying to imagine who could possibly kill himself or herself here. Everything was so precise, pretty, and nice.

The pastoral scene was shattered by an early morning melee of firefighters stomping around, rolling up their hoses, and police detectives combing the house. Other officers kept away the neighbors who shuffled about in their robes and slippers. Lt. Niere marched past the clusters of people on the lawns and driveway.

He could barely see. With the smoke still so thick and dark, a pair of enormous searchlights had been set up. He could hardly hear the patrolman talking to him with the sound of two giant fans whirring like helicopters to clear the smoke from the garage and house.

"Watch out, Denny," a firefighter called out as Niere walked into the garage. "It's so hot in there, the cars caught on fire and their tires melted."

"Wait till he sees it," another firefighter called out.

"You've never seen anything like it before," added a third man, wiping his forehead.

The fans could not cool the intense heat from the now extinguished blaze. Niere squinted, trying to see in the dark as the hot air steamed his tinted aviator-style glasses. He wiped them as he moved on briskly; he had to see what was there. What could be so shocking?

He stood before a dark shape. As his eyes adjusted to what lay before him, his jaw dropped. It took a minute to register.

Smoke curled from the charred stubs of the feet that were sticking high into the air. Niere stepped back to take in the entire scene. Two cars flanked an overturned old-fashioned rocking chair. Strapped into it was the blackened corpse of a nude woman.

Niere felt revulsion, then sadness. His sixteen years with the Ballwin police and two before that in Vietnam had trained him to be professional, but nothing could have prepared him for this sight or the stench of burning flesh. The odor in the two-hundred-degree heat forced him outside for air. Fortunately, he thought, it was cool even for a May day in St. Louis, only about seventy degrees and breezy.

Then, gathering his camera and strobe light, he forced himself back into the garage to methodically shoot his department's set of evidence photos. As he moved about, holding his breath, he realized this was no double suicide. What firefighters had thought was a second body turned out to be chunks of garage dry wall that had crashed in sections onto piles of books.

Was the corpse that of a suicide?

Or a murder?

Niere called his men over. "What do you have on this woman? What do her neighbors say?"

"She's Julia Miller Bulloch," said one of the men on the scene. "They call her 'Julie.' Thirty-one years old."

"We'll still need a positive ID by the family," Niere reminded them, and then: "Her face is burnt beyond recognition. What else?"

"Supposed to be a real nice lady. Kinda shy. A loner. Likes to putter around her house a lot, a real homebody," said another officer.

A detective butted in. "But she's no housewife. Neighbors say she's an executive with the phone company. Big salary. Worked downtown. Just got married."

"Denny, we're trying to reach her husband now," the other police officer said. "He works at Price Waterhouse. He's in St. Paul or Minneapolis on business. Left yesterday. Name's Dennis Bulloch."

One neighbor, Molly Flowers, had told police that she and Julie Bulloch had been close. Close enough to know that Julie had been depressed lately. Detectives had found anti-depressants on her night table.

"She must have swallowed the pills, set the fire and waited in that chair to die," said one officer who had glimpsed the corpse from a distance. No one had seen the body close up.

Digesting all of this, Niere walked back into the garage to the wall behind the cars so that he could face the body. He could make out some material on the body beneath the black coating of the melted tire rubber and the dry wall. The lower face and body of the corpse were wrapped in tape. Neat, even rows bound the arms to the chair. More crisscrossed the chest, leaving the breasts exposed. Yards more were wound around the jaw and mouth. The rows were all as even and precise as if a surgeon had wrapped her up. The only untidy portions were the strips hanging from the legs of the chair, the rest apparently having burned off the woman's calves. Niere crouched down to look at the arms more closely.

He frowned. Large sections of blue tape were wound about each wrist and elbow. What in God's name is this? he asked himself. What was a bound body doing in the garage in a fire?

He strode over to the detectives.

"Julie Bulloch couldn't have killed herself," Niere said. "How could she have taped herself to that chair?"

They nodded.

"Besides," Niere continued, "most suicidal women are not violent. This is murder."

"But Denny," said one of the officers, "we've checked. There are no signs of forced entry—no break-ins into the house or garage. Besides, her husband's out of town. Spouses are the first line of suspects."

Niere shook his head. "Here's this nice girl with a good job. She lives in a nice house in a nice part of town. We have a crime rate here of almost nil. And this lady becomes the victim of some bizarre murder. With lots of tape, no less."

He felt frustrated. There went his family vacation. His wife Brenda and their two children would be disappointed. Although he did not even want a vacation with this case pending, he knew he could not do anything to solve it yet. There was nothing to go on until the medical examiner performed the autopsy and ruled on the cause of death.

A few minutes later, the ME's (medical examiner's) investigator pulled up in his van. The corpse was carried into the driveway for the evidence unit to photograph and examine in daylight. Niere directed some fifteen officers to hold up sheets and blankets, which had been taken from the woman's home, the fire trucks and the investigator's van, to protect Mrs. Bulloch's last shred of privacy as the evidence men performed their grisly chores.

By now it was seven o'clock in the morning and there were

media milling about the front lawn, along with curiosity-seekers and schoolchildren. The police patiently held the bed and stretcher linens until the evidence men were finished. One neighbor likened the linens to the famous "Running Fence," the miles of fabric running along in the West like a billowing Great Wall of China, created by the sculptor Christos in the 1970s. The line of sheets also marked the last time Julie Bulloch, a notoriously private woman, enjoyed any right to privacy. The Fourth Amendment does not extend to the dead, and they lack the additional privacy protections granted their killers.

Julie's next-door neighbor covered her face with her hands and cried as her friend's remains were loaded into the investigator's van and the doors were closed.

Alone, Niere walked through the one-story brick and frame house. It was eerie—silent and dark. All the electrical wires had been cut by the firefighters to prevent an explosion. Niere could see their handprints along the walls, marks they had left when they were forced to feel their way like blind men through the dense smoke. The smoke damage was so extensive that Niere could not distinguish the colors of some of the rooms.

He found the master bedroom cozy but strange. As far as he could tell, it had all been carefully color coordinated and decorated in shades of rose, pale green, and cream fabrics. On the outer wall were a pair of needlepoint gingham dog and calico cat pictures. On one nightstand lay copies of *Fortune* and *Money* magazines, an annotated copy of *The Denial of Death*, by Ernest Becker, and an advanced computer manual. Julie Bulloch's jeans and panties lay crumpled on the floor between her dresser and the foot of the bed. The queen-sized bed was unmade and six pillows were strewn about, with a seventh still plumped up at the head.

Tossed on the daybed and the carpet were a man's white shirt and suit pants with an official-looking, plastic-coated identification badge attached to the belt. What looked like a vibrator and a roll of toilet paper were on top of the television. Niere wondered what had been going on.

In contrast to that mess was the military-tidy second bedroom with its lacy bed hangings and even rows of mint-condition antique dolls. Niere guessed it was Julie's old room, from before she was married. A next-door neighbor, Molly Flowers, had told him Julie had grown up in this house with her younger brother and their parents.

Niere called in officers to check the closets and drawers, while others were dispatched to draw up lists of people to be interviewed: friends, colleagues, relatives, dry cleaners, cleaning women, hairdressers, doctors, former boyfriends, jewelers, anyone whose name appeared in Mrs. Bulloch's meticulous address and engagement books found in her handbag on the kitchen table. Additional forces would canvass the entire neighborhood: Had early-morning joggers or newspaper boys seen or heard anything unusual? A pre-dawn scream, a car screeching, a person running, a gunshot? Arson specialists would determine how the fire was started and what accelerant was used to ignite such an inferno.

Everyone at the crime scene that Tuesday morning, May 6, 1986, assumed that Julie Bulloch had died in the fire.

It appeared that way. No one could have survived it.

The first clue would come from the medical examiner. It would be both a shock and a portent of what was to come.

Two

"A Straight Upper-Middle Class Girl"

May 6–May 7, 1986

As his alarm clock went off Tuesday morning, Carter Miller, Jr., heard the sound of a fire engine. He was getting out of the shower when his sister's neighbor on White Tree Lane phoned. "Carter, something terrible has happened," she said. "A fire at the house."

Shaking, Carter woke up his wife Judy, who drove him to 251 White Tree Lane, where he had been raised and where his newlywed sister Julie Bulloch now lived. The fire was out, but Carter was not allowed inside. Watching the police wind yellow barrier tape across the doors and windows, Carter felt like an outsider. He asked what had happened. There was no answer.

Where was Julie? His former neighbor Molly Flowers came out of her house next door. She went over and put her arms around Carter.

A tall man in jeans and aviator glasses slowly walked over to Carter and introduced himself. He smelled of smoke. He said he was Lt. Denny Niere of the Ballwin Police Department. Soft-spoken and sad-eyed, he told Carter his sister had died. They believed she had been killed in the fire. Carter crumbled in his wife's arms.

It was not until they watched the evening television news that Carter learned his sister had died naked and taped to her bedroom rocking chair. Carter kicked in the television set.

Autopsies of suspicious deaths in St. Louis County usually are performed the day the body is discovered. Usually the following day the cause—natural, accidental, suicide, homicide or undetermined—is released. Ninety-seven percent of the cases are easy. The person died from a heart attack, a fall, a knifing. It is the circumstances that can be hard to determine. In the Bulloch case, the medical examiner himself, Dr. George Gantner, walked into the morgue in the basement of St. Louis County Hospital to perform the autopsy a little before eleven on the morning of the fire.

This would be about his five thousandth autopsy. Dr. Gantner looked at the ghastly sight in the charred chair. He immediately wondered whether a fire had been set to cover up a murder. His curiosity was aroused.

With his glasses slipping off his snub-nose, his shock of straight dark hair tumbling into his round beaming face, George Gantner, an ebullient man, looked like the Norman Rockwell prototype of a genial general practioner who drives forty miles in a snowstorm to deliver a baby. So much for appearances. A specialist in forensic pathology—cases of violent death or unknown causes reported to the police—Dr. Gantner was the highly regarded medical examiner of both St. Louis City and County. Under his aegis, the headquarters of the National Association of Medical Examiners was established at St. Louis University Medical Center, where he served on the faculty.

Having performed the autopsies on about ten fire-related deaths a year in his thirty-year career, the pathologist would know immediately whether Julie Bulloch had died in the blaze in her garage.

But first he would have to get to the corpse. She was so smothered in tape, the lab assistants had to cut Julie Bulloch from the rocking chair in which she had died.

Caucasians who die in fires have telltale pink skin, from the carbon monoxide poisoning. Mrs. Bulloch's skin was not visible, the flesh buried beneath layers of greasy soot or yards of adhesive tape. Despite the stench of burnt flesh and the nauseating odor of soot, Gantner's assistants carefully cut and unwound yards of tape. It was like an archaeological excavation. The body was as precisely wrapped as that of a mummy. Beneath the tape, the unburnt skin of the corpse was revealed. Hers was clean and fair, not the pink complexion of a fire victim.

The doctor and his assistants continued probing the burnt remains. The inferno had literally cooked much of the victim's flesh. It was burnt and split in places like a charred hotdog. The feet and ankles had burned down to the bone. The earlobes and nipples, being of high water content, had popped. The heat had caused the facial capillaries to break, creating a raw-red mask from her nose through her eyes. Fortunately for the investigator, the internal organs were undamaged. There was no evidence of soot in the throat or lungs, which further proved Mrs. Bulloch was dead before she had been dumped into the inferno.

While one technician snapped away, taking seventy photographs for the ME's files, another assistant measured the yardage of the tape. There was forty-seven feet of tape wound on her arms: twenty-nine feet of white one-and-a-half-inch adhesive tape on the right arm along with three feet of vinyl-coated blue tape. The left arm was bound with fourteen feet of the white tape and three and a half feet of blue tape. More than thirty feet of tape were wrapped as neatly as on a Christmas present around the victim's face and hair. The yardage strapping Julie to her chair and crisscrossing her breast in an X-shape went unmeasured.

Some pieces could not be quantified: those scraps hanging pathetically to the legs of the chair. There was no way to tell if the charred stubs of her feet and legs had been taped too. The assistants wondered what the blue tape on the arms signified. And why so much tape?

Dr. Gantner gave the signal to cut away and remove the thirty feet of tape wound about the skull from chin to nostrils. No matter how painstakingly his assistants unwrapped the corpse, pieces of skin and hanks of hair were pulled off on the sticky tape. The ME wondered how a woman could have allowed herself to be wrapped up like that. And go to her executive office at Southwestern Bell the next morning.

As he pried open the jaws of the body, his eyebrows shot up in amazement. Two chunks of white material popped out. They were plumped up, swollen with saliva. Unraveled, they proved to be pieces of ordinary white terrycloth. The medical examiner deduced that they had been forced in under pressure to have come out like that. They were gags that had pushed her tongue so far back that breathing was impossible. The pathologist had his official cause of death: asphyxiation.

Was it murder?

How long did Julie live after she was gagged? The pathologist estimated she could have breathed for a while, depending upon the position of the gags and her head. But if the gags were placed in the front of her mouth and her tongue were shoved back immediately, Julie would have lived eight excruciating minutes before she suffered permanent brain damage and death. That would make her death definitely a murder. She had eight minutes to be rescued by whoever tied her up.

Then there was the ridiculously excessive amount of tape, seventy-six feet at least. Dr. Gantner found the case more than a little challenging. He longed to drive back to his sunny university office, sit beneath his wall-wide collection of primitive masks from around the world, light his pipe, read the forensic literature on erotic fatalities—and think.

This was the first sexual bondage homicide in the metropolitan area, even the region. Erotic deaths, by nature, are rare. Most are autoerotic—some teenager thinks he will have a great orgasm if he partially hangs himself, after which he can safely be released. But the safety mechanism fails.

There were few known cases of erotic deaths with a partner because the latter usually acts as a fail-safe. Julie Bulloch was the first case of a woman's dying during partner bondage—indeed, the first woman ever in America. Whoever was with Julie the night before had fatally betrayed her. And this was more than mere bondage.

It was sadomasochistic for two reasons. The blue tape at her wrists and elbows symbolized shackles. Secondly, the amount was wildly excessive; entire rolls of tape to restrain a woman of five foot two, weighing in at a hundred and twenty-five pounds.

There was no way to tell if the victim had fought the person gagging and binding her. The burning of the body eliminated any telltale bruises or abrasions. The fire also erased her assailant's fingerprints on her skin and the tapes.

What bothered Dr. Gantner most were the gags, more so than bizarre sexual rituals. It was obvious to him that the deceased's mouth was taped last because, once she was dying, her arms would not have swollen as they had. And had her arms been free, she would have freed herself from the gags. Once the woman began to choke, she would have made noises to her partner.

What was this person doing while Julie Bulloch was slowly suffocating?

Was this a homicide—any purposeful death, from self-defense to murder-for-hire? Lt. Niere and the other officers were waiting to find out if they had a case. About two and a half hours after he had begun the autopsy, Dr. Gantner called Lt. Niere.

"She didn't die in the fire. Death was caused by the two gags," Dr. Gantner said. "I'm ruling this a homicide."

The fact that Julie Bulloch died before the fire was not released immediately. Indeed, most of the police officers working the case thought she had died in the fire. Top investigators believed if they withheld that nugget of information, it would help catch Mrs. Bulloch's killer.

As the ME's van had taken the body to the morgue, Lt. Niere had realized this investigation would overwhelm the tiny Ballwin Police Department. In charge of the department while the chief attended a conference, Niere had requested activation of the Major Case Squad, a confederation of three hundred officers from ninety-six police and sheriff departments through bi-state Missouri and Illinois. (St. Louis City Police assists the Major Case Squad, but does not call upon it—the city having its own superbly successful homicide, sex crimes, bomb and arson, and vice departments. Unique for a big city, St. Louis PD is basically uncorrupt and clean.) The Major Case Squad is usually called for felony murder. Very fast, very efficient, the Major Case Squad solves eighty-six percent of its cases, usually within five days. Because of the complexity of the Bulloch case, all thirty-four officers stayed on the investigation for three weeks compiling information.

Before noon, detectives began combing the house at 251

White Tree, canvassing the neighborhood and calling colleagues at Southwestern Bell and the names found in Julie's phone book. Her killer was someone she knew, for there had been no break-in. The police were waiting for more clues from her widower, Dennis Bulloch, a Price Waterhouse consultant, who was out of town.

The state fire marshal, who investigates arson cases, went over the fire scene. There was a rag stuffed into the tailpipe of Julie's car and secured with tape, and two gas cans along the north wall of the garage. The fire marshal also found a metal pot lid filled with burned matter, and wondered what it was doing in the garage.

In the nearby kitchen, police sifted through papers they found in Mrs. Bulloch's handbag on the kitchen table, and other papers there and in the trash. Inside an envelope addressed to Dennis Bulloch were a house survey and a 1984 appraisal of Julie's jewelry for more than $44,000. To-do lists in Dennis's handwriting were tacked onto the refrigerator. His wife dutifully had crossed out her tasks as she completed them: "Peel carrots, refinance papers, check gutters, honeymoon plans . . . P.S. Did you get insurance forms etc. from work? P.P.S. I know I can't think of everything—we've both been through a disaster and should know what to do to preserve it."

Posthumous minutiae of a marriage. Being a detective was like being a ghost who suddenly materializes amidst the most intimate details of people's daily lives.

On the kitchen counter was a cork from a wine bottle. Inside the refrigerator was a corked green bottle of Veuve Clicquot Ponsardin, Brut, 1972. Most of the wine had been drunk. That champagne, Carter Miller had told police, had been one of his wedding gifts, brought back from his own honeymoon, that he had given his sister. Carter was in shock.

Julie's bridegroom, Dennis Bulloch, did not know what to think. He had been in St. Paul since the day before, Monday morning, May 5, when he and several colleagues from Price Waterhouse had flown up for an audit. Married for only ten weeks, he now was a thirty-two-year-old widower.

His boss, Jim Macke, had brought him home on a plane and taken him straight to the police. Hoping for leads, two Major Case detectives, Michael Thompson and Tony Daniele, interviewed Dennis in the squad trailer parked outside the Ballwin Police Department. The officers taped two of the three inter-, views, assuming Dennis would provide the name of a possible suspect.

Dennis Bulloch, in his dark suit, white button-down, and rep tie, appeared rigid, prosperous, reliable; the type who paid his bills in full the day the statements came. What one would expect from a Price Waterhouse man. He appeared the master of self-control. It was appearance only.

DENNIS: (Pathetically) I cried for sooo long. . . .
OFFICER: Dennis, this is a possible homicide. . . . If you would help just a little bit. . . .
DENNIS: (Hitting noises, whining and screaming) You don't understand! You don't understand! (Sixty seconds of piercing wailing like a five-year-old sent to bed without dessert.) Ahhhhh-ohhhh-ah-ah-ahhhh.
OFFICER: (Into recorder) It's 4:39. Interview went kaput.

Thompson and Daniele took Dennis to another room to be more comfortable. Dennis put his head down, refused to talk, and went to sleep. Forty-five minutes later, he was back in control. The police switched on their tape recorder and drove Dennis to 251 White Tree Lane to see if he found anything strange at the crime scene. He noticed that one of the VCRs was unplugged.

DENNIS: Oh it breaks me up. Is it a burglary? . . . (Sobs) A lot of damage? I tried to convince her not to talk to these people. . . .
OFFICER: What people are we talking about?
DENNIS: There's a army guy. She said they're great *friends*. (Sobs) There's a guy named Jim . . . and Mike in Eureka . . . (Sob. Sob. Sob.) A guy who cut the grass.
(Dennis explained that his wife only used first names in referring to her friends.)
OFFICER: Who would she have let into the house? . . .
DENNIS: She didn't say any names. What she said was (sniffles, pause), "If, if you don't want to stay home and take care of me I know somebody who can." . . .
OFFICER: Were there old boyfriends?
DENNIS: She *said* they were just friends. . . .

Thompson tried another tack. Who were her best friends? Again, Dennis answered that Julie never named surnames. He explained, "We spent a lot of time together, the time I was not working. . . ."

While Dennis was unable to provide any names of possible suspects, he suggested that the police hunt for Julie's diary. "If you find the diary, it will provide you insight."

Detective Thompson lowered his voice. "I have a poignant question. Any suicide attempts?"

DENNIS: She talked about pills and carbon monoxide.
OFFICER: Do you know if she ever tried it?
DENNIS: She said (very very long pause), she said she did . . .

"Was it suicide?" Dennis asked.

"Don't blame yourself," said the cop kindly, "it's nothing you've done."

Dennis whimpered, "That's right. That's what I've been thinking all afternoon. That it was."

As the state fire marshal poked around, the police asked Dennis about the wiring to the six television sets and several recorders. Dennis explained he had set the timer to record Monday night's ending of a two-part series Julie was watching. That series was on serial killer Ted Bundy.

DENNIS: Was anything missing?
OFFICER: Any jewelry?
DENNIS: She had gobs. . . . It was in a chestnut jewelry box. (Describes box at length.) Is that missing, too? (Describes costliness of some pieces.) We were trying to consolidate our insurance. (Tone changes.) You say the house burned?

Dennis went on to explain that "*she*" (whom he never called by name or "my wife") had a life insurance policy for $13,000 dollars with Prudential, where she once had worked, in addition to a $39,000 policy at Southwestern Bell, which was commensurate with her annual salary. He told police that they had an $85,000-dollar joint savings account, of which $21,000 dollars came from the sale of his house on Stanford Drive in University City, and $64,000 Julie had inherited from her parents. The detective asked how Dennis knew so much about their insurance.

Dennis snapped, "That was the way I was brought up—security conscious."

Detective Thompson asked who was the beneficiary of Julie's life insurance policies. Dennis said, "She was in the process of changing it over. I don't know exactly. Her brother does."

The detective asked Dennis how he had met his wife and when. Dennis said, "The end of September."

Then, he had a question. "Is this going on much longer? I'm really *nauseous* and I haven't eaten dinner," he complained. The police continued anyway. He said wistfully, "I just thought (long pause) everything was going to work out so nicely." He explained that she did not have a dining room set but he did, so that worked out well.

OFFICER: Any sex aids?
DENNIS: I *know* she had some. A vibrator. She was kind of *liberated* . . . .
OFFICER: There wouldn't be any chance of a hidden side to her sexually? . . . Sex clubs she belonged to?
DENNIS: (Long pause) Not that I know!
OFFICER: We have to ask—any names to go on?
DENNIS: I don't have any names. But she did have (chokes), I can't believe I'm talkin' about this stuff!
OFFICER: (Kindly) Don't worry. We're used to it.
DENNIS: *I'm not.* (Keeps choking.)
OFFICER: We hate to say it. . . . It's part of the investigation. . . .
DENNIS: (Very, very long pause) There wasn't anything sexual, was it?
OFFICER: We don't know. Anything that would help?
DENNIS: (Deep sigh) Sure. *She* had these *books.*
OFFICER: Didn't belong to any clubs?
DENNIS: Not that I know of! As far as I know, she's a straight, *upper*-middle class girl!

Dennis and his parents were eating lunch the next day, May 7, at the Pancake House near the Ballwin Police Station, when Lt. Niere and some detectives wearily filed in to compare notes over food and coffee. Niere was surprised by Dennis's parents. He had expected a distinguished executive with steel-gray hair in a gray summer worsted suit and a frosted-haired matron in proper navy linen dress draped with an expensive silk scarf and accented with heavy gold jewelry.

As preppy as Dennis Bulloch appeared, his family was strictly blue-collar: a father in denim work clothes and a 1950's crewcut which prefigured the retro style, and a mother in a print polyester pantsuit the color of Jordan almonds with little crosses in her ears and a Mamie Eisenhower perm on her dyed, flat-brown hair. Dennis squirmed when he saw the police officers looking at him. He seemed ashamed of his parents.

Overhearing their conversation, Niere was shocked. Using the tone with which teachers lecture naughty schoolchildren, the Bullochs harped at their son: He must invest his wife's estate in stocks and bonds. His mother shrilly added, "You can't just leave that house empty. Sell it fast or it will depreciate in value."

Dennis did not answer. He was not listening.

Three

"Did I Tell You
I Was Married?"

May 7–May 10, 1986

Carter Miller, Jr., rolled up his sleeves. Exhausted and numb, he still had work to do. Because his sister had known her killer—there was no forced entry into her house and the massive taping was too neat to have been done while the victim was under duress—and because he had been in town the night she died, Major Case detectives suggested that Carter take a lie detector test to clear himself. Not that he was a suspect, just to spare him more grief.

From midnight until five A.M., May 7, Carter took and retook a polygraph. The examiner said he had not answered truthfully to the questions: Did you set fire? Did you tape Julie to the rocker? Did you cause her death? Carter kept asking his own questions: Why her? Why that night? Why me?

Finally, Carter passed, but at a horrible price. His answers to other questions eroded his marriage and checked his career.

An early suspect was Dennis Bulloch's first wife, Karen Toks-vig, an executive at Southwestern Bell where his second wife had also worked. Karen's possible motive was the jealousy of an ex-wife.

Within days, the detectives eliminated her as a suspect, but there was no relief for her from the media. Hungry for any nibbles on the crime story of the decade, reporters tracked her down at her grandparents' where she had gone for refuge, and even onto the seventh hole of the golf course where an aggressive reporter sent a message saying it was an emergency. Karen paid a lawyer $2,000 to fend off such attacks.

It was three A.M. and Denny Niere could not sleep. Although it had been past two when he eased himself into bed, he lay there staring into the darkness. He kept seeing the blackened image of Julie Bulloch bound to her chair.

This was worse than Vietnam, where Niere's dead comrades had been mourned properly. Julie had not. Her widower never asked to see her, never asked, as relatives of murder victims do, "Tell me, tell me, did she die in pain? Was it over fast? Did she suffer long?" Dennis Bulloch had asked nothing about his dead wife. Only about her property.

On Thursday, May 8, the Major Case Squad called Dennis Bulloch at his parents' home, where he was staying, for more help. His parents had no idea where he had gone. Nor did anyone else. The Major Case Squad and Lt. Niere gave up trying to find him.

Hating this part of his job, Lt. Niere sucked in his breath and called Carter Miller. Someone had to formally identify his sister's remains.

To ease the gruesome task, Lt. Niere ordered a police car to drive Carter to the county morgue. Carter feared seeing the corpse: This was his big sister, his last living close relative, the person who had always been there for him. How would he react?

He was horrified when the morgue attendant pulled back the sheet and he saw the charred remains. Then his eyes focused on the remnants of the full lower lip, similar to his. Carter felt as though the membrane holding in his grief was ripped apart. He wept in anguish. All alone in the horrible room with what had once been his sister, he cried and talked to her. "Don't worry," he said softly, "you're still my sister and I still love you."

Carter had called his brother-in-law the day before. Even though he did not like Dennis, Carter felt they should get together about the funeral arrangements. Dennis did not want to talk, saying, "Do whatever you want about the funeral."

Too grief-stricken to pick out a coffin for his wife's remains, Dennis found the fortitude to oversee her finances, as well as his own. On Thursday, May 8, he wrote a detailed letter to his parents on how to handle his and Julie's real estate, five bank accounts, stocks and personal property, with a precisely worded power of attorney letter for his parents, and three letters to post offices where he had boxes asking to forward his mail.

While Dennis legally owned the house at 251 White Tree Lane, when the Major Case Squad released it from the crime scene, he was unreachable. Carter was forced to suffer another indignity. He had to make arrangements to have it boarded up and then had to pay the bill. Carter also made plans to bury his sister, mourn for her, and to pay for these rituals.

He sent a bouquet of red roses to the funeral home. He asked the attendants to place a single flower in Julie's hands. Before the wake, Carter went to see his sister for the last time.

Alone with the closed coffin, Carter whispered, "Julie, you get a rose, too. No matter what I have to go through, I want to do whatever I can for you. I want to be there for you the way you were for me."

Dennis failed to attend the wake on Friday or the funeral on Saturday. Dennis's inability to handle his wife's burial horrified Lt. Niere. "Who would miss his own wife's funeral?" Niere rhetorically asked Tom DePriest, the Chief Warrant Officer of St. Louis County. They were sitting in DePriest's office, a spare, immaculate room in the county courthouse in Clayton.

Round-faced and snub-nosed, DePriest, in his late thirties, as was Niere, looked like a Campbell Soup kid grown into an adult who majored in fun at college. People also frequently mistook DePriest for the stereotypical hard-drinking Irish Catholic prosecutor. So much for appearances.

DePriest, a Lutheran, often eschewed the bar scene to coach his son's baseball and hockey teams or help with his homework. The two were close—the boy moved in with the divorced DePriest when he was fourteen. DePriest was hard-working, too. He was always on the phone with a cop or talking to one in his office while several waited to see him in the anteroom, or en route to a courtroom.

As chief warrant officer for the last nine years, DePriest decided who was charged with what crimes after the police presented their evidence. He ran an efficient operation. Straightforward and honest, DePriest showed you what you got, a decent career prosecutor who wanted to make things better. He never processed a case with an eye to political advancement. His ego would fit comfortably in the palm of your hand.

DePriest was fascinated by the Bulloch case. As a prosecutor, he was struck by two facts: There had been no forced entry. And the dead woman had no enemies. There was also an odd coincidence. DePriest, like Dennis Bulloch, had worked at Price Waterhouse.

The case became more interesting to him hour by hour. What were those strange things found in the house? The Major Case Squad had asked Julie's former housekeeper to go through 251 White Tree with Lt. Niere to see if anything was missing; perhaps the murderer had also been a robber.

What was more intriguing was what had been added. The housekeeper pointed out that the three sex manuals—*Joy of Sex*, *More Joy of Sex* and *Making Love Better*—were not Julie's. Indeed, her husband's name had been written in the last one. The books explained how to safely perform sexual bondage. And there were two vibrators in the bedroom. They were new too.

The cop and the cleaning woman then went through the basement. "What's this?" she asked. Hanging on the clothesline was a white slip. It couldn't be Julie's, the woman pointed out. "Why not?" asked Lt. Niere. "Because Mrs. Bulloch was small, a size six or eight," said her former housekeeper. "This thing," she said as she checked the label, "is a size eleven/twelve. And way too long for my Julie." Lt. Niere held the slip up to his six-foot-tall body. The slip came down to his knees. It's big enough for a man, he thought.

No one could figure out the answer to the real question, the one stumping the Major Case Squad detectives, Lt. Niere, and Prosecutor DePriest. What was the nude, bound body of Julie Bulloch doing in her garage? Or, for that matter, in what sexual bondage ritual had she been involved? Tales were told about wild West County parties, sort of bring-your-own-wife clubs; or of roaming sex dungeon clubs with heavy-duty restraints for S & M bondage.

There was another tantalizing clue. The day of the funeral, four days after the body was discovered, Ballwin Detective Steven Schicker found a gray metal file box among Bulloch's possessions. Inside were three color photographs of nude women. One was of Dennis's first wife. The other two were of another woman. She looked quite young. Like a teenager.

In one of the pictures her ankles were bound together.

The prosecutor could talk all day with the policeman about this case, but now Niere had something more concrete than gut instinct and sexual clues.

Jim Macke, Dennis's colleague who had notified him of his wife's death, had not thought anything was awry until Dennis failed to attend his own wife's wake and funeral. After the service, he drove straight to the police and wrote a seventeen-page statement.

Before seven o'clock on the morning of May 6, just hours after Julie Bulloch's body had been discovered, the phone in Jim Macke's hotel room in St. Paul had rung. It was Dennis. "I don't know what family you were with last night, but I was with you, okay?" he said.

Macke asked if he had had a long night. Dennis answered, "Well, yes." Macke assumed his colleague had been fooling around. Then he heard what sounded like traffic noises and a long-distance operator—odd when Dennis was staying at the same hotel.

Notified by Price Waterhouse that Dennis's wife had died in a fire, Macke assumed the woman was Dennis's first wife, Karen. After all, the man had just been divorced. Macke went to Dennis's hotel room to tell him his ex-wife was dead.

Dennis was in the shower. As he stepped out, he yelled to his colleague, "Oh, did I tell you I was married?"

Four

The Bridegroom Takes
the Plunge

May 10–May 11, 1986

The detectives continued their search for Dennis Bulloch on Saturday, May 10. They combed through his desk at Price Waterhouse for an appointment book and called his colleagues. They checked his old house—on Stanford Drive, in University City, a suburb of St. Louis—which he had sold two weeks earlier. No one had any clues as to his whereabouts.

Indeed, the neighbors on Stanford reported Julie had never been there. They had seen Dennis coming in late and staying overnight alone, for days at a time. Some tall blonde had been there over Thanksgiving and Easter. Dennis's parents said they had no idea where he went. But his mother did say that Dennis had taken her car and maybe, just maybe, he was at his sister's grave near Springfield, Missouri. Niere put out an APB—All Points Bulletin—asking police throughout the state to be on the lookout.

The APB on the widower was headline stuff. Hearing the news, his former therapist, who happened to be friends with

Dennis's best friend, warned him: "Lock your doors," he said, "I think he'll hurt someone."

"We've got a lot of circumstantial evidence," DePriest told Lt. Niere. "We know from his colleague Jim Macke how Dennis flew back to St. Paul the morning Julie was murdered. How could he have done it? His coworkers say they saw him there the night before."

While detectives worked on the travel logistics, other investigators logged and read the evidence seized in the Bulloch house. Dennis Neal Bulloch had been a meticulous conservationist. The details of his life were minutely revealed—from his briefcase, his files, his receipts, his bills, his engagement books, his little black book, his torrent of letters, the wedding album from his first marriage.

Like the proud parent of a long-awaited first-born, Dennis recorded every facet of his own life. He rhapsodized over his every "feeling" in his voluminous diaries, of the type novelists do not even think about and even moony-eyed teenagers call "yucky." One diary entry from 1984 was prescient:

Do I run away from responsibility? Yes, emphatically, yes.

Dennis's Day-Timer Telephone and Engagement books were a treasure trove of St. Louis social-climbing history. There were fifty-three single women of varying backgrounds listed, most were well-to-do, judging by their addresses. A few lived on the East Coast. A man whose first wife had left him in May, 1985, who had walked out of divorce court in December, 1985, and back down the aisle in February, 1986, had amassed the names of fifty-three women in nine months.

"Jesus!" said DePriest's investigators, after interviews with some of these women. Dennis had enough recreational sex partners to populate the Houston Astrodome.

Next to the social names, Dennis had methodically written in at what parties, charity balls, or trendy restaurants he and the women had been introduced. For example, an exquisite redhead who belonged to Old Warson Country Club was entered in his little black book with the notation that she was met at Busch's Bar after museum opening, along with the names of acquaintances in common. Sometimes, Dennis described the women's appearance.

The larger their trust fund and the more prominent their

names, the more these women found Mr. Bulloch "the perfect gentleman," as two socialites who belonged to the best country clubs later said. An equal opportunity social climber, Dennis also jotted down prominent men-about-town, such as the businessman-son of a former dashing mayor of St. Louis. He met these people through civic social organizations also noted in his little book.

"Look at these names," said Jack Patty, DePriest's investigator. Dennis dated women whose families were listed in *Who's Who in America*.

Socially, the most impressive of Dennis's dates was Rebecca "Becky" Peabody Cabot, whose family a few generations back had founded a national industry based in St. Louis. Still privately held, the firm had revenues of a billion dollars a year. One relative was named to *Fortune* magazine's 400 wealthiest Americans. The Peabody Cabots could have lived lavishly on the interest from their interest, better than the leveraged buy-out kings of Manhattan's Upper East Side. Their home, the most extravagant palatial spread in St. Louis, including tennis courts, pool, guest houses, carriage house, etc., a brief run in the Mercedes from Neiman-Marcus, cost under $7,000,000 in 1986. But in Becky's family, money flashed was money vulgar. In St. Louis, the very rich often live like the upper-middle class, in keeping with the bourgeois sense of the city.

The Peabody Cabot name was a household word for civic and business power. It would impress Dennis's superiors at Price Waterhouse, who had already noted that he was "very conscious of making social contacts around town."

In his Day-Timer Engagement Book, Dennis also noted what times he went to bed and arose and whether he "got much" from a therapist's session. (Sometimes, he made appointments with his two therapists one day after another.) He reminded himself of the anniversary of nearly every couple he had ever met. He recorded every upcoming party at his tennis club and all his tennis dates. He did not even miss the date of his first wife's leaving, May 9. In 1986, he listed her birthday along with the anniversary of his first date on June 10 with his main squeeze, Christy Meiers. He reminded himself to go to the Land's End outlet when in Chicago.

Several investigators double-checked the booklet; nowhere

did he mention Julie Miller, the woman he had married ten weeks earlier.

Dennis had not met his wife the way he told police, through mutual friends in September. He had lied. Dennis met Julie in a way perfectly acceptable on the East Coast but one that had unsavory sexual connotations in conservative St. Louis.

A stun gun? thought St. Louis County Officer Tom Deakin, as he read the cash receipt from a sporting goods store. It was made out to a "John Mason." What was Dennis doing with a stun gun? Deakin could not ask the shop owner. The store had gone out of business. Deakin discovered the receipt in Dennis's files.

A stun gun is, in the words of a St. Louis police sergeant, a bitch. It can shoot through a leather coat. Most stun guns look like a little black box, the shape of a dollar bill, about three-quarters of an inch thick. A button activates two metal contacts which one places nearly touching the victim's leg or arm. The victim gets an electric shock—a numbing thump—leaving no burns or damage. He or she is rendered helpless by temporary loss of muscle control.

Stun guns were popular in the early 1980s, especially for women's self-protection. Not for he-men like Dennis pushing six feet, who had yellow belts in karate. The gun itself was never found. What did he need a stun gun for, wondered Lt. Niere. Did he hang out at gay bars and fear fights? Did he use it on his wife?

Julie was no wild woman, the police were finding out. Interviewing every former lover they could find (there were six in as many years) they found that the men spoke in chorus. Julie was conservative in bed. She would have made a missionary happy. Her lingerie was the white cotton underwear type. Underneath Ms. Prim was a Good Little Girl.

"Aw," said one prosecutor skeptically, "who's gonna admit he and a dead woman used to swing from chandeliers?"

No, said Niere, Julie was very straight. What you saw in that sad portrait of Julie was what you got: a professional woman who sat for her wedding picture wearing, not bridal finery or even a cocktail dress, but a shirt with a Peter Pan collar and tiny gold stud earrings. Her make-up was the preppy minimalist look.

Carter and his wife had given Julie and Dennis as wedding gifts a fine champagne from their own wedding trip, and the bridal photographs. After his sister had been murdered, Carter received a notice from the photographer that the pictures were ready. When Carter picked them up, he was speechless. Dennis had not gone to the photographer's with his wife.

Except for child abuse cases, Julie was the most pathetic victim the investigators had ever heard. And they had to listen to her audiotape every day. The day after the murder, police had discovered an audiotape cassette, which Julie had recorded in early April, a month before her death. For fifty minutes, Julie cries and begs Dennis to love her and pay attention to her.

"It's the low point of the investigation to listen to it," said one investigator sadly. The others nodded in agreement.

By Sunday, May 11, five days after the murder, the APB and Dennis's picture flashing across the television sets paid off.

Two days earlier, Friday morning, May 9, a bricklayer had spotted an abandoned car parked near the Martin Luther King Bridge over the Mississippi River. Its flashing lights were on. The bricklayer and his two assistants went over to check out the car, thinking it had broken down. They could not get inside to turn off the lights and save the battery. The car was locked with the keys in the ignition. On the dashboard they saw two envelopes. The trio forgot about it the rest of the day, though the bricklayer told his brother what he had seen.

Over the weekend, the bricklayer's brother watched a television interview with a cop who said the police were looking for Dennis Bulloch in connection with his wife's death. On Sunday, May 11, the brother called the police about the abandoned car. A license check showed the blue Bonneville Brougham belonged to Dennis's mother, Ginny Bulloch. A St. Louis City police officer used a slim-jim to break into the car. He then called Lt. Niere, who arrived at 2:42 P.M.

Two St. Louis County police technicians worked half an hour to open the two envelopes on the dashboard without destroying the fingerprints. Inside were a will and testament addressed to a socially prominent attorney in a silk-stocking law firm, a three-page note to Dennis's family, a six-page letter, a one-page list of Dennis's household goods with a photocopy, an engagement book, and his resumé. More light reading for the Major Case Squad.

On yellow, lined paper, Dennis had bequeathed all his worldly goods to his "loving parents" in trust except for $15,000 that was to go to the twins of his best friend, Calvin Porterfield. More interesting, was his allocation of the household furnishings at 251 White Tree Lane and the value he placed on them.

Dennis was the proud possessor of a ruined mahogany Sheraton-style dining room set. Ruined because he had ordered it stripped down to the woodgrain and left unfinished, as if mahogany were Victorian country oak. He grotesquely overestimated this faux pas at $8,000. (By way of comparison, the noted Selkirk's Auction House of St. Louis estimated the value of an 18th-century antique cherry French provincial dining table in exquisite condition at $3,000 to $5,000). Dennis thought Julie's reproduction Louis XIV fanteuil was an antique worth $800, a nanofraction of its value if it had been authentic.

Dennis generously had left his priceless dining room furniture along with Julie's family crystal, china, and silver, totaling almost $20,000, to his first wife's little sister. Instead of inheriting his mother's and great-aunt's pieces, Carter Miller had been bequeathed some den furniture. Dennis's old girlfriend, Christy Meiers, was to receive the goods in the family room and kitchen, worth more than Carter's pieces. Per Julie's request, Dennis had said he wanted her estate jewelry, appraised in 1983 at more than $44,000, to go to Carter's wife. (Later, Dennis gave it to his parents for safe-keeping. Carter never saw any of his mother's jewelry again until 1991.) For some reason, Dennis forgot Julie's late mother's mink coat and mink wrap.

Dennis also left in his mother's car a suicide note, carefully numbered page "1 of 6, 2 of 6," etc., dated May 8, enumerating all his woes. Dennis accused two detectives of emotional police brutality, which, he wrote, had finally pushed him over the edge.

The note was a fascinating psychological profile of self-preoccupation, self-pity, blame, and projection. Dennis blamed other people for his own misdeeds, and he pointedly implied that Julie had killed herself.

He was explicit about how sexually aberrant she had been, claiming that his bride demanded what he called "tender roughness," e.g., spanking. He whined over and over that his life was ruined.

To the very end, Dennis was concerned with appearances. In headline-sized letters, he wrote:

> *Mom & Dad & Gram,*
> *I LOVE you very*
> *much but This*
> *last loss—I just*
> *can't go on with it!*
> *Please forgive me.*
> *Please ask that*
> *Jeff Whitmaier pick*
> *my clothes and*
> *tell the police not*
> *to use hooks if*
> *they don't have to.*
> *I am taking my*
> *final baptism and*
> *hope god forgives*
> *me for all the*
> *stress I put*
> *you through—*
> **God Help Me!**

Part Two

From Teddy Bears
to Bondage

July 7, 1954–May 5, 1986

Five

The Good Little Girl

1954–1973

Julie tiptoed into the den and over to the corner where her father sat in his recliner. She stood patiently and quietly until he looked up from his afternoon newspaper. Carter Miller, Sr., was reading to unwind from the tensions of his day at the office. His five-year-old daughter wanted to curl up on his lap. She wanted him to read the funnies to her as he sometimes did on week-ends. But most of all, she wanted him to hold her.

"Daddy, please read to me," Julie begged.

"Not now," he said. The child walked away, head down.

Trained not to pester him, Julie did not ask again. She was hurt. She felt the only time her father touched her was when he punished her.

He doesn't love me, she thought. This was not true, for he did; he just did not show it the way Julie wanted. She was an easy child to love, an adorable pixie with blond bangs and big round blue eyes who occasionally acted impish, but basically was more than eager to please.

Her father—who had married a much younger woman—now pushing sixty, came home exhausted from work to the demands of two small children. He could not keep up with them, and so

33

withdrew. While others blamed Carter Miller, Sr., for being re-mote and cold, Julie blamed herself. She would have to earn her father's attention. She would become his best little girl.

By nature, Julia "Julie" Alice Miller wanted everything nice and in its place. She kept her collection of foreign dolls, which her father had brought home from his business trips as a buyer for May Co., in military formation. She would clean her room without being asked.

As a teenager, she liked her new neighborhood of colonial-style homes on manicured lawns in Wayne, Passaic County, New Jersey. The Miller family's house was a four-bedroom, two-and-a-half-bath, yellow woodframe with gray trim on a wooded cul-de-sac.

It had not been easy moving from Brentwood, a nice middle-class suburb of St. Louis, all the way across the country to New Jersey and changing schools as a thirteen-year-old. When the Millers first moved to New Jersey, Julie attended parochial schools—Our Lady of the Valley in Wayne and later to DePaul High School. Hating the regimentation, she pushed to transfer to public school, Wayne Valley High School. This was her only rebellious act in the midst of the student riots and radical movements of the late 1960s and early 1970s.

Julie fit in at Wayne Valley immediately. She was uncompli-cated and eager to be liked, facts not unnoticed by her class-mates, for the caption below her photo in her 1972 high school senior yearbook reads: "A very simple book, with very large print, and very easy to read." Her classmates remember her as "real sweet," never cranky the way adolescents can be. She always worried about hurting someone's feelings.

While not that apotheosis of high school popularity—a cheer-leader—Julie was in the second tier, a Color Guard, who marched with the school band during half-time at football games.

She quickly made a best friend, another transfer student named Laura Reeves. Giggling, they would make a point of telling people they were fraternal twins. Living two blocks apart, they were always at one or the other's house. They double-dated frequently, and Laura's boyfriend was best friends with Julie's boyfriend.

In her schoolwork, as with any project, Julie was practical, analytical, organized, and diligent. She was rewarded by entrée into the National Honor Society, made up of the top ten percent of her graduating class of 450.

Julie was good-looking, too. Voluptuous yet petite. She had a home-spun, All-American prettiness, with peaches and cream complexion, blue eyes, and a nose like Sandra Dee's. She wore her blond hair center-parted and long and straight, de rigueur for the early 1970s. Unlike the flower children of the era, Julie was always fastidious about her appearance and belongings. Her face and demeanor seemed to alternate between those of a pixie and an angel.

Julie never acted wild or experimented with drugs or liquor. Or sex. What she felt for her steady boyfriend was not love, not even infatuation. His attention was flattering, but their relationship was more social than deeply meaningful. Julie occasionally dated other boys.

Julie was not looking for a soul mate. All she fantasized about was the All-American Dream as espoused by the girls' and women's magazines of the era: a nice husband, nice children, nice house, and, maybe, a nice job.

Nice also meant no acrimony, no *Sturm und Drang* scenes so beloved by hormonal teenagers. Recalled her brother Carter, Jr.: "When I was in junior high, Mom found a pack of Marlboros and demanded to know if they were mine. They were, of course, but all she knew was they weren't Julie's Salems. Then Julie walked up and said, 'Those are mine. I switched brands.' " She did not reprimand her little brother or demand a favor in return.

Julie was known as "Jules Mills, the fabric fanatic." As she wrote in Laura Reeves's high school yearbook: "Your teaching me sewing and look what became of it." Jules designed conservative skirts, dresses, and suits that she would sew and tailor precisely. Because she loved sewing so much, she took a part-time job in a fabric shop. She liked the independence it gave her, and the extra spending money for sweaters, although the family did not need her income. Julie's sewing was more an outlet for her creativity.

Laura Reeves would often spend the night at Julie's, and the girls would flip through the neatly stacked old *Glamour* magazines in the corner of Julie's bedroom. Julie had redecorated her bedroom herself, whipping up a kelly green bedspread with matching plaid curtains and pillows. When the evening grew late, the girls would climb into Julie's twin beds, turn out the lamps and whisper in the dark about their futures:

Who they were going to marry when they grew up. What they would name their children. How many children they would have. What kind of careers. Julie was vague on specifics, but she daydreamed about everything being nice. The girls drifted off to sleep.

One such night, at about two A.M., Laura heard a clinking noise. She glanced over to see if Julie were awake. Julie had her head up and was looking at the doorway. The two girls burst into giggles. There was Julie's mother, Mary Jane Tracey Miller, standing under a sheet, moaning, with tons of bracelets clanking around her ankles pretending to be a ghost.

The next morning, after she fixed them breakfast, Mary Jane let them try on her jewelry. It was quite a collection for a woman who lived in Wayne rather than the more affluent Short Hills or Montclair. Laura was awed by the respectably-sized canary diamonds, antique gold pieces inherited from Mary Jane's aunt, and the dollops of diamonds on rings, pins, and watches. It would all be Julie's one day.

Mary Jane seemed almost too close to her little Julie, thought Mary Jane's best friend, Pauline Riviers. Whenever Julie had any problem or hurt feeling, she would run to her mother for succor, a practice she continued as an adult. Julie's friends thought her mother overprotected her. Or, was Mary Jane reacting to something sinister?

Julie told another patient in a psychiatric ward twenty years later that something traumatic had happened to her as a child. It changed her entire life, she said. Ruined it.

Mary Jane, who confided her problems to her friend Pauline, never mentioned any disaster, although she did complain that her husband and her daughter did not get along. Reading was their only bond.

Shut out by their too-old father, Julie and her brother became close. Carter senior lacked the stamina to raise small children, said his son.

Mary Jane Tracey and her best friend Pauline Riviers were freshening their make-up in Mary Jane's old bedroom before they went downstairs for the receiving line and wedding reception. Pauline was aware that Mary Jane was not mad for her new husband. "She was dying to get married and have children," Pauline said. "She loved Carter because he proposed," after which she deliberately became pregnant. (As Mary Jane later joked to her daughter, "I wanted to see if at his age he still had it in him.") As Mary Jane reapplied her lipstick, she told Pauline that if her baby were a girl, she would name her after her sister-in-law, Julie.

Carter Miller, Sr., was fifty-two when he married Mary Jane Tracey, who was thirty-three in December, 1953. An Air Force captain during World War II, Carter had come to St. Louis, as a fabric buyer at Famous-Barr & Co. Mary Jane quit her job as office supervisor at Grove Laboratories, now a division of Bristol-Myers Co., just before her small church wedding. The reception was held in the house where Mary Jane had been raised, in Clayton, one of the best suburbs of St. Louis.

Julie was born on July 7, 1954, seven months after her mother's wedding. Carter junior came along in 1958. The marriage initially proved a success. Kind-hearted and good-natured, Carter senior loved Mary Jane and was happy to acquiesce to her desires. She was young and fun-loving, something the childless widower from Ohio needed. Ultimately, he was overshadowed by his wife's ebullience.

The age difference became a source of conflict over time. Mary Jane complained to Pauline that her sex life was meager. Her husband's lack of energy turned into a problem outside the bedroom, too. He became an old man, like someone's grandfather dozing in the corner chair, thought Julie's friend Laura.

To win his father's attention, Carter junior became the family clown, and Julie became the little caretaker cum nurse, keeping things and emotions in their place, making everything nice. Julie never discovered what she wanted to do with her life, and never really tried. All she wanted to do was work—at what she did not know—and then get married—to what kind of man she had no idea.

While her friends went off to college, Julie remained with her

mother and commuted to nearby Montclair State College, a
four-year liberal arts college. Although she was very bright and
made straight A's, Julie soon dropped out of school. She took
the first job she found, at Prudential Insurance Co.

"Her job, handling medical claims, turned into a blessing later
for the Miller family," Carter said. "And a disaster for Julie. My
sister ruined her life taking care of everyone but herself."

Six

"Dying to Get Married"

1973–1985

Julie and her brother Carter sat in the barren hospital waiting room. Both felt as drained as if they had undergone open heart surgery. Carter, twenty, had come home from college for the Christmas break. Julie, twenty-four, tried to juggle her office workload with early morning and late evening visits. Julie and Carter took turns going in and out of the intensive care rooms.

Their mother Mary Jane was dying from breast cancer. Their father Carter senior was debilitated from strokes. The 1978 holiday season seemed like a Christmas in Jane Eyre's orphanage as rewritten by Kafka. There was worse to come.

"What are we going to do?" Carter asked Julie. "Which one should we use?" Julie explained patiently which nursing home she had selected.

The doctors had told them they could not take care of two seriously ill parents at home. They could take Mary Jane, but temporarily needed to put Carter senior into a nursing home. Their parents had been in and out of the hospital ever since last Christmas. It had not been much of a holiday then, but at least they had all been together.

It had been five years since Julie had enjoyed a normal life—

not since the Miller family moved back to St. Louis, in 1973. Julie had not wanted to return to her birthplace, but she gave in and took her own apartment. But the initial thrill of independence wore off quickly. She was lonely. Her high school friends were on the East Coast and her childhood chums were away at college.

Within months, Julie had no free time anyway. Her mother underwent a mastectomy, and Julie spent nights and weekends helping her parents. Then her father began suffering strokes, and Julie was forced to move back home, to 251 White Tree Lane in Ballwin.

From the day she unpacked her belongings, at age nineteen, Julie no longer lived her own life. She became the head of a household of two terminally ill parents and a teenage brother before she could legally vote. There was no dating a variety of men, no trying out a smorgasbord of classes or causes or careers, the things people do in their twenties as they find themselves. No weekends in Chicago, no honeymoon in Hawaii. There was nothing for Julie except her office, her sewing, and her parents. Carter, coming home weekends from college, saw his sister falling farther and farther behind socially.

"Julie never had time to be selfish," he recalled. "Her emotional and sexual development were hacked off in midstream."

Instead of trying on Priscilla of Boston bridal gowns or picking out the baby's layette at Saks as she had dreamed of doing, Julie had bought a beeper so that the doctors could always reach her.

After four years of strokes and heart attacks, Carter Miller, Sr., died from pneumonia in 1979. His wife outlived him, enduring four more years of chemotherapy and radiation treatments. It was an emotionally and physically grueling period for her daughter. The worst part began in 1980, when Julie was twenty-six.

Julie was out of town at an AT&T management training seminar. She had moved to the telecommunications company from Prudential just before her twenty-first birthday. She had foreseen more opportunities to advance at AT&T, and had now been proven correct. She was excited, having just been promoted to management. Her friend, Nora Talcott, another new exec, joined her at the seminar, and, in their free time, the women became giddy having fun.

Julie talked Nora into buying a dog like hers, a Lhasa apso, from a local pet store. Nora kept the teeny puppy in her hotel room and the two women giggled as they tried to train the animal. Julie was her normal perky self.

But then Julie was taken from class one morning. An urgent long-distance call from home, she was told as she raced down the hall. Her mother's breast cancer had metastasized, she was told; the prognosis was not good. Julie began weeping, crying so hard she could not continue with her seminar classes. "She can't cope," thought Nora, helping Julie pack to go home.

Julie was a wonderful daughter to Mary Jane. The true nurse, intuitively knowing her every feeling and wish. As an AT&T manager, Julie would arrange free long-distance conference calls so her mother could talk to her friend Pauline Rivers, now living in New Orleans, and another friend in Memphis. When Mary Jane was better, Julie arranged for a visit to Pauline, and she took in all her mother's clothes after she lost weight from chemotherapy. Mary Jane was forever praising her. Julie never complained about her burden as her mother never complained about hers.

It was a Saturday night. Julie was sitting at her desk at home meticulously taking care of medical bills and filling out insurance claim forms. She did this often; someone had to. A friend had called that afternoon about a double date, but Julie said no, as she did when another friend had asked her to go shopping, and as she did when a colleague suggested a matinee movie. Julie did not want to leave her mother.

Mary Jane rustled in her bedroom and Julie ran in. "Do you need anything Mommy?" she asked. "Can I get you anything to drink?"

"Next Saturday, if I do well after the chemotherapy," Mary Jane began, "let's go look at antique jewelry." Mary Jane fancied a diamond pin she had seen. Julie's friends worried that pushing her mother's wheelchair to the jewelry counter was the outer limit of weekend fun for her.

Julie returned to her desk. She was preoccupied, if not obsessed, with working with the oncologists. She was over-whelmed by details and emotions.

Mary Jane, who had been fun-loving herself, worried that her daughter did not enjoy life. Her last words to Carter were: "Make your sister laugh more," she said with a smile. "We had you for comic relief."

Her last request to Julie was take care of her brother. No one needed to remind Julie of responsibility.

The most emotional moment of Julie's life came two weeks after her twenty-ninth birthday, in 1983. Julie and Carter alternated spending nights camped out in a chair in Mary Jane's private hospital room. Their father had died two floors away.

Tonight it was Julie's turn. Watching the person she most loved, the one she was closest to, her own mother, writhe in pain, Julie felt as though her heart was being torn out. She would go over to Mary Jane, wipe her brow, and say, "It's okay to go now, you don't need to be brave anymore." Then, she would pad down the hall to get the nurses to bring the morphine. Finally, Mary Jane was free of pain and sleeping.

Julie curled up in the chair and dozed off.

Suddenly, she awoke with a start. The sun was coming up. She heard a long sigh. It came from Mary Jane.

"I walked over to her bed and I heard her last breath," Julie told Carter. "I leaned over and touched her. She was gone."

It meant everything to Julie to have been with her mother at her last moment. And she wanted a perfect funeral, too. As they made the arrangements, Julie told Carter how touched Mary Jane had been with his gift of red roses on Mother's Day, so they sent a dozen to the funeral home. Before the casket was closed for the last time, Julie placed a rose in her mother's arms.

It was a gesture Carter would repeat three years later for his sister.

Julie's friends came to the funeral worried about her, but she was extraordinarily calm and composed. Dry-eyed and well-groomed, Julie told Nora, "Mommy would have wanted me to look this way. She would have expected me to handle this."

That night, Julie walked into their house and demanded that her brother come outside. "Look at this," she said, pointing to the shrubbery covered with bagworms. Hours after they buried their mother, Julie and Carter filled buckets with the insects. Julie was compelled to bring order back into her life. Things must be nice, no matter what.

"She never broke down and cried," Nora worried. All Julie said was, "I need to be careful, because I wouldn't want someone to marry me for my money."

Julie returned to being fun-loving, but at the same time doubled her attention to her career, especially how she presented herself at work. The little girl who had worn immaculate little dresses now wore proper business attire: suits conservatively cut by Evan-Picone and Jones of New York, shoes always mid-heel, closed-toe pumps. Her blouses stayed so fresh after twelve-hour days that her colleagues marveled at her appearance. She frequently added a piece or two from her mother's antique jewelry collection, but never anything ostentatious. She always looked nice.

Julie worked hard and was well compensated at Southwestern Bell Corporation, where she had transferred after a blood-letting at AT&T. (Julie needed the sense of cradle-to-grave security of a large corporation.) But Julie considered herself undeserving of her position; she felt that her job just happened to come along at the right time, and that she had done nothing to earn it. Bell, however, disagreed, advancing her quickly.

Southwestern Bell Corporation, one of the Baby Bells, has 125 subsidiaries, and its downtown St. Louis skyscraper is the headquarters for a five-state region covering Missouri, Kansas, Texas, Oklahoma, and Arkansas. Bell is tiered in a hierarchy not unlike the federal government, with management beginning at level sixteen. Julie was at level twenty-two with an annual salary in the high thirties by 1985. She was in a competitive environment of ambitious thirty- to forty-year-olds, and had several colleagues cum friends, such as Nora Talcott, but few friends outside the office.

Nora had not realized how lonely Julie was until one day at lunch. "If I ever get married," Julie said. "I want you to be my maid of honor."

Nora tried to hide her surprise. She thought they had been

only work friends, since they never socialized outside the office. "It hit me how Julie didn't know how to make friends. But it was not that she didn't want to."

Julie, alone in the house she had inherited, felt abandoned. Carter had married and moved out, and it was lonely working by herself all day in a cubicle and then coming home to a three-bedroom house empty except for the yapping of a tiny dog and the tinkle of a cat's bell. Her calico cat, Precious, and her mother's black and white Lhasa apso, Buttons, were all she had. To keep herself busy, Julie went back to sewing and handicraft, cross-stitching a coverlet for her brother's wedding present.

That winter Precious, now fourteen, died, and Julie and Carter took the body to a pet cemetery. Julie was weeping. She had buried her mother less than six months ago, and now this. She turned and said, "Why don't we say something?" She paused. "Thank God for all the joy this animal brought us." Julie stopped crying and smiled. "She became light-hearted," Carter said, "although she had been slammed once more against the wall."

Perhaps fearing or distrusting people, Julie turned to animals. Besides caring for Buttons, she volunteered her services at the local dog pound and at the wildlife rescue center. For her birthdays, per her request, Carter made Zoo donations whereby Julie "adopted" two black rhinoceroses and a seal which she and her brother would visit and feed. Julie wished the outings were more frequent. She was peeved that Carter spent so much time with his wife's family.

With her mother gone, Julie lost her purpose in life. There was no one to whom she could give her affection. Knowing how empty Julie's life had become, a sweet-faced middle-aged neighbor, Molly Flowers, tried to fill in emotionally as one of Julie's several surrogate mothers. Two other older women helped— Mary Jane's friend Pauline Riviers and an executive colleague of Julie's named Jane Muster.

Once, when Julie was leaving her neighbor's house, Molly hugged her goodbye. She stepped back, apparently surprised. Julie returned a few days later and said, "I came back for a hug. That's part of my problem, not showing my feelings."

Julie decided to give her first party. Unfortunately, Mary Jane, too ill for years to entertain, had set no example. Throwing a Tupperware party for the women in the neighborhood, Julie prepared a huge table of food. She was so excited that Molly thought it sad.

Julie had another problem: the proverbial boss from hell. Julie wrote course materials for executive training programs. Her sadistic superior would critique her work by measuring the margins of her typescript with a ruler and by belittling Julie. She would be in tears, and all the long way home the other riders in her vanpool would try to calm her down. Julie did not know how to stand up for herself, let alone fight back.

According to vanpooler Jane Muster, "As much fun as she was, as effervescent as she was, she was very lonely, very timid, and very easily led. Julie at heart was a good little girl who always did what people would expect or want her to do. Anybody with a strong personality could sway her." Her need for approval suffocated any sense of self.

Julie's appearance began to reflect her inner misery. She quit lightening her dark blond hair and opted for the mid-eighties, chin-length, cookie-cutter perm that made drab her small features and pretty coloring. She became, said another executive, "a mousey little girl who always tried to smile."

Julie elaborated on her fantasy of Prince Charming rescuing her from her tower of loneliness. All she had to do was find Him. Then life would be sunny, work easy, and her biggest problem decorating the house for a Martha Stewart Christmas. When she was not fretting about her unadorned fourth finger, Julie fell head-over-heels in love with every new date.

"Tell me a little something about yourself," the radio talk show host said to Julie.

She dutifully recited her vital statistics for the late-night dating call-in show.

"Don't worry," Julie later explained to Nora. "I'm going to be very careful about any men I meet this way. Any man who looks promising will be checked out. And I'll meet them somewhere other than home. I'm not going to let one of these guys in until I know him."

Molly encouraged her to meet other singles at church or community activities. But Julie was too shy to handle strange groups. Her longest relationship had been more off- then on-again for years. And the man was not husband material.

Sometimes, her social life consisted of male colleagues, some of whom were married. Part of that may have stemmed from her obvious lack of social skills. "And maybe that was her way of rebelling," said Jane Muster. "For once, she would no longer be the good little girl."

The single men she dated were no great catches either. "Julie was a lure to creeps," Nora said. "She wasn't discriminating enough. They only had to look good on paper, be professional, nice-looking and earn a decent income. She became fixated over anyone in a three-button suit. The worst part was she would buy them with gifts. After two weeks of dating one single co-worker, his birthday came up. Julie went out and spent three hundred dollars on golf clothes for the man."

Nora pointed out to Julie that if she did not want a man to want her for her money, she certainly used it as a lure.

"She lost her life giving it away," Nora said.

With or without a husband, Julie returned to her nest and began renovating her house. It was a two-and-a-half-year project. At daily lunches with Nora, Julie would display fabric samples and paint chips. "Everything has to be just so," she said. The two women coordinated all the rooms in soft shades of ecru, mint, peach, and rose with dear little touches: Louis XIV-style fauteuils, oils of daisies, needleworked pictures of gingham dogs and calico cats that went perfectly with Julie's adorable collection of teddy bears.

Returning to her sewing room, she would whip up the balloon shades. Watching television, she would embroider and do crewel work. As long as she remained lost in redecorating, Julie's self-esteem was as plumped up as the pillows she made. She never complained about the workmen underfoot for whole seasons at a time.

Julie invited the nurseryman for a candlelight dinner in gratitude for his landscaping work. The next morning she showed up in Molly's kitchen. "I had a wonderful time last night," she said, handing Molly her diary. It was filled with lyrical descriptions of making love with the nurseryman. Dying for affection, Julie savored the cuddling after sex.

But there was no follow through on the part of the landscaper. He was recouping from a divorce and had a business to run, he claimed.

"But we had a relationship," Julie said, "we slept together." She showed up unannounced at his office and called him there repeatedly. Julie's one-night stand told his employees to tell her he was out or busy.

This was a repeat performance of other dates. Julie would cling to them, too. Her loneliness became an abyss. It was like tumbling down a long, dark, cold, wet well. Julie began seeing an employee's assistance program counselor at Bell, who sent her to a psychiatrist.

Doctors do not provide affection and affiliation. Julie would cling to co-workers, crying for hours on the phone at night. One kind soul, Sam Lamonte, tried to help.

"Julie was lonesome, very lonesome, like an animal left alone, like prey," said Lamonte. "You just hoped she wouldn't be taken advantage of. She was very naïve. A smooth talker could snake his way into anything with her. She suffered from the delusion that meeting Mr. Right would solve all her problems. Julie was dying to get married."

Seven

"He Looks Good on Paper"

May–September 1985

How could a career woman like Julie be so naïve, worried Molly Flowers. Julie had come over "for a hug" and was telling Molly about her plan.

"All I have to do to be happy is to meet Mr. Right," she said. "And I know a way to find him."

"I'll run an ad in the *The Riverfront Times*," a gutsy weekly newspaper with a personal *Eligibles* column, she said. She had carefully written her advertisement:

Are you a "Really Nice Guy?" If yes, this "Nice Girl" wants you to read on. I'm single, white and female, 30 years, 5'2", 125 lbs, whose appearance is pleasing to the eyes. My 9–5 life is professional. Other time is combination creative and suburban homebody. I've realized life without a boyfriend isn't all that much fun.

You are the type of man who's emotionally mature, likes himself (but not egotistically), and wants a girlfriend, hopefully, you're 29–36 years, 5'9" or over, weight proportionate, with looks that are easy on the eyes, and no children from a previous marriage. Send brief letter and phone no. Let's meet for coffee & something "really nice" could happen for both of us.

Molly frowned. "Are you sure this is safe?"

"I'll check out all replies first, where they work and where they live," Julie said. "Only then will I meet them. And only then for lunch. I'm not going to bring anyone bad home. What could be safer?"

In her analytical way, Julie thought she knew what mattered in a relationship. Carter feared his sister's overeagerness to walk down the aisle would become entrée to divorce court. "She didn't know what she needed, on paper or in her heart."

Julie was pleased with the many responses to her query. The best one came in early August, 1985, months after she had run her ad in the Memorial Day edition of *The Riverfront Times*. It was from a man with an M. B. A., a career as a senior management consultant at Price Waterhouse, and a house in a respectable suburb. He was a member of the Young Republicans and the Friends of the Art Museum and the Zoo, and belonged to the Classical Guitar Society. He was thirty-two, getting divorced, and had no children. Best of all, his photocopied picture would delight any blind date. He was movie-star handsome.

His name was Dennis Neal Bulloch.

"He looks good on paper," Julie told Molly. "What could be safer?"

To be sure, Julie checked out Mr. Bulloch. She looked up his telephone number on Southwestern Bell's database and tracked how he handled paying his phone bills. When he cleared that hurdle, she called a friend at Price Waterhouse to confirm Dennis was indeed a senior consultant there.

Feeling he was trustworthy, she decided to "take a chance on success" as he called it in his letter. Scared, she dialed his number several times and hung up before finally leaving a message on his home phone recorder. The next day, he returned the call.

They made a date for lunch downtown near their offices for August 14, 1985.

Julie was up extra early the morning of their first meeting, trying on various outfits. She finally chose a different color than she had told her blind date she would be wearing and worried whether that would surprise him.

Julie did surprise her vanpool that morning by discussing her lunch date. Never before had she mentioned her social life. But this seemed so exciting that she passed around Dennis Bulloch's Xeroxed photograph.

"Oh, Julie, he has the cruelest eyes I've ever seen," said one woman, feeling protective.

Stung, Julie replied, "Well, I'm meeting him today to see how he is."

By lunchtime, Julie was so tense she could barely swallow her hamburger. Dennis Bulloch was the clean-cut All-American cliché: nearly six feet tall, with a lean muscular body, and a thatch of strawberry-blond hair sunbleached as if from laps in the country club pool, blue eyes, and even, regular Anglo-Saxon features. He had the looks made for the button-downs and Weejuns he favored.

Dennis was equally impressed with Julie, but for different reasons. He approved of her conversational level and the way she dressed. He could tell she was a professional. Best of all, he was flattered; here was a woman on the same executive level as his estranged wife, even from the same company, who had gone to a lot of trouble to meet him. *She* would appreciate his "potential."

Julie went home and wrote in her diary, "Then lunch at the Branded Bagel on 8–14–85 . . . Then phone calls followed until I said I was going in the hospital. That Thursday night, 9–19–85, you volunteered to come over and talk to me."

When Dennis saw Julie's house, he was impressed. While not like those of the socialites he dated from the poshest suburbs, this was certainly of a magnitude superior to what he had come from. As he began courting Julie, Dennis noticed the extensive and expensive jewelry collection she had inherited from her mother. The collection was appraised at a higher value than his parents' bungalow.

Dennis said the loss of Julie's mother and his sister to cancer drew them together. It was more than that; both outwardly conformed to society's expectations. Hand her a list of things to do from one through ten and Julie would complete it in order. Dennis, however, was a poseur; it was easier for him to follow a role, for he would not know how to behave without one. Appearance was everything.

They both kept diaries, filling them with greeting card maxims and what F. Scott Fitzgerald called the philosophy of popular songs. Their psyches dovetailed, too, in ominous ways. For Dennis, how much was too much? As for Julie, she felt she could not do enough for him. Dennis was unable to trust or to be trustworthy himself, and Julie was too naïvely trusting. Self-absorbed, Dennis was oblivious to the pain he inflicted on others, while Julie was so attuned to everyone else's emotional nuances, she was unaware of her own.

A major value difference was illustrated in why each became a Friend of the Zoo: Julie because she loved animals, with whom she felt a kindred spirit; Dennis because he loved the rich people who attended the annual Zoofari charity ball.

Three weeks after their August lunch date, Julie was discussing with her friends her future with Dennis. Dennis, on the other hand, was not thinking of her. He filled his diary with descriptions of the weather and hotels in California during a trip he made with a girlfriend, and later pasted in his ticket stub from the McEnroe vs. Borg match at St. Louis's Kiel Auditorium on November 15, 1985. There is no mention anywhere about Julie Miller.

Early on in his courtship of Julie Miller, Dennis lunched with his best friend, Cal Porterfield. As he munched on his club sandwich, Dennis told Cal he had met a woman through her newspaper ad who seemed nice.

He said, "She reminds me of Karen," his estranged wife. "Both are bright, attractive, and literally on the same career track.

"Don't tell Karen," Dennis kept repeating.

That was the first and last time Dennis mentioned his future wife to the man he called his best friend. But he refused to reveal her name.

Years later, when he was forced to acknowledge her, Dennis said Julie flattered him. His bloated ego had been punctured when his wife walked out on him. And now this career woman, Julie, with a healthy inheritance who appeared so strong and so self-confident, had only one interest when she came home: taking care of Dennis Bulloch. When she was not paying attention to him, she was running errands for him, dropping off his clothes at the cleaners and picking up his prescriptions at the drugstore.

While Julie devoted herself to him, Dennis was sleeping with, buying gifts for, and playing suitor to numerous other women.

But only Julie would do whatever he wanted, whenever he wanted, however he wanted. She was a copy of his first wife, but one he could control. Julie had even ceased to be Miss Prim, having gone out and bought a collection of body oils with which to pamper Dennis.

By the time he was divorced in December, Dennis thought Julie was "real close" to his long-searched for ideal. She could be the One Who Would Help Him Achieve His "Potential." She was worth more than $300,000. He was not exactly besotted with Julie herself, but her money could be a real boon to his real estate ambitions.

Julie had at long-last found what appeared to be a corporate Prince Charming. Her ideal relationship, she used to say, was one in which the alarm went off at six A.M. and both partners hit the ground running for their careers.

But Mr. Right was not enough. Julie grew more and more depressed. Her insecurity was frightening to friends, although to some non-intimates she appeared self-confident.

Something was wrong, Nora Talcott sensed, as she and Julie made their way through the food mall on the mezzanine of Union Station, where they were lunching in late September, 1985. Julie seemed more melancholic now over her mother's death than when she had died two years ago. Julie was oddly quiet, not even commenting on the new clothes for fall or the hot weather.

The women walked around awhile before deciding which ethnic food to eat and made their way in silence. It was only after they had gone through the lines, ordered their selections and were seated that Julie made her announcement.

"I'm admitting myself into a psych ward," she said.

"Why?" asked Nora.

Julie did not specify. "I'm so miserable," she said. "I've tried everything I know of at work to get transferred from my boss, but no one will listen."

"I walked away thinking, 'Is she doing this to get transferred?' " Nora said. "Then I realized she really was depressed, even if she had hidden it. It had been accumulating for years."

Jane Muster and the vanpoolers were shocked when Julie said she was taking disability leave to enter a hospital. "But if you have a woman who grew up with an uninvolved father and an overprotective mother," Jane pointed out, "then you have a woman unable to cope."

Julie could not always mask her illness. At a jeweler's she and her mother had patronized for years, she dawdled over several pairs of earrings, trying them on, studying them in the mirror. Uncertain what to buy, she turned around and asked:

"Mommy, what do you think I should get?"

The jeweler looked around for Mrs. Miller, then realized she had been dead for two years.

Julie's brother did not believe it when she announced she was going into St. John's Mercy psychiatric ward. "Why?" Carter kept asking.

Julie bit her lip, then said, "Because Dennis thinks it's a good idea."

"Dennis who?" he asked.

Eight

Answers in a Photo Album

September 19–November 14, 1985

"I'm going to throw acid on my face," Julie wept over the phone. She had never become hysterical before, let alone threatened self-mutilation. "I feel so ugly," she cried to her neighbor.

Her neighbor hurried over. After she had been calmed down, Julie called her psychiatrist.

Please put me in a hospital, she pleaded. I want to go somewhere where they'll take care of me as my mommy did and I did for her.

I turned to my brother for help, she explained. He failed to give me what I want, so I got angry and started to mutilate my face. Then I stopped and called my neighbor, who's gone now, Julie told her psychiatrist, Dr. Melvin Meagher.

Not wanting to be alone, Julie phoned Dennis Bulloch, who had been calling her since their first date at lunch a month ago, August 14.

Dennis volunteered to come over. Nervous, Julie scurried about cleaning up the house and showering to make everything nice and presentable. As she finished applying make-up over her red, puffy face, Dennis arrived, carrying a bottle of wine. Julie was touched.

I feel very close to Dennis, she wrote in her diary describing the traumatic night. Dennis was so masterful, so soothing, so in control.

How much did Dennis realize about Julie's weakened condition that night, September 19, 1985? Dennis never discussed her with his friends or therapists, except once with Cal Portersfield. He liked to say he had no idea Julie was deranged until after he had married her. Yet, he took her to the psychiatric ward September 23, according to records at St. John's Mercy Medical Center, where Julie remained for seven and a half weeks. The hospital has a fine reputation. But Julie hated it.

As she walked along the halls, Julie clutched her teddy bear. The stuffed animal was her only solace. And her shield. Instead of talking directly to the staff or other patients, Julie would communicate through her teddy bear. At home she often carried one around, in front of friends, as if to illustrate what she needed. At St. John's, Julie took her teddy everywhere, frequently stopping to embrace it.

After a week of treatment with mild tranquilizers, Julie was put on Thorazine, a strong anti-psychotic drug. She was diagnosed as suffering from affective disorder/depressed. Depression in America is as common as the head cold; major depression is like waking up with a cold, wet army blanket covering one's entire face and body and then trying to get through the day. Affective disorders are characterized by thinking negatively.

Julie suffered them all, the four contemporary Horsemen of the Apocalypse—guilt, anxiety, loneliness, and lousy self-esteem. All are common to depression.

In addition, Julie had hysterical overtones, obsessive-compulsive personality features, and borderline personality disorder features, according to her doctors. Hysteria is gross overreaction, such as mutilating one's face because it is not pretty enough. Obsessive-compulsives both think and act in repeated patterns they cannot control.

When her psychiatrists noted that Julie had traits of borderline personality disorders, they were subscribing to what is a popular diagnosis these days. Borderlines, basically, have unformed personalities. They usually lack firm ideals, goals, and interests.

Borderlines are personality disorders, along with narcissists, passive-aggressives, hysterics and psychopaths/sociopaths. People with personality disorders have chaotic feelings rather than the specific feelings. They feel discomfort and pain but have little idea of what triggered the emotion. They tend to lack the internal rudder that guides and steadies most adults through life. Situational ethics are their battle cry. Many personality disordered patients float between the categories. (In contrast to Julie, Dennis Bulloch was diagnosed originally as a narcissist and later as a psychopath.) Patients with milder non-psychopathic disorders often behave like teenagers; they are selfish and rebellious.

Julie may have been misdiagnosed. Her diagnosis looks like a Chinese banquet menu, with two from the depression column, three from the disorders column—in the words of an internationally recognized psychiatrist on depression. Julie's behaviors were typical of bipolar depression in which all kinds of symptoms come and go. These patients swing violently between melancholia and mania, between deepest despondency and the-sky's-the-limit optimism.

Severely depressed people who are passive and dependent can mimic borderlines. Desperate for attachment, this person says in effect, "I am whoever you want me to be. Just tell me what to do. Just don't leave me." Imagine this patient's psyche as being like a wedge of Swiss cheese. A dominant person can easily move in and out of it.

Julie's friends believe that her weakened condition made it easy for Dennis Bulloch to dominate her. He had longed for a woman he could control, even exploit. Julie and Dennis were made for each other, at least until she became well. She would do almost anything to keep him.

Most women have dated a creep or two who have treated them like a doormat. Afterward, they are immune to this type for the rest of their lives. Julie was murdered before she could learn from her mistake.

Why did Julie tolerate Dennis's abuse? She may have been conditioned early on to such treatment, Dr. Meagher believed. Julie attributed her problems with self-esteem to her job at Bell; her doctors did not. She was too repressed to realize how unhealthy her family had been. Dr. Meagher called her relationship to her father "disturbed."

He also said Julie held "deep-seated, unresolved feelings" about her mother over the last three years of Mary Jane's life. While nursing her dying mother, Julie had perpetuated her dependency. Even after she had buried Mary Jane she was afraid of expressing herself.

In summary, Julie had three major problems: She was too close to her mother, too far away from her father, and her own identity was blurred and embryonic. All three problems intertwined. The more her father ignored his daughter, the more Julie felt worthless and the more she fled to her mother's lap for comforting. The more her mommy cradled Julie, the more helpless she felt. Feeling inadequate, Julie crumbled at her father's neglect.

There may have been an uglier side to Carter Miller senior's emotional abandonment. Dr. Meagher believed her father may have sexually abused Julie. Mary Jane's overprotection may not have been inappropriate, says one doctor. How would most parents treat a violated child?

It was not certain whether Julie had been molested as a child and whether her father did it. Sexually abused children often bury the incidents so completely that decades later only flashes of recognition become conscious. Dr. Meagher believed that someone in the family did something awful to Julie. She was killed before she could resurrect the memory of who it might have been.

Had Julie been abused, that meant she would have been less able to resist Dennis. Abused children are violated in their psyches as well as their bodies. Their ability to trust can be devastating. And, they may be unable to build fences to keep out dangerous people. Which makes them prone to exploitation. Being exploited further erodes self-esteem, which limits the ability to assert oneself against brutality. That leads toward more helplessness and passivity.

After Julie's first week in St. John's psychiatric ward, her neighbor Molly Flowers came to visit her. Her neighbor was pleased that Julie seemed so ebullient. "Dad really did love me," she proclaimed. "All I have to do is look for the ways he showed it."

But, as the doctors had warned, she crashed about ten days

after hospitalization, around early October. Fifty milligrams of Tofranil, a tricyclic anti-depressant, was prescribed. Julie became incoherent, talking in symbols and riddles. Often she spoke through her teddy bear. When Julie was lucid the message was frightening:

"How dare my doctor assume my daddy did something to me!" she cried to one nurse. To another she confided, "The only contact I had with him was when I was punished." After which she cried and added that what she wanted most was for her father to hold her.

Julie became psychotic.

One morning, a nurse walked in her room as Julie turned the radio on. She began sobbing, then looked up at the nurse. "The song is crying," she said. "The radio station KS-94 FM has special meaning. The FM stands for father and mother along with motherfucker," she told a staffer.

Despite her illness, Julie maintained her good grooming, with manicured nails and appropriate clothes. She was eager to please even when hysterical, the nurses noted. No matter how mad she was, Julie at age thirty-one remained the good child. She even referred to herself "as a little girl even though I know I am not."

She saw the staff as *in loco parentis*. A nurse noted, "She wants us to tell her what right things to do so she can get our approval, do it right, and never have to return here." Julie assumed they had all the answers. She expected unconditional mothering from the women and direction from the men.

"I need discipline to help me open the emotional doors," Julie told a nurse. She drew a heart on the blackboard in the sitting room and wrote beside it, "Because the children need love." She said she wanted the staff to approve of her and "the other children."

Yet, Julie hated how they treated her, telling her housekeeper that she lacked privacy—the nurses were always eavesdropping on her, always watching her. Her housekeeper knew how much that must have bothered Julie, who was so private that she had not even told the woman the name of her new boyfriend. (Julie was not being paranoid. The nurses checked up on her every two hours and kept copious notes of everything she did and said.)

The most pathetic image is that of Julie the successful professional in her thirties clutching her teddy bear as she went to therapy and meals; she carried him everywhere, day and night, even on passes. She would cry into the stuffed animal and hold it the way she wanted to be held herself.

Desperate for love, Julie's delusions became grandiose. She was overheard saying on the phone, "Mr. President [Reagan]— he's like a big brother to me and I need a brother-to-sister talk. I'll mail the letter today by Federal Express or maybe Air Force One can get it." Julie spent hours on the phone with friends and family, alternately crying and laughing.

Frequently she called Dennis at Price Waterhouse, leaving messages for him and saying she was in St. John's. The receptionist recognized her voice. Dennis frequently took Julie out on passes. And, to cheer her up, he sent her signed cards which Julie proudly flashed to friends and her housekeeper.

By late October, Julie was both manic and psychotic, suffering delusions of being a prophet of God. Dressed in scrubs and red high heels, Julie proclaimed that she and another female patient were "soul sisters" who were writing "a cosmic book" together. She wanted Carter to have her favorite cross because "Pope John XXIII gave it to me personally."

Her doctors wrote, "She has bizarre preoccupations with religious, sexual, lesbian, and grandiose thoughts, incoherent psychotic statements about herself and the world and her family." All signs of the manic stage of bipolar depression.

Another symptom of mania is sexual acting out, inappropriate sexual behavior. The Poor Little Match Girl was transformed into the Vamp, who came on to male patients and staffers, including one insufferable boor who assumed he was a real stud. With a younger patient, Julie stood at his door holding hands with him while gazing into his eyes. With a male visitor, Julie pulled up her blouse and exposed her midriff.

Julie said she had done "kinky" things in bed, "that her sexual behavior had gotten her in trouble," but never described it. It may not have been all that decadent, at least according to her former lovers. Was it sleeping with married men? Oral sex? Bondage with Dennis? Bondage would not have been her idea, having once told her housekeeper how "gross" she thought leather and chains and all that stuff were. This femme fatale

image does not fit with the Julie who had been terribly embarrassed when her housekeeper found a photo in a bedroom
drawer. In the picture, she wore a black nightgown.

Julie's counselor at Bell—through their Employee Assistance
Program—came to see her and tell her she seemed fine and
should return to work soon. That night, Julie had another psychotic episode.

Julie was kept on Tofranil, the anti-depressant, but was per-
mitted passes. An anti-psychotic drug, Stelazine, was added. By
Halloween, 1985, when she had been institutionalized five
weeks, Julie was not allowed off the floor unless supervised. She
was to be dressed in scrubs and tied down and strapped to her
bed, if necessary. She would refuse her medicine. As the nurse
gave her the drugs, she screamed, "You're doing Dad's dirty
work."

Her condition worsening, Julie was transferred to 5C West, a
locked ward. Drugs were to be given without her consent. She
became suicidal. She was quite mad. After staying up all night,
she waved a plastic wand, saying, "It reminds one of borderland," and danced down the hallway. Julie never explained
what "borderland" was.

Calmer the next day, she sat sobbing and hugging her teddy
bear. Her crying continued for an hour as she begged for help, "I
need a magic tranquilizer." After a mega-strength dose of anti-
psychotic medication, Stelazine, Julie hurried into the dining
room and wolfed down paper napkins. Manics sometimes believe that there are dangerous messages on paper, which must
be hidden.

Despite these symptoms, Julie was given passes and left the
hospital on November 1, which another psychiatrist said is
"bizarre medical treatment, terrible medicine." Taking Haldol, a
potent anti-psychotic drug precludes leaving the hospital, the
physician said. Did Meagher not think she might hurt herself
while in this manic state? Such as picking up a Mr. Goodbar?
Going out and buying a new house? Marrying a wacko such as
Dennis Bulloch? Allowing herself to be tied up?

Julie said she was "attempting to put the pieces of the puzzle
together." She believed the answer to why she was so depressed
lay in the family history. When Mary Jane's brother visited, she

would question him about the lives of her parents. One evening, Julie excitedly returned from a day trip home. Along with her ubiquitous teddy bear, she was carrying a family photo album.

"I'm looking for the answers in a photo album," she said. "The key to my emotional problems."

She proudly showed the album to one of her new friends, Mike. He smiled at the pictures of a seemingly normal family of father, mother, daughter and son, everyone happy and laughing into the camera.

The Julie turned a page. Everybody suddenly looked like zombies, Mike thought.

"Why such a dramatic change?" he asked.

"Something terrible happened to me when I was a little girl," Julie said. "That explains why I'm here." But Julie never would explain to anyone what had taken place.

One evening, while talking with a nurse, Julie spoke nonstop, "crying and grieving the loss of her father." Julie said the photos of Mary Jane in her album showed that her mother watched over her.

She always was throwing out these clues to friends visiting her. Julie confided to one woman that what had happened caused a particular personality trait of hers. But she never explained what it was.

Mike believed the clue to some deep trauma lay in the photos. The pictures told a story. If someone could translate it.

Julie's religious delusions persisted. She talked of crucifixion and a scheme of rebirth requiring twenty-five years of therapy, which is long even for psychoanalysis. "There are sublime messages coming from the static in the TV, especially cable." Julie said she was psychic not psychotic. And she said she had total control over TV programming. Something station managers do not even have.

By November 11, nearly seven weeks after she had entered St. John's Medical Center, Julie was better, back in the land of the semi-rational. She remained enchained by the dead; indeed, Julie never broke her pitiful attachment to her dead mother. Not only was she transferred to a regular ward, she was allowed out again. She visited her parents' graves on Veterans Day, November 12, in Veterans' Cemetery at Jefferson Barracks, an army post dating back to the Civil War. Eleven days after she was to be tied down on her bed, if needed, Julie was allowed to come and go as she pleased.

After fifty-two days of hospitalization for depression, Julie was sent home November 14, armed with her anti-psychotic medicine and a list of appointments with Dr. Meagher. It was noted that Julie would do anything to avoid abandonment. "She seems loose and disconnected, but not dangerous," her psychiatrist wrote. If psychosis is no big deal, what is? questions an expert.

But the danger was not from within.

Nine

"She Was Like Prey"

Thanksgiving, 1985–February 21, 1986

A few weeks after she was released from St. John's Medical Center, Julie was not only considerably less depressed, she was excited about the upcoming 1985 holiday season. She would no longer have to face Thanksgiving, Christmas, and New Year's Eve alone. She had found somebody who cared for her and took care of her. Dennis had been so solicitous during her psychiatric ordeal; he was both the old-fashioned Prince Charming and the New Sensitive Man.

Julie planned to introduce her new beau at a family holiday dinner at her aunt and uncle's. Dennis must have been impressed, for the house stood in a posh suburb and Julie's cousins were all professionals, as was her brother. Yet, he did not mix. Carter found Dennis stiff, distant and aloof, uninterested in both the people and their conversations. But Carter's wife was thrilled for her sister-in-law. "What a catch," she said. "He's so successful and so handsome."

Molly Flowers agreed when Julie brought Dennis to a neighborhood Christmas party. He was so clean, neat and well-dressed, and well-spoken, just like her little Julie. "Why, if they get married, with all their stocks and real estate, they'll have it made," she told her husband. "What a wonderful asset to our community. This is someone Julie deserves."

Julie sat quietly while her hairdresser trimmed her perm. She had been going to him for nine years, following him whenever he changed shops. Equally loyal, the hairdresser was worried about her. Before her breakdown, Julie had been ebullient, chatting and laughing with all the regulars in the small Clayton shop. Now she was so incoherent and jumpy from medication, he wondered how she could have driven over.

"The medicine they gave me in the hospital made me do crazy stuff," Julie said. "I'm very frightened," she told him. She gave no details.

Julie sat at her desk at Southwestern Bell. It was her fourth day back at work full-time and already she felt claustrophobic in her cubicle. She could hear muffled voices down the corridor, which made her feel isolated from other people.

It's hopeless, she thought. I feel as though I'm trapped in a cage. While running errands last night for Dennis, she had fantasized about driving her car into a pole or a wall. I know that's sick, Julie thought, and told Dr. Meagher, her psychiatrist.

"I'm so lethargic, too," she said during her next appointment. "All I want to do is sleep."

"How much do you sleep?" he asked.

"On weekends I go to bed between four and six in the afternoon," she said, "and don't get up until seven or eight the next morning."

Julie was hospitalized again for severe depression—a week during Christmas at St. Luke's West Hospital. She was given lithium carbonate, the standard treatment to alleviate the mood swings in manic depression. Julie felt safe at St. Luke's, safe enough to confide:

"I twice tried to escape from St. John's Mercy locked unit," she told them. "Depression runs in both sides of my family. My mother had suffered it when her own father had died. My father's mother died in a psychiatric institution.

"My life has been uneventful," she told the social worker taking her history. "I am a person to whom things happen.

"I have no interests other than sewing and crocheting. I wish I could find some direction to my life but I don't know what I want or where to begin," she said. "There are only four people in my life—my brother, my sister-in-law, my dog, and my boyfriend," Julie told the psychiatrist. "My boyfriend is very concerned about me," she added.

"My problems all began a decade ago, 1975, when both my mother and my father became terminally ill. When my father died, I couldn't cope. Mommy always protected me from everything, even while she was dying.

"Nursing my parents had become my excuse to avoid the dating scene."

As always, Julie worked diligently on her diary, a "journal of my feelings." When one of her friends visited her, Julie started to give the woman her diary for safekeeping, then said, "No. Not now. *But if anything ever happens to me, read my diary.*"

The staff found Julie to have good insight and fair judgment. Melancholic as she was again—Julie told a therapist she was "fighting for her sanity"—she was in better shape than during her first hospitalization: She realized she needed to find a new job and to socialize more.

Julie tried to make new friends. A female nurse about her age came into her room. Sitting in her chair, crocheting, Julie began talking about being a single thirty-one-year-old woman.

"I'd like to know where I could go to make new friends," she said.

"Try a Catholic singles group," suggested the nurse.

"When I get out, could we get together, go for lunch on our days off?" Julie asked.

"No," said the woman, "it's a bad idea for patients and staffers to have relationships outside the hospital." The nurse was more concerned with the oddity of Julie's request than what her brusque rejection would do to the patient's feelings.

Despite Julie's handicaps in relationships, Dr. Meagher felt she was quite sociable, capable of give-and-take and empathy, but just too dependent. Her method of handling conflicts was immature. Her temperament was one of sensitivity, persistence, and intensity. Other strengths, the doctor noted, were being very bright, very artistic, very creative.

What was a creative woman doing, then, in conforming corporate America? Julie had worked in Southwestern Bell's marketing department—briefly with Dennis's first wife—a creative place said to be fast-moving and high-risk. Too much so for Julie, who may have had the talent but not the personality for it. She later transferred to internal communications, called the "golden handshake:" good pay, good benefits and near cradle-to-grave job security. Julie's dependency was at war with her need for self-expression. Creativity lost to security.

What caused this second breakdown? Perhaps Julie had not recovered from the first or had been mismedicated. Dr. Meagher believed that Julie had suffered possible psychological neglect and abuse along with unresolved Oedipal confusion, possible scapegoating in the family, and possible sexual abuse.

Friends and relatives came to visit Julie and she was allowed frequent passes. On Christmas Day, 1985, with Carter at his in-laws and Dennis supposedly skiing, Julie had trotted over for-lornly to her next-door neighbors, the Flowers, for the holiday dinner. At least that is what she told Molly Flowers, who felt sorry for her. Dennis probably told Julie he would be gone for the holidays to excuse his crowded calendar of society balls and holiday suppers.

However, when Julie returned late Christmas night to St. Luke's, she told a staffer that she had been at Molly's and her aunt and uncle's and she had seen her boyfriend. Was she trying to make things sound better to be judged ready for release? Or was she merely embarrassed? Was she acting ma-nipulative with Molly Flowers for sympathy? Or was she fanta-sizing that she was wanted and loved?

When Julie was released from St. Luke's, her prognosis was "fair." She was to take her medicine and see Dr. Meagher five times a week. Her assigned goals sound eerie in retrospect: Learn to assess other people and yourself. Establish your own set of values, own identity, own self-worth.

After Julie returned home, Dennis stayed over (when he was not out of town). Suddenly, Julie was afraid of living alone. She could hear someone walking in the backyard at midnight, crunching on the snow. What if the prowler broke in? she asked friends, who never doubted something was going on. They wondered whether Dennis was playing *Gaslight* with Julie, who was heavily sedated. Was this connected to the anonymous phone calls she had received last fall?

Julie repeated that she would feel safer with a big dog around, in addition to her beloved Buttons. Dennis vetoed that idea. Instead, he convinced Julie into giving Buttons to her brother Carter. Until the day she died, Julie constantly begged him for "when there might be a dog." Dennis never gave her an answer.

Julie never fought back. As she wrote in her diary, "I have no self-esteem, self-confidence, especially sexual self-confidence. The drugs make me feel different." Even the smallest tasks were hard; food tasted differently. "But most of all, I am paralyzed with anxiety about my future."

In late January, Julie was tidying up the desk in her study at home. What's this? she wondered when she discovered a pocket pad of phone numbers. "It's not mine." Looking at it, she realized it belonged to Dennis. When he was at her house he made calls from this desk, with the door closed.

Doing what most people do, or at least think about doing, Julie opened the Pandora's box of Dennis's little black book. I wonder if I'm in his book, she thought, thumbing through the "M's" and found "Julie Miller." Relief. I am important to him, he does love me, she thought at first.

Oh, my God! Next to her name were her two Fidelity Investment account numbers. Trembling, Julie pulled out her own files. The numbers checked out. She looked further. Carefully written over his ex-wife Karen Toksvig's name were her Visa and Master Card account numbers.

Julie was reluctant to confront her lover because she had invaded his privacy. When she did mention it—as recorded on the fifty-minute audiotape she made for him in early April—rather than being outraged, Julie groveled and apologized. I shouldn't have snooped. I should have brought up my dastardly deed earlier. Oh, please, please forgive me, she whimpered. She pleaded with Dennis to tell her what issues they should keep private and where in her house she could smoke. Julie was both enthralled by and in thrall to Dennis.

Her friends tried to get her to go out more. One evening, after work, Julie and three women from Bell went to see a psychic. As

Julie walked into the woman's room, the psychic sensed that she did not like herself.

Neither Julie nor the psychic—who had known Dennis Bulloch for decades and found him dangerous and evil—realized they both knew Dennis. Instead, Julie called him by another name and described him as "an investment counselor."

Julie asked the psychic what the cards literally held for her, especially concerning her boyfriend. The psychic shuffled her deck of regular playing cards and spread them out.

"As I read them, a fear came over my heart," the psychic said. "I looked at the man in her cards and saw that he looked like the devil. I told her not to continue seeing the creep.

"I said, 'If you marry him, you'll be dead by May 8.' "

Dennis was pushing Julie to get married; he had been divorced December 20. He told her he did not approve of his sleeping over at Julie's (although he had lived with his first wife before their wedding).

"He thinks it looks bad," Julie told her brother and her friends. "He's scaring me, too," she added. "He says if I don't marry him, he'll leave me."

On Valentine's Day, a Friday, 1986, Julie was promoted at Bell and received a handsome salary increase. Thrilled, considering her misery with her former supervisor, she told Dennis that night. His response was to propose marriage. After a decade of waiting for this event, it did not feel right. Julie neither said yes nor no.

The following week, Julie and her colleague cum friend Terri Sacher were nibbling on club sandwiches at lunchtime.

"I don't know what to do," Julie confided. "I don't feel that he really loves me. I don't understand why he's so adamant I have to wear a wedding ring when he won't." She sipped her coffee and lit a cigarette, ruefully commenting that if she married Dennis she would have to quit smoking for him.

"But what bothers me the most is that he wants me to transfer all my inheritance into a joint account with him."

Terri looked up wide-eyed.

"I feel like he's just marrying me for my money."

Dennis had promised to contribute to the joint account, but it would be a fraction of Julie's more than $64,000—about $23,000.

Julie's house alone was worth $90,000, according to tax appraisals in 1985, in addition to her blue chip stocks and bonds. No mention was made of Dennis putting Julie's name on his stocks and bonds or on his real estate.

Julie was reluctant about the merger. But Dennis prevailed.

On Friday, February 21, Julie climbed into her vanpool with some startling news. "Dennis and I are getting married tomorrow," she announced.

The vanriders had been together for years and shared confidences during the ninety-minute rides every morning and night. They prided themselves on doing things together, like a family. When the group recovered from the surprise engagement, one man asked Julie if they were invited to her wedding.

"Dennis wants it private," Julie replied sheepishly. To change the subject, Jane Muster asked what she would wear.

"Oh, my light blue suit," Julie said. Nothing new. Jane asked about the flowers she would carry.

"Dennis doesn't want to spend the money," Julie said with her head down.

"We all felt terrible for her," said Jane, who gave the bride-to-be a dusty pink rose corsage that she had worn that day to a retirement party at Bell.

"Julie always said, 'Dennis doesn't want to spend his money.' But he did not mind spending hers." Dennis did not pass muster with Jane.

Julie also announced the wedding plans that day to her brother Carter and his wife Judy. Carter was shocked. "Julie had always dreamed of being a bride with all the trimmings, including a priest." Scurrying for gifts, Carter and Judy gave the bridal couple a gift certificate for bridal pictures and one of the three bottles of champagne they had bought during their honeymoon in France.

Touched, Julie told him: "Dennis and I will save this for a special occasion."

Dennis later said they drank it the night she died.

Ten

"Something Nice Will Happen"

February 22–April 2, 1986

Carter and his wife Judy waited with Julie the next morning, February 22, 1986, at the wedding chapel. It was called, ironically, considering Dennis's betrayals, the Church of the Open Word, and was, ironically, in Creve Coeur, French for "broken heart." The chapel was generic Protestant and impersonal. Carter was seething: How could Dennis pick an old converted farmhouse, so inappropriate for the celebration of one of life's major rituals? Julie was embarrassed.

"Dennis wants a small, out-of-the-way ceremony," she tried to explain. He had invited no one.

"Why does the wedding have to be so fast?" Carter asked. "No engagement ring. No wedding showers. No long white gown with veil."

"Dennis says it's a good idea and there's no reason to put it off," Julie replied. Carter felt sorry for her and asked no more questions.

While they were waiting in the chapel, a few miles away in

University City, Dennis and his ex-wife Karen Toksvig were wallpapering their house for sale. Karen was not amused when Dennis stopped midway, saying cryptically he had to leave. Karen wondered why he was all spruced up in his good navy blazer on a Saturday morning, reeking of Brut aftershave and wearing a carnation, of all things.

En route to his wedding, Dennis bumped into an acquaintance. "I've been having a lot of trouble dating since Karen and I split," he said.

As Dennis pulled up to the chapel, Julie was telling Carter and Judy why Dennis did not want a double-ring ceremony: If he wore a wedding band, it might catch on something and hurt his hand. The emergency rooms are packed with married men who lost their fingers in wedding band accidents.

The bridegroom walked in nonchalantly and said, "Let's get this going." He rushed his bride through the already brief ceremony. Carter and his wife took the newlyweds for a wedding luncheon at a Cajun-Creole restaurant nearby. There had to be some celebration, Carter thought.

After ordering blackened redfish, but offering no toasts, Dennis left to make a phone call. When he returned, he told Julie, "We've got to get going." He showed no emotion, but smiled to himself. When he left again to make another phone call, Julie, shamefaced, said, "There isn't any time today to have the wedding pictures taken." The bridal couple would have to go the studio for the shots. Dennis returned and herded his bride and the best man and his wife out the door. There was to be no honeymoon; Dennis could not spare the time away from work.

His bride was bubbly, thrilled she had caught up with the rest of the world. She was pleased that she had found a bridegroom so much more traveled and worldly than she, she wrote in her diary.

That day, all that Dennis noted in his engagement book was that there was a party in the evening at his private tennis club, 6:30 to 10:30.

The next morning, Julie phoned Nora Talcott. "Guess what I did this weekend?" she said.

"I was flabbergasted," Nora said. "He took her out for day trips while she was hospitalized and the next thing is she's married to him. I asked when the wedding pictures would be ready. Julie explained, 'Dennis didn't want photographers there.' "

Nora, horrified, asked, "Do you know what you are doing?"

"He saw her as instant victim, instant money. It was better than the lottery."

Molly Flowers and her husband also were appalled. Julie called Sunday afternoon, February 23, saying she wanted to show them something. Molly expected Julie to walk in with an engagement ring. "Instead, she was wearing a little dinky, measly wedding band," Molly recalled ruefully.

Two days after the no-frills wedding, Dennis picked up his bride at her office and took her to lunch. It was no romantic tête-á-tête over paté and champagne. They grabbed sandwiches and went to Julie's bank and a notary public to change her financial documents to read, "Dennis and Julie Bulloch." Dennis never added his wife's name on anything of his. He refused to give Julie a key to his house in University City, saying his ex-wife was too jealous. Karen said she never knew he had remarried.

By mid-week, Julie lost her normal effervescence. "She got real quiet, sealed up like an envelope," said Jane Muster. "We had to work on her just to visit with her in the van during the long rides."

Instead of lavishing his eager bride with affection, Dennis would nag and berate her. Because he could not dominate in the world of men, he had to control women. He ordered Julie to fire her housekeeper; he did not want to spend the money on her.

With her housekeeper and her beloved dog Buttons gone, and Dennis away so much, Julie felt overwhelmed with loneliness and fear. She would drag her bedroom rocking chair into her walk-in closet where she would rock for hours, cuddling her teddy bear.

I feel more like Dennis's roommate than his wife, Julie thought. Why does he have to sleep in the other room when he spends the night? He says he needed to sleep alone to sleep late. Maybe he doesn't find me appealing, she said in an audiotape.

On her late mother's birthday, in March, Julie wrote to Mary Jane. She wondered if she had married for the wrong reasons.

She worried over her inability to explain what she wanted from her husband. Julie said she felt like a "second-class citizen" on the outside and inside she was a timid toddler.

"What's in a name change?
Sharing and trust . . .
Am I too scared to trust?
Yes—when I'm not accepted for what I am."

Shortly before their wedding on February 22, there had been a pregnancy scare for Julie. Dennis himself had *two* that month. One with Julie and one, he claimed, with his girlfriend, Christy Meiers. He said Christy had an abortion after which Dennis wrote her how "no one else would I let have my children."

It is not clear what happened with Julie's pregnancy, but it is obvious from the fifty-minute audiotape she made that Dennis failed her miserably. Frightened of him, Julie relied on letters, diary excerpts, and this tape to talk to Dennis during their brief marriage. She made and gave him the tape six weeks after their wedding, sometime in early April. It is not known if Dennis listened to all of it. Julie cries throughout:

> [Paraphrased] *Dennis, what about when it looked like I needed an abortion? Maybe it was just a bunch of cells to you, but to me— well, my mother deliberately became pregnant with me before she was married, that's how much she wanted me. So I couldn't see a possible baby as just some cells.*
> *What really was a knife in my heart was, here was the hardest day of my life. Very, very traumatic. I wanted you there, I needed you there with me. But you found other things more important to do. Maybe—I won't always be number one. Please tell me, though. What is more important?*

A minute later on the tape, Julie switched to how lost she would have been during her breakdowns without him. And then, as the good wife she was, worried because he had left his overcoats at home. What was he wearing to keep warm in Denver in early April on his business trip?

But Dennis was not on any business trip, then or later; he had just disappeared. Julie became frantic when Dennis became unreachable. And he often was—claiming he had to travel for Price Waterhouse. He refused to give his wife phone numbers and hotels where he allegedly was staying. Dennis told his wife he would be gone on business trips when, in fact, he stayed at his home in University City. Sometimes with other women.

For his bride, it was like living with a man wearing roller skates. One night, he would romantically light candles before her, carrying her off to bed to gently make love, and then the next morning he would disappear for parts unknown until he surfaced ten days later as though nothing had happened.

This was a betrayal and perversion of Julie's American Dream, her schoolgirl fantasy of the handsome husband who lived in a nice house with his sweet little bride and cared for her. The only thing Dennis was attentive to was money.

He was thrifty—with his money. He would tack lists on the refrigerator, reminding Julie to name him the beneficiary on her life insurance policies and to buy various things for him which he could have just as easily picked up and paid for himself.

Flashing Julie's charge cards, Dennis outfitted himself that spring in the finest men's shops. He ordered the basics from preppy catalogues: Jos. A. Bank Clothiers for black-tie shirt, braces, studs and tie; turtlenecks from J. Crew; as well as silk rep (which Dennis spelled "repp") ties and shorts from Lands' End. As Julie complained to a friend over lunch in March, "I always have my wallet open."

Dennis never wore his new black-tie ensemble escorting Julie to charity balls. Nor did he take her to any Price Waterhouse functions even though the company made it clear: If your husband works for P-W, you work for P-W, too. "When you marry, the first person you tell isn't your mother. It's Human Resources at Price," explained a former Price CPA there.

Dennis never notified anyone at Price he had remarried. Ironically, Dennis's superiors rated him as "good" on integrity on his evaluations in the fall of 1985 and winter of 1986. His "professional image and appearance" were ranked as "good" and "exceptional." Dennis was the master of appearance over reality.

While Julie never had a honeymoon, her bridegroom enjoyed one. With another woman.

In early March, 1986, less than two weeks after his secret

wedding, Dennis telephoned Nina Honeywell, a socialite he had been dating since August. He said he had recently gone out of town. He had been thoughtful, though, sending her a Valentine's Day card. Nina and her group welcomed the prodigal escort back into the bosom of their exclusive country club for dinner on the first Saturday in March.

The group fell into planning a trip. Most of them enjoyed much free time, toying at jobs. Nina and her best friend, Margaretta "Muffy" Spencer, spent more time at the luggage carousels in airports than hunched over papers at the office. The gang voted to go skiing in Jackson Hole for a week in mid-March. They would stay at the condo belonging to Muffy's mother. Dennis liked to say that Nina had called and invited him.

The morning they left for Jackson Hole, Dennis picked up Nina, which surprised her friends, who wondered why he had not just spent the night. As they were unpacking in the condo, Dennis opted to room with one of the men.

That prompted one of the guys, Luke Jackson, to ask Dennis on the ski lift: "Hey, I'm curious. What are you and Nina up to?"

"Well, I just got divorced and all I want to do is play the field," Dennis replied. He had then been remarried less than a month.

Dennis behaved oddly, continuing his old obsession with his body. He was always fully dressed or covered, even to use the one bathroom the guys all shared. He slept in his sweats. When they all went to a bath and tennis place with steamrooms, saunas, and whirlpools, Dennis left for the day and bought a present for his old girlfriend Christy Meiers. His wife got nothing. Another time, the group took their bathing suits and trooped off to hot tubs. Dennis went skiing alone and called Christy, but never his bride, according to phone records.

One night in Jackson Hole, after dinner and drinks, the gang played a new game. It was "How to Host a Murder." Dennis's talents really shone; he came out of his shell that night for the first and only time. When they finished the game, he wanted to go another round.

On the flight home, the group faced a long layover in Denver where they had planned to take advantage of a fabulous ski sale. They had avoided splurging until then. Except for Dennis, who had bought a very expensive set of skis in Jackson Hole—his second set—for more than a $1,000. "Dennis wants to appear rich," Luke Jackson commented dryly to another of the guys on the trip. Dennis did not understand the Old Money dictum that less is more than enough.

On their return to St. Louis, Dennis spent the weekend at his house in University City in order to take Nina to a Young Republicans party. Being an outsider, Dennis could not foresee his downfall. His bride was better connected than he knew. There is an old saying in St. Louis: Everyone knows everyone else, although Nina's crowd liked to point out, "We do not really know anyone who lives as far out as Ballwin."

Julie had a cousin in Ladue, to Dennis the best of pricey suburbs. The cousin and her husband went to dinner one night with their old and dear friends who just happened to be Nina's aunt and uncle. Julie's cousin announced that Julie had a brand-new husband.

Nina's aunt announced that Nina had an eligible beau; good news for Nina, a decade past her debut, and still no diamond solitaire on her left hand. The women compared names—or name, as the case was.

Nina was dressing to go with Dennis to the Young Republicans party Saturday evening when the phone rang. It was her aunt. With some very bad news. The sort every single woman fears. Nina was badly shaken.

The doorbell rang. It was Dennis in a tweed jacket and a splash of Brut aftershave. He said he needed to use her phone. While he was on hold, Nina asked, "I heard you're married. Are you?"

"He didn't give a verbal response, he just gave me a gesture— through his eyes and just a shake 'No.' " Nina believed him. They partied for six hours. Nina felt relaxed on the way home.

As he took her to her door, Dennis turned to Nina, and said, "I have something to tell you." Realizing he could no longer fool Nina, Dennis confessed:

"I'm married. I had to," he said. "She kept leaving suicide threats on my answering machine, saying that she'd kill herself if I didn't marry her. I don't love her. She's not very attractive. I don't even live with her." As with the police, Dennis never called his wife by name.

Dennis told Nina he could not bear to see another human

suffer the way he had when his sister had died and his first wife had left him. Dennis looked so wounded Nina felt sorry for him.

Beleaguered Dennis added that he was terrified Price Waterhouse would discover his marriage before he could have it annulled. The "stress" was driving him to a therapist, he said, although he had actually quit months earlier.

"Didn't you think about this beforehand?" Nina asked.

"I make decisions without a lot of thought," Dennis replied. Nina was surprised. As she said later, she always had the image of Dennis as a typical Price Waterhouse man following through on his "commitments."

Marital vows meant little to Dennis. To him marriage was one long bout of casual sex with the same partner.

Another woman also had no idea she was seeing a married man. Christy Meiers flew into St. Louis from Washington, D.C., the weekend after his last date with Nina, to spend Easter, 1986, with Dennis in his house in University City.

Dennis began his favorite ritual, sexual bondage. Normally, Dennis would tie Christy's arms to the bedpost and then proceed to oral sex and intercourse.

But tonight Dennis wanted something a little different. Hogtieing. Bending Christy over a chair, he tied her right wrist to her right ankle and her left wrist to her left ankle.

Then, he went too far: He tried to blindfold her. Christy protested. He tried again. She said no. He pushed harder. The third rejection so angered Dennis, he flounced into another room where he spent the night solo and sulking. Fortunately, the ties were loose enough for Christy to free herself.

Easter Sunday, Dennis drove Christy to his parents' home. "This is the girl I'm going to marry in August," Dennis told his folks as he put his arm around her.

Monday morning, as Christy was leaving, Dennis cried. "I don't want to lose you. Please don't abandon me."

His bride of five weeks spent Easter alone.

Three days later, April 2, 1986, Julie returned to the psychic she had seen in January. It was nine-thirty that night when she rang the doorbell. She was frightened. Once comfortably seated on the sofa with the psychic, she confided, "I can tell Dennis's mother likes me. But I have a lot of questions in my mind. My husband tells me to be at certain places at certain times or else! He doesn't like regular sex and I don't like what he likes. He's trying to get me to put everything I own in his name."

But it was too late.

Eleven

The Perversion of the American Dream

March 12–May 5, 1986

Ten days before Dennis told Nina he intended to annul his marriage, he had manipulated his bride into signing over complete control of all her property. Dennis had called one of the top downtown law firms, the silk-stocking partnership where the impeccable former CIA Director, William Webster, also the former FBI Director and federal appellate judge, had practiced.

The partner handling random call-ins that day was the son of one of the four most powerful men in the metropolitan area. His family had been members of St. Louis Country Club, the most prestigious social club, since its inception. Had Dennis realized his attorney's connections he would have cultivated his friendship. The lawyer socially far surpassed anyone listed in Dennis's Day-Timer address book.

The attorney, a decent man, told Dennis that what he wanted—a letter of power of attorney and a simple will—was boilerplate legal stuff that any lawyer could draw up and would charge less than a partner in this firm. But Dennis wanted the best.

At noon on March 12, 1986, Julie was sitting dejectedly at her office desk. Her phone rang. Her husband was waiting for her in the lobby. Delighted, she flew downstairs.

Stone-faced, Dennis told her he was in a hurry: He had to leave town for Price Waterhouse. In fact, he was en route to Jackson Hole with Nina. They must rush over to a notary public to sign some papers, Dennis said.

The papers turned out to be a power of attorney. Dennis would have the ultimate in control—all of Julie's real estate, bonds, stocks, bank accounts, even her mother's jewelry. Julie tried to protest but felt overwhelmed by Dennis's arguments. She did not want to embarrass him with a scene.

By April, Julie discovered her husband had lied to her: Dennis had instructed his lawyer to draft the papers weeks before he picked her up at work on March 12. She told Dennis in her audiotape:

> [Paraphrased] *You said you had gotten those forms in that envelope that morning. But I saw that envelope before—in your car the morning we got our marriage license. Somehow, I feel slightly betrayed. You always say honesty is essential.*

Julie tried convincing herself it was not true. A bank vice-president had said to her when she withdrew her money to open a joint account with Dennis, "Oh, Julie if you could have seen the way he looked at you. So adoringly." (The way a pet dog watches its owner eat a steak.) Alone again, Julie would recite the woman's words like a mantra.

When Dennis and his ex-wife wallpapered their house in University City together in early April, he mentioned he might get an AIDS test. Since his ski trip to Jackson Hole, he had been sick, he said, with a high white blood cell count that was unaffected by medicine.

That same weekend the fifteen Southwestern Bell vanpoolers and their spouses gathered for a baby shower. When Jane Muster opened the door, there was Julie, all alone, head down, like a little waif.

Julie sighed, "Den can't make it. He's been called out of town again."

Everyone felt sorry for her. "We got the picture real quick-like; something was real, real wrong," Jane said. "He didn't act like a bridegroom; normally, new husbands can't get enough of their wives. I call it obsessive bonding."

Julie would try to explain to Jane how Dennis stayed at his house in U. City to safeguard against break-ins.

"Why don't you go stay with him?" Jane asked.

"He's afraid someone will break in my house," Julie answered.

Sometimes, Julie would call Dennis at his house, saying, "I want to come over—we could go to lunch."

But Dennis would reply he was too busy cleaning to leave.

"If only he gets his house sold," Julie would cry to friends. "If only, if only he would sell that house."

Julie cried to Dennis in the long tape she made in April while he was gone again:

> [Paraphrased] *Dennis, I guess I still idolize you so much that it's hard for me to believe you wanted to marry me. Sometimes, when we're lying in bed, after making love, being so close to each other, I can't believe I'm really married. I hate to say it. I know it's not your fault, but marriage isn't what I thought when you're gone all the time—three weeks of the last six weeks we've been married.*

In April, seven weeks after her marriage, Julie horrified the vanpoolers. She quietly climbed in one morning with her head down. Normally, she wore her hair brushed back. Today, she had combed it over her face like a curtain. Normally, she wore only a dab of lip gloss and a flick of mascara. Today, she had a thick pancake make-up. It failed to conceal what appeared to be cigarette burns on her face. Four or five of them. Her new hairstyle could not conceal the thinning hair around her face, as though hunks had been yanked out.

Another morning Julie hopped into the van clutching a handful of travel brochures she had picked up in Bell's travel department. Dennis had promised her a honeymoon and she fantasized about Maui. When are you going? asked one of the riders a few days later.

Julie looked down and smoothed her skirt. "Dennis thinks we should save money and go later," she said. "He's right. We need to invest the money."

Julie told her colleague Terri Sacher that while she liked being held, Dennis did not like holding her. Julie repeated that comment to her neighbor Molly Flowers, who had come over when she saw Julie pulling weeds in her backyard. The two women sat in the warm April sun and talked.

"I'm beginning to think I made a mistake," Julie again told Molly.

"What's the problem?" Molly asked.

"I resent his going off and not telling me where he is, or when he'll be back."

"What are you going to do?" Molly asked.

"If only he would change jobs, everything would be better," she answered. "Then he'd be home more and we wouldn't fight so much."

Julie was sitting quietly in the chair as her hairdresser sectioned her hair and rolled it for a new permanent. It was April 19 and she had not yet told her hairdresser she was married. He wondered why she was so silent. Then she flatly made her announcement.

"There was no joy, even when I congratulated her," he said. "She didn't have to say this was a mistake. All she had wanted for the last seven years was the whole package, the All-American package of white picket fence, the house, the kids. She had been boy crazy. She just wanted to love and be loved. She had been dying to get married."

Her hairdresser wondered why Julie had made such a decision only two months after her last breakdown. "I assumed she did it while taking all that medicine [Haldol, Thorazine, Stelazine, lithium carbonate]. Sometimes, when she came to the shop here in Clayton, she seemed so doped up I wondered how she could function."

Dennis and his ex-wife Karen finally sold their house April 22, two months after his secret wedding to Julie. Dennis no longer had an excuse for not living with his new wife and for not returning to his former wife her share of the furnishings.

As the movers uncrated her old bed, Karen shrieked. Hanging from the mattress cover and sheets were huge pieces of electrical tape. Dennis claimed he had been tired of the mattress cover slipping off and had taped it on.

The night Dennis moved out of his house, he called his best friend Cal Porterfield, saying he was lonely. Flopping onto the Porterfield's bed to watch television with Cal and his children, Dennis said he had not decided where to move.

"I've met a woman I'm considering living with and she lives in West County," he said. "It's perfect. You know that mahogany dining room set I have? Well, she needs one!"

Anticipating a windfall, about this time, Dennis asked a real estate agent about rental properties he could buy. He said he had $100,000 he wanted to invest. The woman was puzzled: Karen, Dennis's ex-wife, had told her Dennis's net worth was no more than $25,000, counting his share of the three properties he and Karen owned plus stocks.

By late April, Nora saw a good sign. The old Julie bounced in for their lunch. She had started getting her strength back. She was lively and fun, and enjoying her new job.

To her other pal, Terri Sacher, Julie seemed to be emerging from Dennis's control. She said over their hamburgers one day at the end of April, "I'm thinking about divorcing him.

"All he wanted was my money. Dennis should stop spending my money and start spending his own. He's not living up to the agreement he made before we were married."

There was another change, too. Instead of her dress-for-success suits, Julie slid into the vanpool one May morning in a fluid two-piece black dress with a tiny red and green print. She looked so pretty, everyone complimented her on her new sophisticated look.

While she had more realistic expectations of marriage, Julie wrote she did not know how to achieve them. She still was afraid; frightened that if she failed, she would become more depressed:

> [Paraphrased] *Every morning, I lie in bed, afraid to throw off the covers and get up. Afraid to confront Dennis. Afraid I'll make mistakes and fail.*

Dennis moved in with Julie on their two-month anniversary, April 22, 1986. Julie was thrilled. There was more good news:

Interco Incorporated had offered him a job, one with minimal travel. There was only one more business trip. Dennis announced Friday, May 2, that he was leaving Monday morning, May 5, for a week-long trip to St. Paul.

The last Saturday of her life, with Dennis playing tennis, Julie took her long yellow legal pad and pen to a nearby restaurant to eat, smoke, and write. She had been married to her idol now for ten weeks:

[Paraphrased] *Although he says he loves me, it doesn't feel right. Most of the time sex with Dennis is not the mystical union I dreamed of, but some hormonal act. So impersonal. Is it him? Or is it my lack of femininity? Does he really love me or am I just a warm body lying there in the dark?*

[Paraphrased] *But then sometimes we fall asleep all curled up together like puppies in a basket. And he's so gentle. Or, is that to compensate for when he's rough and makes me cry? I feel the child inside me is sobbing now. Someone, Mommy, Daddy, please save me. I wish I could save myself. But how?*

Julie's only company that day was Carter and his wife. They came by briefly; Dennis had told Julie to have them drop off their copy of her safe deposit box key. Where was her husband? she worried after they left.

The next day, Sunday, May 4, alone and lonely again with Dennis playing tennis, Julie took to her telephone. It had been ages · since she had spoken with her best friend from high school, Laura Reeves, now Laura Edwards, who was still living on the East Coast.

"Jules said she had gotten married. Her life was finally turning around," Laura said. She worried that Dennis was less Julie's soulmate and more the bridegroom on top of the wedding cake.

One of the women who had gone to the psychic with Julie in January had a strange dream: Something dreadful was happening to Julie. The friend had moved to Atlanta and had not talked to Julie in months. She called that weekend to warn her.

Sometime that weekend, Dennis insisted on something different in bed. Something that hurt Julie as she lay face down. She told him to stop but her husband refused. She cried in pain, but Dennis continued. *He* was enjoying it.

Julie grabbed a robe and fled to the kitchen where she sat smoking a cigarette at the table and wept. She waited for Dennis to come in and apologize. She waited and lit another cigarette. She looked up; he was there at the doorway.

"You're just going to learn how to like that. You'd better get used to it!" he screamed. As he walked away, Dennis turned around and chided her for smoking.

Julie was devastated.

They spent Sunday night, May 4, together. Dennis watched a television movie about one of his pet interests—mass murderer Ted Bundy—while Julie puttered around, avoiding the violence.

On the phone again, she told a friend in Florida, "I'm afraid of my husband. I'd like to throw him out. But if I push for divorce, he could have me institutionalized. He has power of attorney. I couldn't bear that."

On Monday, May 5, Julie lunched with Terri Sacher, and told her about how Dennis had hurt her during what Terri assumed was anal sex. The woman commiserated; she was concerned about another matter, too—Julie's money.

Julie was anxious about a deposit Dennis was supposed to have made the previous Thursday into a joint account they had set up at Mercantile Bank. Julie said, "This is his last chance to come through with his promise to deposit money into a joint account because at this point I'm the only one who has money in the accounts. He promised me he would deposit his paycheck."

The two women finished their sandwiches and hurried over to the downtown branch of Mercantile bank. There was no record, in part because the banks were not connected.

Julie became distraught. Hands shaking, she dialed the West County Mercantile from her office. Dennis had made no deposit. Julie called Terri and said she intended to bring it up that night when Den called from St. Paul.

Julie was back to her old self, thought Terri. Angry and ready to fight. Indeed, fed up with Dennis, Julie dumped some of his shirts and sweaters into a black plastic garbage bag that evening.

Earlier, the two women had discussed Julie's reluctance to be alone at home. "Why don't you come over tonight," Julie asked. "Dennis is going out of town and we can go out for pizza and talk. We haven't had the opportunity to do that very much."

Terri replied, "I have to catch an early flight to Dallas tomorrow morning and my clothes aren't ready."

"Ohh."

"I'm watching a movie, the second part of a movie on TV. It's about Ted Bundy."

"Well, you can't come over anyway because I don't watch that kind of stuff."

The night of Monday, May 5, Julie Bulloch went home alone.

Part Three

The Potential
of Dennis Bulloch

November 30, 1953–January 3, 1986

Twelve

An All-American Guy

1953–1979

Dennis Bulloch was All-American handsome with the kind of physique you see in beach blanket movies. Dazzled, Dinah Moltke watched him slam the door of his green Corvette convertible and strut onto the high school tennis courts. She was thrilled when he came over and asked her out. What did this twenty-three-year-old premed student want with her, a sixteen-year-old virgin who was still in high school?

After they became engaged, six months later, Dennis introduced Dinah to sex. After she turned seventeen, Dennis showed her something different, something Dinah had never heard of.

A new ritual to heighten his pleasure.

While her parents were gone for the evening, Dennis led Dinah into her bedroom. After he undressed her, he picked up her ankle and using a shirt, tied her to the bedpost. Dennis was so gentle that Dinah agreed to sexual bondage then and at other times and in other places. Even her parents' living room. He became aroused tying her up. He himself did not want to be bound. Dinah would do anything to please him.

She had to. Dennis broke up with Dinah a total of five times during their three-and-a-half-year relationship. He said he could not "commit." Each time she took him back.

Dinah's parents, at first, had been impressed with Dennis. Such good manners. Every Sunday he and his family attended the nearby United Church of Christ. Dennis was so devout that the ministers had wanted him to be ordained. He was a member of the PTL (Praise the Lord) Club at Illinois College, in Jacksonville, Illinois. And he tried so hard to fit in with Dinah's family.

He showed up once as the Moltkes were sitting down to dinner. "Why don't you join us?" Mrs. Moltke asked.

Dennis came into the kitchen where she was scooping the vegetables into bowls."Oh, you don't need to do that," he said. "You can put the pots and pans on the table. It's just us family."

Dinah's parents were worried what his revolving door behavior was doing to their teenager, but she was smitten.

How could Dinah resist those bouquets of flowers he regularly sent? Dennis made the boys Dinah's own age look like oafs. Instead of hanging out in some pool hall, slurping beer with the guys as they talked baseball, this man drank wine or scotch as he described his exquisitely delicate feelings. He said he was so soft-hearted, he could not bear to dissect his biology lab frog, let alone experiment with live ones. Dennis abhorred the local pastime of fishing, with squirming worms suffering on the hook and the bleeding fish fighting for their lives. The other local sport, hunting, was anathema to Dennis. He told Dinah that taking the life of an innocent animal was unconscionable.

Dennis analyzed his feelings in a cornucopia of letters, poems, and cards to Dinah, and always, in his multi-volume diary. Dennis's diaries were not merely for private reflection; he expected his *pensées* to benefit humanity. So, he kept them in a safe deposit box. He needed to, for he expected to be remembered by history.

That would not be hard. Dennis expected to be another Kennedy, he wrote in his diary. He would toy with his investment portfolio and sit on the boards of the museum and zoo. He would relax at the snootiest country club. Maybe he would run for high office, "Senator Bulloch," he told another teenaged lover. Dennis felt he was entitled.

The constant refrain in his diaries was to achieve his potential. He was so talented, he wrote, in medicine, science, business, the arts, charming people. He had always found women to see his "potential," beginning with his beloved Gram, Ginny's mother, then his first fiancée's mother, and now his second fiancée, Dinah.

Dennis enjoyed describing his dreams to Dinah as they zipped along in his Corvette. He did not want to end up like his parents; they were not good enough for him. They were useless, Dennis wrote. But what could he expect from people who held such menial jobs. They could not comprehend their son's socioeconomic potential. Dennis admitted telling lies to impress his social superiors or to get what he wanted. To him, there was no line between truth and lies. "There is to me," Dinah complained when he lied to her.

She said she did not understand why he refused to set normal, ordinary, reasonable goals. The rules did not apply to him, he told her, for he was special. Dennis saw nothing wrong in exploiting people and then dropping them.

Looking at him, people had always thought Dennis had it made. He had cultivated the image since high school, where he was considered handsome, bright, and well-mannered. He was arrogant too, an unacceptable trait in St. Louis, unless, of course, one has gobs of Old Money.

Growing up in a small town, such as Arnold, provides youngsters with an advantage. The small fry are bigger fish. Dennis had the opportunity to excel where he would have been only average in an academically competitive school in St. Louis County filled with high achievers. Dennis was bright but not skipped-his-freshman-year-at-Harvard-he-had-so-many-Advanced-Placement-credits bright.

In retrospect, one teacher believed he was a budding Dr. Jekyll/Mr. Hyde. "While he had a silver tongue, it was slit." Another instructor thought that his mother knew and protected this duplicity. "She always babied him," the teacher said. "But she'd tell me, 'He'll take you for all you're worth and give nothing in return.' "

Dennis was a chief in his Cub Scout den and a patrol leader. "He always followed the rules and responsibilities," recalled Ed

Schollmeyer, later one of his two loyal friends. "He'd make us do the dishes first before we could play. He was regimented by his mother to do things right."

Another of Dennis's Boy Scouts remembered Dennis teaching him to smoke pot and tie knots.

Despite his wholesome appearance, there was something odd about Dennis, even as a small boy, according to a fellow Boy Scout. "He always slept in his scout uniform pants. He never said why. He wouldn't swim naked or shower with us other boys either." In high school, after working out with the wrestling team, Dennis would wait until they had showered before he would enter the area. Same thing in college. From childhood until he arrived in jail, Dennis Bulloch never appeared naked before his own sex. Unless one counts the alleged orgies.

In second grade, Dennis allegedly urinated on a little girl. Some say he must have pulled his penis out and aimed at her, for the urine splashed on her socks and shoes. The child became hysterical and now says Dennis was forever embarrassed in her presence.

In high school, Dennis was on the student council and the wrestling team, where he later claimed to be captain but was not. Dennis had switched to wrestling from football because "he did not like being hit hard. He wasn't that aggressive," his former coach said. He was such a good boy that on Senior Skip Day, while the rest of his classmates cut classes, Dennis showed up.

He was admitted into the National Honor Society and won a full scholarship to college for a Science Fair experiment in which he deafened mice to study the effect of music on their nervous system. Ten years later, he admitted to his first wife that he rigged the data to win. But for now, Dennis appeared to be the all-around, All-American good guy.

But that was at Fox High in Arnold, which then sent only twenty-four percent of its seniors on to college, and which Dennis painfully understood to be in the boonies of St. Louis. His background would not serve as a social passport. Not only did Dennis want to belong to the upper crust, he wanted to devour it.

Recalled a family friend, "From childhood on, he made his parents take him to expensive restaurants. He got his mother, who worked in a grocery store, to buy him them foreign runny smelly cheeses and that smoked fish that Jews eat."

Where did Dennis learn about brie and Nova Scotia in a small town with no gourmet foods shop? When his mother would not cater to him, the eight-year-old would pack up, leave her a note and stay with his grandmother, Gram.

He was equally fussy about his clothes. Dennis wanted to appear as though he and his father and his father before him had all been outfitted at Brooks Bros. His mother's ironing had to be exact or he redid it himself. He hated the family dogs whose hair got all over his fine attire. Unfortunately, his father wore a suitcoat as though it were an army blanket and his mother adored polyester because she could toss it into the washing machine. His parents did not comprehend the importance of appearances. Dennis did, and that saved his life.

Thirteen

Upstairs / Downstairs:
St. Louis County /
Jefferson County

1960–1980

What Dennis Bulloch never understood was the essential character of St. Louis. A newspaper editor called St. Louis the biggest small town in America: "There are really only a hundred people in St. Louis. They just change masks so you think there are more of them. Given twenty-four hours, anyone well-connected can place you."

The city founded by the French in 1764 and briefly owned by the Spanish is historically too old to be considered middle western. Said another editor, "St. Louis is the sidedoor to the East, backdoor to the South and a window to the West." East Coast moxie is considered obnoxious; Southern gentility affected; and West Coast looseness downright looney.

St. Louisans like to think of themselves as being mostly Eastern in appreciation of cultural amenities, but socially the city is Southern. Missouri was admitted as a slave state in 1821. Indeed, slaves hauled up the Mississippi in riverboats from New Orleans were sold on the steps of St. Louis's Old Courthouse, where Dred Scott was led away in chains. As a border state Missouri flipflopped during the Civil War. Cotton is still grown two hundred miles south of St. Louis near the Arkansas border. The Daughters of the Confederacy remained very active in St. Louis into the 1960s.

The social history makes sense once one accepts that social St. Louis is a series of contiguous upper-middle-class small towns, some with upper-class areas, along Highway 40. The two essential questions natives ask to place a person are about family and position: "What is your mother's maiden name?" and "What school did you go to?" The questioner is not interested that one might have matriculated at Yale. What he or she wants to know is what high school, public or private, did one attend.

Other ways to be accepted are to marry into society or arrive as the chief executive officer of a Fortune 500 corporation based in St. Louis, such as Southwestern Bell, Emerson Electric, Monsanto, or Ralston Purina. Even then these high positions do not imply that the person is "from St. Louis." People move to St. Louis and think they fit in because they have joined some clubs and boards and their neighbors and colleagues include them in parties, but these people neither belong nor understand what that means. Belonging takes a good three generations. And if one really belongs, then one need not do anything else in life, save perhaps play polo well at St. Louis Country Club.

One way to find the natives is family-tree climbing: Anyone in St. Louis more than three generations usually has a German ancestor (Protestant, Catholic, or Jewish); more than five, a French; and beyond that, a Native American.

"That's because the French weren't racist over here. They immediately intermarried with the Indians and even the Irish," said a judge with a French forebear. "The French would poke anything." Nineteenth-century St. Louis had more intermarriages than the East Coast, much to the horror of the Wasps who arrived to establish the banks and railroads as soon as the fur-trading settlement made money. "There wasn't much choice," explained a very social matron. "Unless one wanted to marry her first cousin."

At the end of the nineteenth century, St. Louis was one of the four largest cities in America and expected to soar to the top. And why not? Known as the Paris of the New World, its intellectual and economic dynamism developed the symphony, botanical garden, and Washington University.

But fin de siècle was fin de Saint Louis. Today, it is locked in a time warp. It could not now develop those old institutions which make St. Louis such a civilized place to live. The attitude is, "We haven't done it that way, we won't do it that way, keep your ideas to yourself." Which made St. Louis the perfect place for a man of unlimited ambition but limited talent, such as Dennis Bulloch.

Corporate transferees happily say, "It's a great place to raise kids," because St. Louis is a throwback to the 1950s with its paterfamilias president, *Father Knows Best* solutions, and June Cleaver next door making chocolate chip cookies. St. Louis may claim Washington University with its first rate medical school, the world-class Missouri Botanical Garden, a fantastic Zoo, one of the best American symphonies, and the internationally acclaimed Opera Theatre (the only new institution), but in its social attitudes, the revolutions of the sixties and seventies happened on television.

As of 1990, there was no woman sitting on the federal district bench, let alone federal appellate court, and none in high government office. The distaff side does not head up anything except the League of Women Voters.

There are outbursts of social progress from time to time, but more like death rattles than birth pangs. St. Louis is the cradle of the Pro Life movement. And the birthplace of Phyllis Schlafly. This was the city that banned the Baby Brother doll because he replicated baby brother's outdoor plumbing. City aldermen kept St. Louis *Hair*-free when that Broadway show with "nekkid people" tried to go on. In St. Louis, several religions make a cottage industry out of the whore-madonna complex.

This misogynist miasma surrounded Dennis Bulloch's murder trial. It saved his life and made a mockery of his wife's death.

How could Dennis have comprehended the nuances of St. Louis society when he was from a lower-class neighborhood in poorer Jefferson County?

The drive from St. Louis south through Jefferson County is

picturesque. The verdant rolling hills and valleys along the Meramec River are immensely appealing. Some of the people are not. The historic marker before the county courthouse says it all: Jefferson County was settled around the time of the Civil War by migrants from the Old South and immigrants from German farms. The marker needs to be updated for the newer immigrants—the biker gangs and the hillbillies. Rural Jefferson County has a white-trash element for whom family reunions are a great place to meet girls.

"Hillbillies come up here for the cheap land to raise a passel of kids and some ponies," said Capt. Ed Kemp of the Jefferson County Sheriff's Department. "The problem is the authorities have to forcibly remove the kids and ponies because of abuse and neglect."

Wife beating is endemic: A popular song has been, "She broke my heart and I broke her jaw." A standard phrase printed on those ubiquitous baseball cap bills is, "My wife ran off with my best friend. I sure do miss him."

In Jefferson County, as of 1990, there were no public libraries and no bookstores. There were quick shops and displays of five flavors of chewing tobacco hung beneath T-shirts emblazoned with "Freedom or Die." "It's not liberty they're talking about, but license," noted a former reporter. Capt. Kemp explains, "The rednecks like to come into town on payday for three things: To get drunk, to fight the sheriff's deputies, and to get laid. In that order."

"Once you cross the Meramec River [dividing Jefferson County from St. Louis] you're in a completely different world," Kemp said. "It may be pastoral, but it 'ain't' no Eden." And it would be redundant to say one is from Jefferson County and non-ethnic white. When Dennis was a tot there were a dozen Klu Klux Klan Klaverns to chose from, but no places to find books.

Dennis's father, Robert "Bob" Bulloch, was "raised and schooled," as he said, in Victoria, "a stone's throw" from the Jefferson County seat and not far from the Ozarks. Bob's father was a chronic gambler and boozer from Georgia. His mother was chronically depressed. When Bob came home from grammar school, his mother would still be in bed, forcing him to raise his younger siblings.

Dennis's father used Southern expressions—"I 'bout bit a nail"—and odd tenses—"He could have ran"—and talked with a drawl and dropped his "g's", as in "walkin'." "A sweet man, a gentle man, he was," said those who knew, "a few sandwiches short of a picnic."

He embarrassed his son, who wanted a flashier role model with a Wharton M.B.A. who eased his Lincoln town car into his reserved executive parking place at McDonnell-Douglas Aircraft executive offices. Dennis was humiliated by a father with a GED (General Equivalent Degree) who carpooled to the McDonnell-Douglas plant where he was a shift-worker airplane mechanic. Dennis fancied a father who enjoyed the cocktail hour before the maid announced dinner, not one sprawled for whole evenings on the plastic slipcovers before a television screen watching "The Beverly Hillbillies" and "Hee-Haw."

As a teenager, Bob met and married go-getter Ginny Wiemann. She had been born and bred on a truck farm where her mother sold produce near the Anheuser-Busch brewery where her father worked.

When they were twenty, Bob and Ginny's first child, Dennis Neil (by age thirty, Dennis would spell his middle name "Neal" because he thought that it was classier) Bulloch, was born, November 29, 1953, in Hollywood, California. It seems fitting that Dennis was born in the land of contrived images. The Bullochs lived in Los Angeles while Bob worked as a mechanic at Lockheed Aircraft.

Bob and Ginny moved back to Missouri, to be close to their families, when Dennis turned four. When their daughter Cynthia Louise—named for Ginny's mother Louise Wiemann—arrived in 1958, their family was complete. Ginny's friends marveled at how protective she was of her babies, washing her children's toys after the neighbor kids played with them. "She behaved like a real mother tiger, especially about Dennis," commented one friend.

In contrast to quiet, passive Bob, Ginny yapped and pushed, always telling Dennis what to do. She reminded people of their third-grade teacher, the one in a starched white blouse that never wilted in the September heat and who rapped her students' knuckles with a ruler.

Ginny could go the teacher one better: using a quarter word when a nickel one would do. When asked about her son's release from prison, Ginny pursed her lips and said, "We're elated." In the home state of Harry Truman, plain speaking is the norm, especially for plain folk.

During the Kennedy era, the Bulloch family moved to Arnold in Jefferson County, settling in a $13,000 home on Judy Drive. Arnold was then a bucolic vista of farms and pastureland and woods, an ideal place to raise children. When Cindy began elementary school, Ginny took a job as a check-out clerk at the National Supermarket nearby.

Arnold lost its sublime prettiness. From the end of Judy Drive there sprouted a Drury Inn, a Pit Stop, several fast food shops, and a Walmart Super Center. Judy Drive was a short gravel-mixed road flanked by a dozen aluminum-sided "ranchburgers" with wading pools or pick-up trucks parked on the front lawns. The rear windows of these vehicles were filled with tens of tiny stuffed animals, mostly puppies, some with bobbing heads.

Judy Drive became "the avenue of the lawn animals." Flanking the door to one house, for example, were a swan, a donkey with a wheelbarrow, two frogs under an umbrella, a mother hen with three chicks, a fawn, a Madonna in blue robes, a rooster and nine other miscellaneous concrete creatures. And that was just the left side. The plaster menagerie meandered on the right. Years later, Dennis did not bring his friends from posh country clubs home to Arnold.

The Bulloch home was immaculate and unadorned: The hedges always trimmed as though a protractor had been used. The grass always clipped as short as a Cold War crewcut. The drawn Austrian shade in the picture window was folded like a flag. The interior, however, was a mess, with piles of things in the living room. The house was worth about $45,000 by the mid-1980s; about as much as the jewelry collection of Dennis's second wife.

The Bulloch family appeared so wholesome. What could be more All-American than a family fresh from a cover of *The Saturday Evening Post* by Norman Rockwell—Mom, Dad, two much-loved, healthy, bright, blond children who would go further in life than their parents ever imagined? Dennis Neal Bulloch was going to be his mother's fulfillment of the American Dream. His father was partial to his daughter Cindy. Nothing unusual about that.

But Dennis liked to claim that when he was a teenager his father threw him across the room, striking his head against the wall. No one who knew the family believed the tale, unless, as one relative said, Dennis had hurt his sister.

People preferred Cindy. Men and women smile, recalling how pretty and sweet she was, her nicknames being "Cookie" and "Sugar" and, en famille, "Sugie." Insanely jealous, Dennis would be so mean to her, she would temporarily stay at a friend's house.

Ginny seemed blinded by her son's fair-haired radiance. "To her he was always the grandest thing," said a friend. Until he moved in with his third fiancée, Dennis lived at home in his all-black bedroom. He demanded black wall-to-ceiling carpeting but Ginny refused. Angry with his mother, he did not talk to her for months.

In 1979, Cindy, aged twenty-one, was diagnosed with leukemia. She died twenty-six days later. Her parents were numbed with grief.

Ginny turned to her remaining child and blamed him for her daughter's death: "If you hadn't hit her so much . . . " Then, she began to smother him with love. Bob never recovered from seeing the coffin of his baby being lowered into the ground. He turned inward, withdrew from life, and died in spirit.

As Cindy lay in her casket, Dennis said, "She got what she deserved." He told a friend, "She's where she belongs—six feet under." Unable to face the funeral service, he fled. Ginny made his excuses for him, saying he was in the Missouri Ozarks, and that he sat on Cindy's grave for four days and four nights. Dennis later told girlfriends how heartbroken he was. Sometimes he wept.

As his parents were disposing of Cindy's things, Dennis asked his fiancée Dinah Moltke to buy his sister's car with him. She gave him $1,000 but Dennis never bought the car. When Dinah questioned him, he said that he was in trouble, that he owed money for gambling debts, that he was responsible for his little sister's death. He never paid her back. Months later he left Dinah for his next teenage fiancée.

Ever sentimental, Dennis kept the photographs he had taken of Dinah. He had liked the teenager to disrobe for his camera. He had tied her ankles together and photographed her. He filed that Polaroid of Dinah, naked and in sexual bondage, in his gray metal box along with other nude photos of other women.

That single picture almost sent him to Death Row.

Fourteen

"Blue Skies and Butterflies"

December 30, 1979–May 9, 1985

Dennis was euphoric. He had met True Love. With her, he could reach his "potential." He was starting a new decade, the 1980s, he wrote in his diary, and a lifetime of joy. It would be all "blue skies and butterflies."

For once he would unleash his feelings and not try to control them on his lover, he wrote in his diary. He recorded his idyllic meeting of Ms. Right the day before Christmas Eve, 1979, at the home of family friends. Dennis seemed unconcerned that he was still going with Dinah Moltke at the time.

Like his two fiancées before her, new love Karen Toksvig was a teenager. Eighteen to his twenty-six. She was all curves, with thick wavy hair, a generous mouth, and a full figure. Dennis enjoyed catching her in the nude and photographing her.

Unlike him, Karen did not waste time discussing her "potential." At seventeen, she had begun college carrying twenty hours a semester as a business major, in addition to working full-time, so she could graduate in two years and begin her ascension into management. Karen moved swiftly and spoke and thought even faster. She was much quicker than Dennis. Yet, she was the patient listener Dennis had been craving.

He told her remembrances of every past love, no short list. He literally cried on Karen's shoulder over the deaths of Cindy and his first fiancée's mother. Confession was a near fatal mistake; Karen later recalled every detail to the police.

Believing in his religious teachings that masturbation was unnecessary, Dennis had taken lovers continuously since his junior year in high school. The steady girlfriend or fiancée usually was a younger girl. There was one exception, when he was twenty—a woman of thirty-seven who publicly bragged about fellatio: "I don't get down on my knees for just any man." She also lavished money on Dennis, who regularly visited a psychic to divine how much money a woman had and whether he could "make" her.

To Karen, Dennis appeared to offer stability and security. Karen was in her early teens when her parents divorced. She felt it was her fault. She went to live with her father, a successful subcontractor in Imperial, near Arnold. That was a fiasco. On her seventeenth birthday, they had a terrible fight. Karen's father kicked her out as she cried hysterically. Timid and insecure, the girl could not resist a man who had all the answers when she did not even know the questions. And Dennis was so sensitive, too. He wrote her yards of poetic lines about making love on a beach with waves crashing over the climactic scene.

At first, sex with Karen was idyllic. Each time he could make her respond to a new technique, Dennis would commemorate the event in his diary and write her some saccharine sentiment.

But within months, by spring, 1980, sexual differences began snaking their way into Eden. Dennis became so self-conscious he could not perform after the first round of sex. He wondered if he could not connect sex with love. When Karen tried to reassure him, Dennis would dwell on the problem and become impotent.

"It's your fault," he would yell at her, "You know what I want and you won't initiate it."

Dennis wanted her to find him irresistible, so that she would do anything, anything he wanted.

That included anal sex. "When he'd try that, I'd tell him to stuff it and laugh, which would anger him," Karen said. "Sex with him was very serious business. Never playful, never ever funny." When jealous and angry, Dennis would pin her arms down in bed. Karen would bellow at him and he would roll over. She believed he was too intimidated by her to suggest bondage.

Dennis chronicled every febrile fluctuation of his romance several times each day in his diary: Karen was a garden of earthly delights; she was an ungiving prude. She adored him; she was flagrantly flirting with other men. He sent her a card reminding her she was first and foremost in his life "*even* before myself," all the while complaining that nothing she did was enough. Without her he was unfulfilled and empty, he wrote. Only she made him feel alive and gave his barren life meaning. And only *she* would be allowed to bear *his* children.

Obsessed, when he was not writing about Karen, he was writing to her—letters, cards, quotes of love poems. In one card, he said, over and over, how he needed how she made him feel, he needed her presence, he needed her to be free.

Despite his dependence on her, trusting Karen became a form of Promethean torture. For five years, Dennis stood sentry for signs of infidelity. A few weeks after they began dating, Karen went on one last date with an old beau while assuring her new love she would rather be with him. Dennis rifled through her things, and found ammunition, her Christmas card to a male friend, which he copied down. Over and over in his diary he asked how could he trust her?

He berated her for giving him a venereal disease, even though her gynecologist diagnosed it as only a common yeast infection.

Karen was visiting her uncle, a professional photographer; Dennis went there. Trying out a new lens, the uncle was photographing his niece. He told Dennis to leave. Furious, the next day Dennis demanded to know what time Karen had left her uncle's. Was her blouse unbuttoned in the pictures? How could she think that he, Dennis, would go along with such provocative behavior? Why had she not thought of him when she posed? Convinced that the photos were suggestive, he ordered Karen's uncle to turn over the film. When he refused, Dennis was in agony.

"If you really loved me," he told Karen, "you would do what I want."

Obsessed with Karen, Dennis lost interest in college, even

during finals. "Why?" Karen asked. "I think our relationship is more important," he answered. This may have explained why his term papers were patchworks of plagiarism.

By the time he was graduated from college in late 1981, Dennis and Karen were living together. Yet, he remained, in that buzzword of the eighties, "uncommitted." It was Karen's fault; her love had limitations, he said. She failed him in bed by denying him whatever he wanted. He wrote her he would do anything to keep her close. And he expected the same.

Then he threatened: Other women found him irresistible. How would Karen feel if he cheated on her? he asked.

Later, in 1981, when they were twenty-eight and twenty, Dennis and Karen moved to the most elite suburb of St. Louis, Ladue, where she was an *au pair* for two doctors. While Karen cared for the children, and cooked and cleaned for money and board, Dennis did nothing except list the Ladue address on job applications. He was ecstatic about using the coveted 63124, the Ladue zip code, instead of Arnold's designation. To him, one implied multi-million-dollar estates, the other, trailer courts.

When the story of Ted Bundy hit the media, Dennis became fascinated and tried to find out everything he could about the All-American-looking handsome serial killer. His mother worried he was obsessed by Bundy. Dennis would say, "I wonder what it feels like to kill a woman," and then practice karate.

Dennis had always worked out. Long before it was in style, he exercised at Vic Tanny's three times a week besides regularly playing tennis and racquetball. This was not to alleviate stress or stay healthy. Dennis's concern was centered solely on his appearance. To achieve his potential he must first create the perfect image. He lay under a tanning bed, avoided drugs, and stocked up at health food stores, all to look younger. Dennis was terrified of growing old and, worse yet, looking his age. Within a few years, he would begin lying bout his age, even on bank loans.

By age twenty-eight, Dennis felt his youth was gone. He had expected a future filled with brave new worlds. Time had run out. It was not his fault: he had no one to guide him. For all his talk about "potential," Dennis had yet to define what it was. He was not advancing at work in the laboratory. He had few business contacts and fewer friends, two to be exact.

All his free time and all his thoughts were centered on Karen. After a two-year courtship, they were married on Valentine's Day, 1982. She was twenty and he was twenty-eight.

The morning of his marriage, he wrote in his diary, Maybe now I can find my potential.

The wedding took place at the United Church of Christ in Kirkwood, an established, Waspy suburb of St. Louis. Their wedding was a traditional ceremony with Karen dressed as a bride in a long white gown with a veil. She had made the down payment on her own engagement ring, as well as writing the check for the honeymoon, because her bridegroom was in graduate school. About a hundred guests attended the reception at a nearby church hall. The bridegroom was hung over, which did not surprise the bride, who was used to Dennis's heavy social drinking. After the wedding rehearsal the night before, Dennis and his high school pal Ed Schollmeyer had made the rounds of the local taverns. Ed carried him home and Dennis spent the night before his wedding passed out in the bathroom.

A friend of Karen's was surprised at her choice; Dennis was violent: As Karen had climbed into bed one night, she said something Dennis did not like. His arm swung out with such force he knocked her out of bed and across the room.

Karen could not reconcile his violence with the soft-hearted lover who was so inconsolable when their cat died that she had to dig the grave and bury the animal herself.

Dennis's friends thought Karen was a sister substitute. Karen believed he was continuing with her the love-hate he felt for his sister, mother, and grandmother: "I love you for taking charge; I hate you for running everything," as one friend said. As Karen blossomed professionally at Southwestern Bell Corporation, she became less the insecure malleable teenager Dennis had met and more an independent woman.

In one area, Dennis remained in charge. He became the trustee for Karen's money when they married, telling her that because she was underage everything had to be in his name. Then, he refused to tell her where he hid her bank account.

On another issue Karen was firm. She announced before the wedding that she would not change her name to Karen Bulloch.

In retaliation, Dennis announced, "When she takes my name, I'll wear a wedding band." Friends on both side of the aisle saw the exchange of vows as a prelude to a power struggle.

Dennis wrote little in his diary the first year of marriage. As his M.B.A. graduation neared, he worried that prospective employers would find him too old.

That the promising premed student of 1972 was now far behind his peers punctured Dennis's inflated pride. Dennis had put off "reaching my potential" eight years earlier and now he suffered for it. In 1974, realizing that his grades were no entrée to Harvard Medical School, he had dropped out of Illinois College in his junior year.

His fiancée then, another teenager, Wendy Meadows, was unsympathetic to his angst. Her mother, Marilyn, believed in him, which Dennis desperately needed: He could not fulfill his destiny unless he had a supporting woman behind him, he acknowledged in his diary. Marilyn and Dennis became very close.

But then Dennis's future mother-in-law died suddenly. For a decade after, Dennis would write in his diary and tell girlfriends how bereft he had felt when Mrs. Meadows "left" him. He told Wendy he wanted to postpone the wedding until he finished college, which he was making no move to do. When Wendy went to visit relatives, he fooled around with other women. When Wendy found out, she left him.

Three years later, in 1977, Dennis, now engaged to Dinah Moltke, returned to Illinois College, majoring in biology. His mother was happy with the idea her first-born might still become a doctor. Dennis spent his off-hours at a literary society and the PTL (Praise the Lord) Club. After a few years of lab work, he tired of research. He had met his future first wife, Karen Toksvig, and wanted to go into business, as she had done.

In 1981, college diploma in hand, Dennis began the M.B.A. program at the University of Missouri at St. Louis (UMSL) while working part-time in the computer center. Dennis made a friend there, Jasper "Jas" Kossuthski, who became a pass into the country clubs Dennis aspired to belong to. Karen, with whom he was living, and whom he married in 1982, thought the snobby clubs a joke.

With his M.B.A., Dennis found his golden staircase to corporate America. He was hired by Price Waterhouse in 1983 at a salary of $23,500 as a staff consultant in their Management Consulting Services. Price was the elite of the "Big Eight" national accounting firms, the whitest of the white collars.

Karen, meanwhile, had been promoted into management at Southwestern Bell, and at age twenty-two was out-earning her husband at $35,000 a year, without an M.B.A. Her salary did not faze Dennis; what hurt was their home life. While he wrote cards "Sunsets + Jello, Den" to tuck under her pillow, the new executive was nose-deep in her briefcase. Or she would not be home at all—out-of-town again at some training seminar.

Dennis was insanely jealous of all the men Karen worked with. He also thought Karen's pro-ERA stance could hurt her. At another level, he was pleased with his wife's financial success.

Karen's income enabled Dennis to play the real estate market during the boom years of the early eighties. Those profits provided the down payment for their first house. It was in one of the nicer old suburbs ringing the city of St. Louis, called University City, with its streets named Swarthmore, Yale, Tulane, and Stanford. By moving into U. City—although it was not one of the top neighborhoods—Dennis was inching his way up the social ladder.

Their address on Stanford Avenue would not cause embarrassment at a Price Waterhouse party or at Saks Fifth Avenue. Ironically, U. City, with its base of academics from Washington University, is very liberal, sophisticated, and integrated. It is doubtful that Dennis, a member of the Young Republicans, knew U. City had gone for McGovern in 1972. It is unlikely he realized that the most cerebral bookstore in the metropolitan area, Paul's Books, and the leading highbrow film theater, the Tivoli, were now within walking distance of his house.

On moving day, his parents came up from Arnold to help. Ginny, in a tube top and shorts, cut the grass and Bob pulled weeds. Karen was inside unpacking as Dennis unloaded his car. A neighbor stopped by to introduce herself and asked who the older couple was. "They're some people I hired to put my lawn in order," Dennis said.

Dennis was especially pleased with his tiny, nondescript house. Part of an estate sale, it was chock full of starter furnishings, machine-made Oriental rugs and eighteenth and nineteenth century-style mahogany reproductions.

Dennis sent the Regency-style dining room pieces to be stripped from a mirrorlike finish to the natural wood-grain. "He had the concept but missed the details," sniffed a neighbor, "though he knew enough to put the TV in the bedroom."

Then the dread of every homeowner hit. The furnace conked out. After Dennis ordered a new furnace installed, he found a cheaper one. He removed the new furnace and returned it. Karen was cross for weeks. "He was always obsessed about money, about getting the best deal regardless of who got hurt," a friend of hers recalled.

In his pursuit of Mammon, Dennis fancied himself the future Donald Trump of St. Louis, though he was never as vulgar. He took real estate courses, stocked up on how-to books, and hung a large wall map of metropolitan St. Louis in his study at home into which he stuck colored pins identifying pieces of prime real estate. Besides the house on Stanford, he and Karen had bought another one in University City for rental, as well as a time-share condo in New Orleans. Dennis had a private telephone line with a recorder installed so that he would not miss any hot deals. He hired a part-time secretary. Although he had a realtors license, he sent other agents out scouting. His investments netted (after buying out Karen in 1986) about $23,000 on Stanford, just under $6,000 on the second house, and the time-share remained unsold as of 1991.

Dennis, now frantic about reaching his "potential," thought that get-rich-quick schemes might make him an entrepreneur before he was too old. Karen thought his wheeling and dealing silly and told him so. She laughed at his jockeying to impress his colleagues. Dennis joined the Friends of the Art Museum and Friends of the Zoo and had the mailings sent to his office.

"Dennis knew the value of appearance," said a colleague who knew both of them well, "Karen did not care to impress. She concentrated on hard work on the job to get ahead." Dressing for success vs. work ethic. Style vs. substance. Potential vs. delivery.

Sex continued to be a problem. Dennis complained his wife refused to be a sex object because of the ERA. He criticized her lack of passion, which, of course, did not send her sizzling off to bed.

Dennis wanted Karen to satisfy his strange fantasies. If he could not reveal his "kinky" side to her and have it satisfied, he wrote, he would be frustrated and lonely. He could not live with her "prejudices."

"Why don't you want to bite my neck?" he asked.

That was the least of what he wanted. When they took a shower together, Dennis tried to give his wife a golden shower, urinating on her. Karen would scream and stomp out of the bathroom. He constantly talked dirty in bed, which was about as tantalizing to Karen as changing a baby's diaper.

Karen usually handled her husband's bullying by ignoring him. Sometimes the only one who paid attention to him at home was the live-in student cum cleaning woman. Dennis liked to refer to her as his "housekeeper" to his colleagues at Price Waterhouse. She was a messy, overweight woman whom he liked to taunt. She titillated his morbid curiosity, he told Karen. He wanted to read her love letters. He wondered aloud to his wife what she would be like in bed. Dennis and the student ultimately romped in her bed beneath his wall map of prime St. Louis real estate sites.

Fifteen

"Fulfilling My Potential"

1983–1985

In his diary of the yuppie years, 1980–1985, Dennis reported his plan to dedicate himself on the altar of High Art after making his fortune. Yet, there is no mention of major or minor exhibits or special concerts, books, or films in his writings.

How Dennis would become rich seemed vague: He was obsessed with the goal rather than the process. He could not take the tension of meeting deadlines at Price Waterhouse, and had to work longer hours than other consultants to keep up. Frightened, Dennis filled his diaries with self-help clippings from magazines and sloppy slogans exhorting himself to be happy with himself, be himself, not imitate others, and, lo and behold, he would be a "success"!! Dennis wrote with numerous exclamation points and underlinings.

Dennis was a peon at Price Waterhouse. The corporate hierarchy has "a pecking order like a prison," said former Price CPAs. There are fixed stages along the career track, each with a role of rigidly codified behavior. In Dennis's area, Management Consulting Services, that hierarchy consisted of staff consultant, senior consultant, manager, senior manager, and then partner.

A master at playing roles, Dennis had the Price look: gray or blue pinstriped suits, white shirts, styled hair, and clean-cut face. "And he acted the part," said a former colleague, Leslie Jefferson. "All he ever talked about was the same things the partners were into: money, the stock market, real estate. No charm. No wit. And he talked sooo slowly. Sometimes, we wanted to scream at him, 'Just say it, Dennis.' "

Dennis enjoyed drinking with his colleagues after hours, downing Margueritas. At office parties and other gatherings he would consume up to ten drinks over a long evening, beginning with mixed drinks and by the end switching to wine to avoid appearing drunk. As he became more a Price man, he took to scotch.

"You're supposed to drink it," he told Karen who hated the taste. "Scotch is more upper-class." Dennis rarely if ever drank at home; he was strictly a social drinker.

Dennis reveled in the moneyed atmosphere at Price Waterhouse. "But he didn't know he really didn't fit in," his colleague Jefferson said. "He went pink with pleasure at a partner's Christmas party in a million-dollar house in Brentmoor Park. Dennis didn't understand the connections you need to bring in the money to buy that kind of mansion."

Dennis was thrilled with the firm's annual fall semi-formal dinner dance, nicknamed "The Prom," usually held at the most expensive hotels. He liked the fact that Price encouraged its men and women to attend social functions.

"They want you to go to charitable and social affairs and bring in business," Jefferson explained. "It's more important to be social than brilliant. Some partners are not all that bright, but they sure know what to say over the endive at the Zoofari." The firm so encouraged joining clubs that often the partners would deliberately choose different country clubs, in order to swim in different pools of prospective clients.

To his chagrin, Dennis was not yet eligible to attend the Price alumni dinners for former colleagues held at the Bogey Club, in Ladue, the most exclusive club in the metropolitan area. Bogey has only sixty-three members at a time, most of them CEO's of major corporations. Nearly all *haute* WASP. Bogey's nine-hole golf course borders the equally beautifully landscaped nine-hole golf course of the Log Cabin Club, the arrangement allowing members of both clubs an impressive eighteen-hole layout.

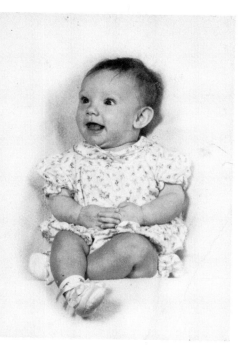

Julia "Julie" Alicia Miller. She was a much-longed-for baby by her mother. (Courtesy Carter Miller, Jr.)

Julie, aged seven years. She was confirmed as a Catholic, like her mother. (Courtesy Carter Miller, Jr.)

Julie, aged thirteen. By junior high school, she was a pretty girl, popular with her peers and their parents for her proper manners and her sense of fun. (Courtesy Carter Miller, Jr.)

Julie, aged sixteen, as a member of the high school color guard. This is her brother's favorite picture of her, one he keeps over her favorite antique, an oak roll-top desk which he now uses. (Courtesy Carter Miller, Jr.)

Julie, aged twenty-seven, at her tenth high school reunion. Despite moving back to St. Louis, Julie remained close to her friends in New Jersey. As a young executive, she was still bubbly and fun. (Courtesy Carter Miller, Jr.)

Julie, aged thirty, 1984. In her company photo for Southwestern Bell, Julie appeared more professional. And more depressed. After the recent death of her mother, Julie became anxious to fill the void. Marriage, she thought, was the answer. (Courtesy Carter Miller, Jr.)

Julie Miller Bulloch, late winter, 1986. Jubilant upon becoming Mrs. Bulloch, Julie did not seem to mind that her bridegroom not only refused to have any photographers at their wedding, he also would not sit with his bride for a wedding photo. So Julie went alone to the studio for her portrait, a gift from her brother and sister-in-law. (Courtesy Carter Miller, Jr.)

Dennis Bulloch

Dennis Bulloch, high school
freshman. He had that clean-cut
All-American look his entire life.
(Courtesy Fox Senior High School)

Dennis Bulloch, high school senior.
Popular and bright, he was in the
National Honor Society and on the
student council, varsity marching
band, and the wrestling team.

The Bulloch family home in Arnold, Mo. Always ashamed of his roots, Dennis spent his life social-climbing. He never brought any of his St. Louis friends back home, certainly not those who belonged to country clubs. (Photo: Ayse Erenmemis)

Julie Miller's house, 251 White Tree Lane, Ballwin, Mo. Even with the police barrier up, Julie's house was pretty and of a much higher level than anywhere Dennis had ever lived. Dennis insisted that Julie put his name on the title.

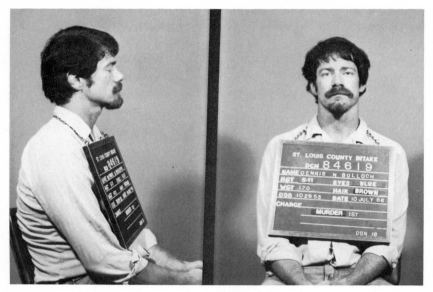

Although he had his hair dyed and grew a beard while in California, Dennis could not escape the criminal justice system. This police mug shot was taken just after he was brought back in handcuffs from California. (Courtesy St. Louis County Prosecuting Attorney)

Now clean-shaven, hair still dyed, Dennis was forced to stand in a police line-up for witnesses to identify him. The other men are prosecutors and police officers. Dennis is second from right. (Courtesy St. Louis County Prosecuting Attorney)

St. Louis Country Club, Ladue, Mo. To walk through the doors of the most elite country club in the metropolitan area was the main ambition of Dennis Bulloch. (Photo: Ayse Erenmemins)

Lt. Dennis Niere, Ballwin Police Dept. Since the predawn hours of May 6, 1986, Lt. Niere has labored to find evidence against Dennis Bulloch. (Photo: Guillermo Gomez)

Tom DePriest, Prosecutor. DePriest issued the murder warrants against Dennis and pursued him through two trials. (Photo: Guillermo Gomez)

Tom Mehan, Prosecutor. He seconded DePriest in the first two trials. The two prosecutors were affectionately nicknamed the "Toms" by the defense team. (Courtesy Thomas Mehan)

Art Margulis, Criminal
Defense Attorney. A former
FBI agent and prominent
defense lawyer for decades,
the Bulloch case was the
most shocking and intriguing
he had ever seen.

John Ross, Prosecutor. Ross
broke Dennis on the witness
stand during the third trial.
Appalled by the evidence,
photographs of Julie's corpse,
Ross was most shocked when
Dennis ordered multiple
copies of his wife's remains.
(Photo: Guillermo Gomez)

Bill Grant, Margulis's
partner. A friend of the
prosecutors, Grant faced
them three times in court
over Dennis's charges.
(Photo: Guillermo Gomez)

This evidence photo shows what
Dennis Bulloch did to his bride. Her
body, especially her arm shown
here, was wrapped with clinical
precision. The dark pieces of tape at
the elbow and wrist symbolize
shackles. This is the least gruesome
of all the evidence photos. Dennis
himself ordered many copies of the
most horrifying ones.

How conservative was Price Waterhouse then? The army of three thousand white shirts stuffed into dark pinstriped suits was commanded by a contingent of white male officers. No women partners, no black partners, a few token Jewish partners—so good at tax law, you know.

A woman CPA at Price looked out her window at a pocket park on a nice spring day and decided to eat lunch al fresco there. Down she went in the elevator carrying her orange, when it stopped at the next floor and a senior partner joined her. Glancing at the piece of fruit, he asked what she was planning to do. "I'm going to sit on a park bench and eat it," she replied.

"Next time, make sure you hide it in a brown paper bag and make sure no one knows where you work," he sniffed.

By late 1984, although Dennis, now thirty-one, had been promoted to senior consultant, he felt something was missing. Why did he always want to be more than he was? he wrote in his diary. What did he need to make him happy? The answer was odd: "A little girl (as in picture of an unknown child pasted on next page) full of happiness and love certainly would make me happy."

While Price seemed satisfied with his work, it became clear Dennis was no potential partner. And at Price, it was "up or out."

Around this time, friends noticed that Dennis was less than honest with them. While Karen would say he was from Arnold, Dennis claimed he was from Fenton, in St. Louis County. Fenton is next to Arnold geographically, and, to Dennis, superior in status. When confronted, he claimed his superiors at work told him to say he was from Fenton.

Karen worried why her husband used aliases, keeping a list of them on a legal pad: Dennis Block, John Block, Dennis Toksvig, John Mason, Jonathan Dennis (many included John or Jonathan). The names "John" and "Jonathan," Dennis told Karen, were associated with successful men.

Dennis hated his surname, with its bovine connotations. "Bullock" is an Old English diminutive form of "bull," in addition to meaning "young bull or gelded bull," according to the *Oxford English Dictionary of Etymology*.

Her husband's lying became more sinister to Karen. One

night, as she pulled into the driveway, she could see Dennis standing at the window. He was not smiling. When she got inside, there was no one home. She was positive she had seen him, and began to feel she was living in the world of *The Turn of the Screw*.

Beginning in early 1985, Dennis would not come home until the wee hours or not at all, and would refuse to say where he had been. Or he would ignore his wife altogether, while she cried that she had become frantic because he might have been hurt. His favorite excuse, when he bothered to give one, was that he had been looking at real estate. "At four A.M.?" Karen would shriek.

Karen's friends were concerned about her safety with Dennis. One male executive from Bell, Sam Lamonte, who befriended Dennis's second wife, met Dennis at St. Louis's Lambert Field when he and Karen were to fly to Dallas for a training seminar. "I met this straightlaced type in a London Fog, Weejuns, starched blue jeans, and white shirt and reeking of Brut after-shave saying goodbye to his wife."

Karen and Sam were buckling their seat belts when she said to him, "I want to run something past you. We're having problems, but I don't want it out in the office. Dennis has the tendency to beat the hell out of me."

"You've got to be kidding," Sam said.

"No, I'm not," Karen said. "I'm afraid of him."

"You'd better move out or get a gun."

Dennis was so jealous that, after he had downed a few drinks, he would grab Karen by the wrists, slam her down on their bed and, while pinning her, would shake her hard, accusing her of adultery while he himself had been untrue. "I think the more Karen grew at Bell, the less Dennis felt he could control her, and the more he needed other women," said a colleague.

Dennis was having an affair. Karen's friends reported seeing him in a red car with another woman in the Moorlands area of Clayton. Nothing else is known about this infidelity except that, a few months later, Dennis opened a savings account with an address on the same street in the Moorlands area, although he lived on Stanford until April, 1986.

The affair broke up when the woman announced she was going back to her lover or husband. Dennis copied a letter to her in his diary. He wrote little about his love, mostly about his "potential." Dennis believed himself so talented, he just could not decide which area to focus on.

"Dennis is acting real weird," Karen confided to a friend as they walked out of final exams in the M.B.A. program at St. Louis University in the spring of 1985. "He removed the wall in the kitchen last week, leaving this huge, glorious mess, and expects me to clean it up." Karen made it clear she had not time to help between studying for her finals and being swamped with work at Bell.

The next morning, May 8, she lingered over coffee to tell Dennis she had an office softball game that night. As one of the few female account executives at Bell, she emphasized it was nearly mandatory to bring one's spouse. "It's at six tonight. There's a picnic afterwards."

Dennis blew up. "You need to come home and clean up this mess," he screamed. Not wanting to fight or be late to work, Karen left.

He called her at her office four times to check on their plans for that evening. "What do you think I'm doing tonight after I explained it all to you this morning?" Karen snapped.

"There's a going-away party for someone at the office," he retorted. "And I'm going."

"I'll be the only female account exec at the picnic without a husband," Karen wailed. "Be at the park at six." Dennis never showed up.

After the game and the picnic, the Bell group went to a nearby bar. "When I got home," Karen recalled, "it was maybe midnight. Den's car was in the garage, but no lights had been left on, which surprised me. I expected to find him awake. I decided not to wake him and took off my clothes at the foot of the stairs. I tiptoed up, holding the banister in the dark." She went into the master bathroom.

"I was brushing my teeth in the dark. Afraid that closing the bathroom door all the way to turn on the light would cause creaking. Then, all of a sudden I realized I could see the bathroom sink. Before I could turn around to see who had turned on the light, a hand yanked my toothbrush out of my hand and pushed my body around. I was petrified."

Dennis glared at her and bellowed, "Where the hell have you been?"

Karen said, "Look, Dennis, you know where I was."

He accused her of having affairs. He claimed he could smell "the sexual aroma" on her. He began pushing her on the chest, harder and harder. He grabbed her arm and twisted it. He hit her hard.

Karen said, "I fell back and hit the back of my head on the tile wall and fell on the floor. He got on top of me with one hand over my mouth, telling me not to scream because the neighbors might hear, and he had one hand raised up in the air. I thought, 'Oh, my God, he's going to kill me. The last thing I will ever see is the pink bathroom tile.'

"Then, it hit me. 'Wait. If I have time to think. I have time to get out of here.' I pulled away and ran down the stairs in my underwear. He stood at the top of the staircase and said, 'If you leave, don't *ever* come back.'

"I yelled, 'No problem.' I threw on my shirt and jeans and grabbed whatever I could from a pile of clean laundry and ended up running out of the house with two pairs of pantyhose. I drove to the nearest quick shop to call my mom.

"I was shaking as I dialed her number. 'I'm coming home,' was all I said."

Dennis could not believe a woman would ever leave him.

Sixteen

"I'm Fitting Into Society"

May 9–December 31, 1985

The next morning, Karen could not move her arm. Bruised and sprained, was her doctor's diagnosis. She went to the Women's Self-Help Center for battered women. Therapists there told her that abused women usually feel that they caused their beatings. Karen was relieved, having thought Dennis's violence was her fault, as was her parents' divorce.

Karen's counselor explained that Dennis was a psychopath. Psychopaths use aliases, lie, exploit others, lack close friendships, make misogynistic sexual demands, steal, are violent, and feel no guilt or remorse.

During their next conversation, Karen told Dennis, "You're looney."

"I have a chemical imbalance in the brain," he replied. "I just had tests at St. Mary's [Health Center]." As Karen said later, "It was as if Den saying, 'I have a note from my doctor excusing why I was so mean to you. Please come back.' "

Still guilt-ridden, Karen went with him to their minister for counseling. She quit when the minister implied that she had triggered the outbursts. Dennis began seeing two therapists alone, a social worker and a psychologist.

117

Dennis would endlessly analyze with their friends, Cal and Tina Porterfield, what his therapists had said and what Karen had done. He could not get over the fact that she had slammed the door on their marriage. He complained that he had done nothing to provoke her. Dennis neglected to mention that he had fooled around with other women and had beaten his wife.

How long does it take for a man to recover from a divorce? Answered an attorney whose bread-and-butter once was divorce work: "If the divorce was the man's idea, maybe three weeks. If she threw him out, maybe never." Later, this lawyer became Dennis's criminal defense attorney and saved his life.

Karen's recent promotion at Southwestern Bell only exacerbated for Dennis her leaving. She was now earning $48,000 a year to Dennis's $31,500. Eight years younger and without an M.B.A., Karen was showing the "potential" he had craved. His wife had become the man he had wished to be.

He projected onto Karen his infidelities. What a "hypacryt [sic]" she was, he wrote. Convinced that Karen had a lover, he went too far.

Three weeks after Karen had left him, she flew to Washington, D.C., to play tourist and visit an old friend. Dennis found out where she had gone.

Karen recollected: "He called my hotel room at midnight, desperate. I called our minister long-distance to try to get help for him.

"The next day, I was out sightseeing all day. My friend dropped me off in the hotel lobby, and when I walked in, there seated next to the potted palms was Dennis.

" 'Where have you been?' he said. 'I can't live without you.' Dennis is nothing if not melodramatic.

"It turned out he had been waiting in my hotel room. He had told the hotel manager he was there to surprise his wife. Fortunately, I took too long to return."

Prostrate with a badly bruised ego, Dennis called in sick, sometimes several times a week, to Price Waterhouse. He took a leave of absence for the month of June, traveling to New England with a new girlfriend—while Karen and he tried to reconcile.

Reunion was only possible, Dennis wrote his wife, if she

accepted and loved him as he was. He needed unconditional love.

When he returned, Karen told him she wanted a divorce.

While they were dividing up the property, she gave Dennis her engagement ring, a one-carat diamond, to be appraised. Dennis told her he lost it and filed an insurance claim listing himself as beneficiary. Later, he told her he found it. He never notified the insurance company.

Just before their divorce on December 20, 1985, Dennis called his estranged wife. "Come on over," he said. "I have a nurse here at my house to give you a physical for a life insurance policy. I'll pay the premiums," he added. The policy was for a quarter of a million dollars. Dennis would be the beneficiary.

"Should I go?" Karen asked her friend, Tina Porterfield.

"Do you want to die?" Tina answered.

Dennis brooded over the divorce, writing in his diary endlessly. What hurt most was that Karen had decided on divorce "without consulting" him.

Karen had told Dennis she did not consider him a good person. Why? He had asked.

"Because you steal—towels from hotels and schools all the time—and commit insurance fraud," she had said. "You're always trying to screw someone out of something."

She believed he had stolen the family silver from Karen's mother back when they were dating.

Dennis felt Karen should forgive these trespasses. He wrote her how committed he was to their marriage. How committed he was to their church.

Karen no longer responded to his manipulations. Nor did she care that he had a new girlfriend.

Dennis had found comfort and solace in Christy Meiers, whom he met in June, 1985, while auditing the U.S. Department of Agriculture in Washington, D.C., a Price Waterhouse client. A big-boned Rubenesque red-head, Christy provided a maternal quality Dennis said he needed. They saw each other through work several times a month. They spoke over the phone twice daily, from office and home, Dennis using the alias "John Mason."

They enjoyed a very active sex life, which starting in July, 1985, included the gentle art of bondage. The first night, Christy did not know what he was doing as he tied her wrists together with his silk ties and then tied her arms to the bedpost in her bedroom. He proceeded with oral sex and intercourse. Dennis had tied her up so loosely she was not afraid.

For her birthday on August 9, Dennis sent her a book on car repair and a woman's floppy silk bowtie. The card read, "Maybe we can find a different use for this."

As Christy became used to bondage, Dennis added little twists—hogtying, blindfolds. He believed Christy exhibited the abandon he had always sought and never received from his wife.

Did this sexual practice really incite Christy to ecstasy or was it that Dennis became aroused knowing he could manipulate this wholesome woman from the Wisconsin dairyland into sadomasochistic perversions? Control was the ultimate turn-on for Dennis.

Despite his libidinous pursuits, Dennis continued writing to Karen or about her, up to fourteen times a week. At four A.M., on the morning of Christy's birthday, August 9, 1985, he wrote his estranged wife how he hated her. Dennis claimed he hated Karen because he could not trust her. He could not trust her because he loved her. Such conflicts were irreconcilable, he wrote. But if he could not resolve them, the pain would kill him. Dennis wrote Karen:

> *May you burn*
> *for what you've done!*

On August 9, the day that Dennis wanted to see his first wife burn, and had sent his lover a bowtie for bondage, he answered the lonely hearts ad of an Alton, Illinois, registered nurse. And around that time, Dennis made his first date with his next wife.

While dating, Dennis went from parsimony to maniacal spending sprees. He stopped paying his bills only to run up higher ones. His multiple MasterCards hit $5,000 each in charges. He treated himself to beaches and ski resorts; he had a current passport for wherever. In St. Louis, he dined formally at a top French restaurant in Clayton, a well-to-do suburb, or informally at trendy bistros in the chic Central West End. Befitting his new status, Dennis hit the singles bars. He loved to dance and then cool off with a scotch on the rocks. He did this all on $31,500 a year while making mortgage payments on two houses and a condo, and a $300 a month car payment.

Of all the fifty-three women Dennis was seeing, for whom was he buying mail-order lingerie from Frederick's of Hollywood? The company's phone number and address in Hollywood are listed in his annotated little black book, although there was a branch store twenty minutes from his house. Frederick's was the only retailer he listed.

In his search for Ms. Right, Dennis dove into the rich mother lode of women from the Highway 40 corridor, where money and power in the St. Louis area were concentrated. His new criteria were rich, social, and pretty, the latter negotiable depending upon the former. Most of the women had never been married; Dennis could not take the competition.

His favorite socialite was a former deb, Nina Honeywell, a brunette with a catlike face who was an alumna of the best private Catholic schools. Perennially single at twenty-eight, she had just broken up with that Eighties cliché, a man who could not commit. These facts were not lost on her friends, who hoped that the newcomer would change her unlucky love history.

Women like Nina may have been attracted to Dennis because he was not a well-to-do, nice Catholic boy. Many proper Catholic boys make love like they are sixteen-year-olds in the back seat of a car getting away with a sin, or like acolytes at a transcendental experience, if they are sober enough to perform.

Dennis could attract so many women of so varied backgrounds for one reason: He was a con artist with protean talents to appear in any desired role. For example, many women love what they can mother. Out came the stories about Dennis's poor dead sister and how bereft he was. Out came how his wife betrayed him. It was I-am-wounded-can-you-heal-me? Women love challenges, and Nina offered high tea and sympathy. And then, to clinch the conquest, there was his siren song to single women who were pushing thirtysomething: All I want is to be settled in a nice house with a family.

Dennis fashioned himself into what women's magazines herald as the New Post-Sexual Revolution Man—sensitive and open. He did not want to be like his father, closed off to life. He much more admired the women in his family, he said, like his mother and his grandmother. Dennis told Nina he wanted to be the best he could be.

A woman involved with Dennis Bulloch usually felt insecure, and therefore all the easier for him to control. But the more they matured, the more they pulled away from Dennis. Something he ruefully learned from Karen.

What Dennis felt for Nina was less love or sexual lure and more awe of what she could provide—money, family connections, and friends at "the club." Nina and her crowd of big names offered entrée into Old Warson Country Club and St. Louis Country Club.

"I'm fitting into Society," Dennis crowed to Karen one Saturday morning as they were fixing-up their house for sale. He was to meet Nina's crowd at the St. Louis Country Club.

This was the club that a generation ago asked members married to Jews to resign. It had been so Old Money that the late beer and baseball baron August A. "Gussie" Busch, Jr., CEO of Anheuser-Busch Brewery and the St. Louis Cardinals, was blackballed. In the pecking order of those who care, St. Louis C.C. is like an eighteenth century Chippendale-style piece; Old Warson C.C. the Baker copy; Bellerieve C.C. and Westwood C.C., *the* Jewish club, the Henredon reproductions. The rest are Thomasville and Broyhill copies, and so on. While there are many liberal Democrats who belong to country clubs, most clubhouses are bastions of Royalists and Republicans.

Dennis drove along meticulously following the directions to the club. It was so tucked away—in the heart of the ritziest suburb, Ladue—that if one did not know where one was going, one would miss the entrances in that lush shrubbery lining the roads. The area looked like a tamed rural Jefferson County. Except that multi-million-dollar estates were hidden behind the berms and banks of trees. Here were the "out-of-sight rich" defined by Paul Fussell in *Class*. Somewhere among the greenery were inconspicuous little white signs reading, "St. Louis Country Club" and "No Trespassing."

Dennis found the open gate and swung his Honda Accord onto the clubgrounds. There were no markers pointing the way to the main building, only mansions barricaded behind four-story high trees on multi-acre lots. The roads in the club were named after famous golf courses. Glen Eagle, St. Andrew's,

Braeburn, Pine Valley. People living on the club grounds knew where they were; they did not need tacky reminders such as "Country Club Drive" to engrave on their notepaper.

There were so many trees of different types and colors that the grounds looked like an arboretum that just happened. It did not occur to Dennis that a landscape architect had designed acres and acres of quiet good taste. The golf course, he could see, was superb. What appeared to be a second golf course turned out to be the polo field, where members could sit under yellow awnings on the terraced patio and sip bloodies and gin and tonics while watching the matches. Dennis pulled up before the white stucco clubhouse with its Palladian-style windows, black and white awnings, black shutters, and clay tile roof. Today, I found my goal in life—to be at one with the plutocracy, he later wrote in his diary. He strolled in.

Dennis joined Nina's crowd, which included a descendant of a St. Louis First Family and two heirs of industrialists plus a Busch beer relative. The sort who have downtown streets named for their forebears. It was Dennis's practice with this crowd to arrive and leave alone.

With few exceptions, everyone else had grown up in the group. Together they had passed through all the proper rites of passage, learning to swim in country club pools, suffering through fortnightly dancing classes, and attending debuts and cotillions. Nina and friends took trips together as a group.

Dennis was relieved that in Nina's crowd only the appearance of erudition was enough. While the rich are more sophisticated, they are no more intellectual as a class than the folks of Jefferson County.

Dennis reveled in playing paddle tennis and dining at the club with Nina's crowd. But it was obvious to them that he had no idea which fork to use in eating escargot, nor did he even know what escargots were.

"We all assumed he was not our kind," explained Nina's old pal Luke Jackson. "Dennis never revealed more than he was at Price Waterhouse, had received his M.B.A. from University of Missouri at St. Louis and was in the process of becoming divorced. But we didn't ask questions, because we knew he would not connect. But if he married the girl, that would be fine. One tries to make the best of these things."

Nina's male friends noticed something strange about her new friend. Dennis never showered or used the locker room facilities after the guys' racquetball and tennis games. He was always fully dressed.

Dennis was shameless in his adoration of clublife. It became a joke: While he lunched with a colleague, a mutual acquaintance walked through the restaurant and said, "Dennis, guess where I'm going today?"

"I dunno," said Dennis through mouthfuls of hamburger, "where?"

"St. Louis Country Club," said the man. "That's all you want out of life—to belong to the club."

He chortled. Dennis did not understand that even going to the club as a parvenu on a pass was not the same as belonging.

Dennis continued his marathon pick-up practices. He was catholic in his tastes in women, ecumenical when it came to those with trust funds. Many of these relationships were casual, such as the one with a West County woman he dated in October and November of 1985. Dennis gleefully told her the details of every wild party he attended. Too gentlemanly to name names, he told of Mazola parties, orgies in which men and women rubbed Mazola salad oil over their nude bodies. He partook, he said, of gatherings which became sadomasochistic.

In his socializing frenzy, Dennis turned to his high school pal Ed Schollmeyer, Jas Kossuthski from grad school, and Cal and Tina Porterfield.

Dennis most preferred being with the Porterfields, coveting the life they led. Calvin was an academic with a trust fund, Tina a graphic designer. Her style was reflected in their Creole-style house filled with Pierre Deux fabrics and choice eighteenth-century French provincial walnut and pearwood pieces from Selkirk's, the old established St. Louis auction house. Mixed in with all the ladderbacks and armoires were a Joseph Albers lithograph and an early Francis Bacon sketch.

The Porterfield twin girls were adorable angels who never interrupted their parents' parties. Tina always had a tendency to take in strays—dogs, cats, the newly divorced or widowed, and, in the fullness of time, Dennis. The Porterfields seemed to

have a magic circle of largesse that extended to whoever walked
through their persimmon-colored Provençal front door.

They included Dennis in their parties because Tina's college
classmate Karen worried that he was in need of companionship. The Porterfields were aware that he was unable to mix. At
parties Dennis would be off to the side, hugging the bannisters.
The worst evening occurred when he showed up at the Porterfields' in black tie for a simple buffet and proceeded to alienate
the guests and isolate himself. "He always had to make a point
instead of party talk," Tina explained later. Yet, Dennis could be
so charming at times.

One Friday night, when the Porterfields were entertaining
Tina's clients, Dennis volunteered to tend bar. After the scotch
ran out, Dennis left quietly to buy more liquor without telling
his hosts. He refused repayment. The next morning, he showed
up on their doorstep with three longstemmed red roses, one
each for Tina and the twins, "Flowers for my girls," he said with
a smile.

At other times, he would say to the girls, "Don't you want to
come live with me and be my daughters?" Tina found this eerie.
Sometimes, the girls were afraid of him.

Many times, the Porterfields felt besieged by Dennis. He
would show up at seven-thirty in the morning on weekends,
asking, "What's doing today?" He would tell them, "You're my
only real family." He made a barnacle of himself to them as he
had to Dinah Moltke's family and to that of a high school
sweetheart.

As generous as Cal and Tina were, Dennis could not resist
verbal sniping at his benefactors. After Tina had spent a fortune
refurbishing the sitting room in Brunschwig et Fils linen toile,
Dennis pronounced, "Your decoration would have worked if the
colors in this room went together." He frequently pointed out
Cal's spreading bald spot. Dennis would chide Tina for her
weight gain: "Teen, you're getting a double chin. Best to drop a
few. You're getting faaaa-ter."

"He's certainly not the gentleman he pretends to be," Tina
complained to Cal. "Dennis's fine manners are only an appearance that will crack with time and exposure," Cal replied.

Dennis mystified the Porterfields. As much as he was at their house, as much as he reiterated his feelings about Karen, Tina and Cal never felt they knew him.

On sultry summer nights, Dennis would sit in the Porterfields' gazebo with Cal and cry. "He would say, 'All I wanted to do was meet someone nice like Tina and have a family and be settled,' " Cal recalled.

"I'd tell him to relax and let it happen.

"Den would cry and say, 'No, I can't find anyone.' "

Dennis thought that if he could have the life of the Porterfields, he would achieve more. He really did not want an independent-career wife, like Karen. He needed a prop to keep up his appearance. Someone he could control.

One rare night home alone in late July, 1985, Dennis relaxed in his easy chair. He carefully read through the personal ads in old copies of *The Riverfront Times*. He did this often, responding to women with a photocopy of his picture and varying biographies. One ad from the late May edition was especially appealing. The woman sounded compatible. Her ad read:

> Are you a "Really Nice Guy"? If yes, this "Nice Girl" wants you to read on . . . Let's meet for coffee & something "really nice" could happen for both of us.

Seventeen

Making Violent Love

Christmas, 1985–January 3, 1986

The difference between a lady and a flower girl is not how she behaves, but how she's treated.
—Eliza Doolittle in Shaw's *Pygmalion*

By Christmas, 1985, Julie Miller was appealing more and more to Dennis. "She really flattered my ego," he later said, "running my errands." While Nina Honeywell and Becky Cabot had gobs more money and those idyllic country club connections, they were not about to play lady-in-waiting.

Nina and Becky presented a sexual dilemma, too. With former debs, Dennis could hardly expect to dominate them and indulge his fantasies of golden showers or other perversions. He did, though, with a woman who did not run in such divine circles.

Nina and Becky and other rich girls presented a financial liability. Their grandfathers and fathers had seen to it that their trust funds were tied up tighter than any of Dennis's bondage partners. Without the principal, Dennis lacked the capital to expand his real estate empire. Rich girls would be even less

127

malleable than his first wife. Dennis could never compete with their fathers for power.

One winter night, Cal answered the door. There was Dennis resplendent in his tweed Chesterfield over white tie and tails. Cal wondered why he had not rented an appropriate cape or coat.

Dennis was saying he had gifts for the twins, two puppets and two $50 bank accounts. Cal thought Dennis really had come by to show off his ball attire. Dennis was en route to pick up Nina to escort her to the Fleur de Lis Ball where Catholic debutantes are presented to the Archbishop of St. Louis. Cal could not wait to tell his wife about the social faux pas of a tweed coat over white tie.

Dennis had already gone to the fanciest ball in St. Louis, the Veiled Prophet Ball.

Back when he was growing up, every St. Louisan knew about the Veiled Prophet Ball and Parade and its Queen of Love and Beauty. Little Dennis may have been among those huddled masses who lined the wintry streets to watch the V.P. Parade pass by with its ethereal floats of His Mysterious Majesty, the literally veiled prophet, and His Queen and Her Court in their fairy-tale, spun-sugar ball gowns.

No one missed the extensive television coverage of the ball. Each debutante was formally announced, as was her lineage. She would walk down a long runway to make her nose-to-the-floor curtsey to the Veiled Prophet. Crowding around the tube to oh and ah was a regular St. Louis family ritual. The following morning, many little girls would bow and scrape around the house, trying to curtsey. The two newspapers heralded the debs with front-page color pictures and full sections about who their parents were, and what they, and the former queens and special matrons, wore.

The debs presented in the century-old V.P. Ball have mostly been part of a self-perpetuating group. Their fathers must belong to the Veiled Prophet Foundation and pay an initiation fee and annual dues which are far less than those levied by the prestigious country clubs. ("It's far cheaper to run the V.P. Ball for one night than maintain the golf course at the club," a member of the foundation and various clubs explained.) The father must be active in the community to belong to the foundation, someone with deep pockets who empties them on prominent charity boards. Some poor schnook from Velda Village with a wad of dough from his muffler shop is not going to get his baby into the V.P. Ball. The father must be sponsored and elected to become a member of the foundation; that is, he can be blackballed. Foundation members take turns swathing themselves in chiffon as his Mysterious Majesty, the Veiled Prophet of Khorassan.

Their fathers' memberships entitle the women to become one of the thirty or so maids of honor. The four or five Special Maids and the Queen are selected by a secret group of men. The elect almost always are legatees of sisters, mothers, and grandmothers who were Queens of Love and Beauty; the V.P. prides itself on continuation, but money makes it possible. Most of the royals are Wasps; for example, the 1990 Queen—from the roots of her Saxon flax hair to the tip of her vestigial nose. She just happened to be a first cousin to President Bush.

A place in Society was once mandatory to put a *peau de soie* pump on the ball floor. There were no black debs at the V.P. until 1990, and few ethnics. An exception: Baseball Hall of Famer Stan Musial's daughter was introduced at the Ball a generation ago. The first Jewish girls came out in the mid-1960s, and each year the handful of Jewish debs at the ball grows larger. "They aren't all Sephardic or German, either," sniffed one horrified Jewish socialite. Many wealthy Jews are uninterested in V.P.

The 1985 holiday season was the best that Dennis of Arnold could have asked from Santa. It began with the V.P. Ball and was followed by a holiday repast with his V.P. date's family who also had invited one of their closest friends, a Really Old Name. Dennis spent Christmas dinner at another socialite's family— forsaking his own along the way. Lastly, there was the Fleur de Lis Ball before New Year's.

The last ball was Dennis's swansong to High Society. While he was with Nina, he ran into the Old St. Louis Name who had met him over Christmas dinner with another former deb. The Name was not amused that Dennis was two-timing his family friend.

Dennis saw his long-coveted social position being knocked awry and begged Cal not to betray him. Cal pointed out a skeleton in Dennis's closet more frightening to his new social set. "What are you going to tell them when they ask where you went to school, Dennis?" Cal said.

In St. Louis, high school alma mater is a measure of social standing: There is an apocryphal story about a young bride introduced to an older woman at a tony party. "Well, dear, did you go to Mary I. [Mary Institute, a private day school for girls]?" the woman asked.

"No," said the bride, who had been graduated from one of the better public high schools.

"Burroughs, then [John Burroughs, a private coed school]?" "No," replied the bride who started to explain where she had gone.

"Maderia [a very social boarding school in Virginia]?" questioned the woman, somewhat impressed that this might be the answer.

"No, I . . . "

"Villa [Villa Duchesne, an expensive private Catholic school for girls]," the woman said firmly and exasperatedly, thinking that the groom, the scion of an old Wasp family, had married a practicing Catholic.

"No," whispered the bride.

"Well," said the woman as she walked away, "I guess you didn't go to high school, did you?"

"Dennis freaked out over exposing his roots," Cal said. "He always got scared when anyone tried to pin him down."

Cal found it strange that Dennis never brought his dates around. A detective later told Cal that Dennis had a classic case of street smarts: A slick operator has five friends, each of whom sees a different side of him. But they don't know each other. He never gives the friends enough information that, should they meet, they could piece his stories together. Criminals do it all the time, the cop said.

Eventually, however, the jigsaw puzzle about Dennis was assembled. A third socialite discovered that Dennis was seeing Nina and Becky in December; and Nina found out in March that Dennis not only was still seeing Julie Miller, he had married her. Faster than a hot stock tip, the word went out at country clubs everywhere that Dennis Bulloch had committed a social felony.

When Becky Cabot heard the news she felt awful. "I had no

idea," she told a friend, who replied that maybe the wife wasn't always the last to know. Weeks later, Becky heard that Dennis had been charged with murder.

"He made such a nice appearance," Becky said, shaking her head.

Julie Miller's ad in *The Riverfront Times* had been one of about a dozen Dennis answered. To the less financially fortunate, Dennis revealed a different identity. He would rather wear a lime green polyester doubleknit to the Club than admit to hobnobbing with the hoi polloi. While he did not understand the French phrases with which some socialites larded their English, Dennis was not about to be seen with women who thought the plural of "you" is "youse." In his less social incarnation, Dennis was not quite the "perfect gentleman," as Nina called him.

Barbara Villiers, a registered nurse, had also placed a personal ad in *The Riverfront Times*. She could not wait to meet "Dennis B.," as he called himself. Handsome as all get out, she thought, looking at his picture. And successful; he said he was with Touche Ross & Co., a Big Eight public accounting firm. Dennis sent her his home phone number with his standard line, "to take a chance on success" and call.

After several unreturned calls, Barbara was about to give up. Then "Dennis B." picked up the phone. They talked for more than an hour and a half—Barbara paying the long-distance rates from Alton, Illinois—about families and feelings.

Barbara was most impressed when this new man discussed the dreaded "r" word—relationships. "If I ever make a commitment to you," Dennis said, "I would see to it your brain did not vegetate and that I always would respect you for who you were." Dennis said he loved the aggressive Modern Woman, adored it when they made the first move.

They decided to meet the following night. Dennis said he would be coming from work; Barbara responded how attractive she found men in coat and tie.

"I'll wear one if you take me out for a nice dinner," Dennis said.

Instead, they met at 10 P.M., at Ted Drewes, a famous frozen custard spot. Barbara slid into his Honda Accord and sat admiring Dennis's clean-cut good looks, styled hair, pricey ski sweater and lovely manners. Such a gentleman, she thought; he never cursed or swore. They talked for two hours. He was so attuned to her feelings, sympathizing over her dying grandmother.

It was now close to midnight. Dennis, hand on her leg, asked Barbara how far it was to her house. Touched, she thought he was concerned about her driving home safely.

"I'm going to be real bold," he said. "Do you have any wine at your house?"

Barbara said she did. He followed her home. After wine and a few kisses—mouths closed, Dennis left at 2:30 A.M., saying he really wanted to see Barbara again and to call him any time.

She did, a dozen times. During one conversation, Barbara asked his last name. "Bender," Dennis said. He could not give her his address because, he said, these ex-girlfriends keep dropping by. To see him again, Barbara hinted she had a rare German wine and cheese. Dennis did not appear to respond. She bought him a Christmas present but returned it.

A month later, Barbara's doorbell chimed. It was midnight. Frightened, she slowly opened her door. She could smell the scent of Brut. There was Dennis Bender, smiling.

"The wine and cheese were too good to pass up," he said.

"A warning bell went off in my mind," Barbara later told police, "and what flashed was, 'Do I know this man well enough to let him in?' "

As he took off his coat, Dennis said he had been drinking at an all-night lounge in East St. Louis. Barbara brought out her wine—Blue Nun Liebfraumilch—rare only in a dry county in Texas. They drank that bottle and began a second. Dennis grew relaxed and talkative, unaffected by the liquor.

Together, they watched the porn film *Blue Lagoon* on cable. Dennis dimmed the lights. They sat closer on the sofa and began necking, Dennis again avoiding French kissing. He undressed Barbara as she unbuttoned his shirt. In minutes, both were naked on the sofa. Barbara wanted to move to her bedroom.

"No, it's more exciting here," Dennis said.

He moved up on the sofa so that his chest was even with her face and told her to bite his nipples.

"Bite me, hard, so that it hurts," he said.

"I don't want to hurt you," she said.

"You won't hurt," he urged, "harder, harder. Claw my back with your nails so that it hurts," he demanded.

Dennis began sucking on Barbara's nipples, so hard it hurt her.

Barbara pulled away and stretched out on the sofa with her head on the armrest. Dennis went behind her, moving the end table. He pulled her—her head upside down—toward him to begin fellating him.

A long time passed. Barbara wondered why he had not ejaculated. She felt like she was going to choke. Dennis stopped, saying he was getting too excited and began sipping his wine.

"You're quite good at this," he complimented her.

Barbara stretched out on the sofa again. Dennis walked around toward her. He began caressing her body all over, from her shoulders down to her hips. Oh, good, she thought, feeling his hands and breath move over her body. She closed her eyes in anticipation of deeper intimacies.

Instead, she felt a bolt of pain searing through her neck into her skull. Then another.

Barbara opened her eyes in shock. Dennis was standing over her, his teeth gritting. He was slowly and methodically striking her with karate chops to her neck. There were three blows to her neck as Barbara struggled to push Dennis away and scream.

"I was screaming as loud and hard and long as I could. I have never been more terrified in my life.

"Then I felt his hand over my mouth. Just as suddenly and unexpectedly as it had started, it stopped."

Dennis, nude, sat on the floor "like a little boy in his own little world."

"I didn't mean to scare you or hurt you," he said with tears in his eyes.

Barbara nodded, afraid to set him off again. "My mood is broken," she replied. She put on her sweatshirt and jeans and opened the door, motioning him to leave. It was freezing as the January wind blew into the room.

Instead of taking her cue, Dennis sat naked and motionless, looking confused and sorry. "I thought he was a little boy who needed someone to protect him and tell him what to do," she said later. Dennis apologized again.

"I'm bad and I should be punished. Will you spank me?"

"The spanking can wait til next time," she said. It was now two in the morning. Dennis continued sitting nude on the floor.

"I thought you would enjoy being hit," he said after a moment's silence. "I was only trying to intensify your pleasure. When I'm getting my hair styled— I've read in women's magazines that women become very excited when hit on the face and neck. I thought that sex and violence go together for women.

"I'm worried I haven't satisfied you or brought you to a climax," Dennis Bender said. "Let's go back to the sofa to finish."

Barbara shook her head, suggesting they wait until the next time.

"I know I should have asked you first about striking you, but I never would ask you to do anything you did not want," Dennis said.

"I haven't had it [sex] like that since May," he added.

Barbara was afraid to ask him directly to leave, fearing he could swing back into his own perverted world. Dennis asked to put on his clothes and to finish his wine. There they stood for three hours talking until five o'clock about raising children, careers, grandmothers. Your average post-coital, post-karate chop conversation.

"By the time he left, I was amazed at how much our opinions meshed," Barbara said. "Were we that much alike or was he incredibly good at saying what I wanted to hear?"

Part Four

Admissible Evidence

July 1986–May 1987

Eighteen

How She Caught
the Bridegroom

May 11–July 3, 1986

Barbara Villiers, like other former dates of Dennis Bulloch, did not believe at first that Dennis was involved in his wife's murder. The whole scenario of events made no sense. The burnt remains of Julie Bulloch were found bound to an oak rocking chair in a garage fire on Tuesday, May 6, 1986. Dennis had been in St. Paul on business for Price Waterhouse at the time. Then, around the time of his wife's funeral, Saturday, May 8, which he had failed to attend, her widower had staged a suicide leap into the Mississippi River.

Dennis had left not only a carefully thought out will (he had told police he was brought up to be "security conscious"), but also a lengthy suicide note in which he asked that no hooks be used when dragging the big river for his body (he had long been concerned with his appearance). None of the police believed Dennis had jumped into the Mississippi River. They began a scavenger hunt for clues that day, Sunday, May 11.

"There's no way he'd kill himself," Ballwin Police Lt. Niere told Assistant St. Louis County Prosecuting Attorney Tom De-

Priest the next morning. "We have no indication except his word, and we know that's no good. What's more, he's a coward. It takes courage to jump."

DePriest nodded. Niere continued: "While the evidence guys were unsealing his letter, I paced the bridge on both sides. There are no footprints, no wallet. You know jumpers usually empty their pockets before they go."

DePriest agreed, and on May 14, 1986, eight days after Julie's death, issued a warrant charging Dennis Neal Bulloch, aged thirty-two, with first-degree murder, meaning premeditated murder. Conviction carried the automatic penalties of death in Missouri's gas chamber or life in prison without probation or parole.

Dennis was placed on the Ten Most Wanted Fugitives List of St. Louis County Police with his litany of aliases: John Mason, David Bender, David Johnson, David Mason, and John Masterson. The U.S. Attorney of Eastern Missouri, in St. Louis, became involved, too, charging Dennis under federal fugitive warrants with fleeing the state as a murder suspect. This unleashed the long tentacles of the FBI.

At first, Jim Macke and Leslie Jefferson were Dennis's only colleagues at Price Waterhouse who believed him guilty. Indeed, when Leslie heard the radio news driving to work on May 6, that the wife of Dennis Bulloch had been killed in a fire, she assumed Dennis had done it. Most other Price employees said Dennis was too smart, too organized, that he would have planned the murder better. The partners, however, were said to be scared to death about the adverse publicity of the case.

When Carter Miller went home at night, the first thing he saw was his sister's little dog Buttons wagging his tail. It made his loss more poignant, but Carter was grateful that at least the family pet was spared the fire. Buttons brought back memories of Julie and their parents. As if Carter could ever forget.

Luke Jackson, the socialite who had gone skiing with Dennis only seven weeks earlier, was so unnerved by the news of Dennis's flight and the murder charge that he moved from an apartment in Clayton to a condo in Ladue. Somewhere his old friend would never find him.

Jas Kossuthski, who had introduced Dennis to the merry

pack of socialites, had no idea what was going on. He was deep in a jungle, having been shipped out by the Peace Corps just before Julie's corpse was discovered.

Karen Toksvig was frightened and angry. Six months after their divorce, Dennis was still using a joint credit card and she was being billed. Her ex-husband had charged more than $300 at the Payless Cashway in Columbia, Missouri, midway between St. Louis and Kansas City.

Lt. Niere noticed that the date on the charge slip coincided with the rape of a schoolteacher there. From her description, Niere thought her attacker might be Dennis. But the young woman had not gone to a doctor immediately after her assault, so there was no physical evidence, such as semen or hair. Niere planned to drive halfway across the state to interview the rape victim, but just before he left, the Columbia police called him to report the woman had been so traumatized she had left town, no known address.

"Julie would have been better off picking up some guy in a bar," Niere told DePriest. "All he would have done is break her heart."

Dennis's parents were calling Karen: This last tragedy was beyond bearing; their only surviving child charged with the heinous murder of his secret bride. Only they said they believed Dennis had jumped to his death. Ginny Bulloch would never believe the truth about her fair-haired boy, thought her former daughter-in-law. Ginny's whole life had been based on denial.

Bob Bulloch told Karen, at first, that he thought Dennis had killed Julie. Bob said Dennis was "off his rocker" and that what he had done was wrong. How much did the Bullochs know then? Phone records show they called a now unlisted number in St. Paul looking for their son when he disappeared May 8. They phoned Branson, Missouri, near the Ozarks, where the family visited and where Dennis had fled in 1979 when his sister Cindy died. They had a long talk with Dennis's old flame Christy Meiers in Washington, D.C., May 10, the day of Julie's funeral, telling her he had disappeared and his wife was dead. Christy assumed that was Karen, not knowing her lover had remarried.

Ten days after the murder, the Bullochs called Christy again with more bad news: Dennis had been named as the murderer.

Three days after the Bullochs had phoned Christy, Dennis himself called her, the woman he had spurned for money and position. First, he called her parents' home in La Crosse, Wisconsin, at 9:15 P.M., May 13. Her sister Cissy answered. A man said he was John Masterson of Price Waterhouse and had dated Christy under the name John Mason while he was in Washington. "I'm trying to find her now," Dennis added.

Frightened, Cissy called the St. Louis Police at 9:30 P.M. that night, saying she was worried for her sister's safety. The St. Louis Police contacted the Ballwin Police, who contacted the FBI.

The next day, May 14, Dennis called Christy in her Washington, D.C., office. He thought (erroneously) that the police could not tap government phones. (They do not need to in many cases; tracing calls is faster, requiring only about half a day's notice to set into motion. Wiretaps require affadavits and federal court orders. For a tracer, FBI agents or the local police ask the phone company to use its computer system to trace all phone calls to a particular number back to their source.) By summer, the FBI had put a tracer on Christy's office phone.

During his first call to Christy since the murder, Dennis was upset, but rational. He said he was having black-out spells.

Dennis kept repeating, "I didn't do it. I've been set up. I can't come back 'til I find out who did it."

"Where are you?" Christy kept asking him. She was shaking with fear.

"I can't tell where I'm at," Dennis answered. "I need to get out of the country. What kind of extradition agreement does the U. S. have with Canada?"

Another time when he called her at home, he asked, "See if Ed Schollmeyer [his friend from high school] knows anyone who could find me a new ID, such as a street person's."

Dennis usually kept their conversation brief, but he wrote Christy poetry and long loving letters. In his new persona.

Before, Dennis had played the role of the New Sensitive Man with women. With men he had portrayed himself as the Price Waterhouse Man With Potential. In his latest incarnation, Dennis transformed himself into the Romantic Outlaw. A Byronic Jesse James. By 1990, he would reshape the image into Political Prisoner.

[Paraphrased] *Dearest Darling,*

Why did this have to happen to me? I want to go back but political enemies have made it obvious what my parents and I would suffer if I went to the judges.

What sorrows me isn't what has happened to me. I am heartbroken over what may happen to us.

But I know your deep capacity to love. I know your strength and endurance. What is this short moment apart when we face our entire lifetime joined? Say yes. Say yes. Say yes to keep me going. It is your strength that I rely on.

I know it is dangerous to call you and write you. But without you what am I?

You alone love me for myself. Because I am Dennis. Not because I am handsome, smart and successful.

What new role had Dennis assigned to Christy? She was to provide the Love of a Good Woman who gives the outlaw sanctuary and helps him redeem himself and reach his "potential." As Dennis repeatedly explained, what he needed was "unconditional love."

Dennis phoned Christy seven more times while he was on the run, never saying where he was. At one in the morning, May 29, he talked for two hours without even hinting where he was hiding. Christy thought he was in the same time zone, for when he called, she, half-awake, had asked what time it was and he said, one A.M. Dennis was irrational during this conversation, swearing someone had set him up and giving free rein to bizarre sexual fantasies.

Later he wrote her:

[Paraphrased] *Yes, I made a mistake, it was a large one. But don't we all?*

Although he did not acknowledge it during these phone calls and his letters while he was in hiding, Dennis had been involved with Christy for a year now. After his first wife Karen had left him, in May, 1985, he had turned to Christy for love, sex, and companionship. He had continued to see her during his courtship and marriage to Julie. Several times, they took vacations together. And when Dennis had been in Washington, D.C., on a business trip, or Christy in St. Louis, they had stayed in each other's homes rather than hotels.

Dennis and Christy had spent all holidays together excluding Christmas, 1985, when he said he must stay in St. Louis to be with his ailing Gram. Having been with his parents several times, she was convinced they had not known he had remarried when she saw them last at Easter, 1986. Ginny and Bob, had they known about his secret wedding, were too straight to have been so open-armed then toward Christy.

And at Easter, 1986, Dennis and Christy had talked about getting married, agreeing she would move to St. Louis. Everything had appeared so normal then, although Dennis did not call her afterward. Christy had phoned him that she was coming to St. Louis for a business trip May 4–6.

But Dennis had said they could not stay in his house in U. City as he was moving in with Gram. He had been noncommittal about getting together.

Now, in late May, however, while he was hiding from the police, Dennis was planning a lifetime spent in wedded bliss with Christy. "There is no other to bear my children," he wrote her. The abortion he allegedly convinced her to have in February was now forgotten. Dennis later remarked that while he was not certain that the child was his, he had paid for the procedure.

After professing in a June, 1986, letter to her: 'I promise to be open to you. Openness is ever so important,' Dennis carefully crafted the ultimate lie: He said he had never slept with Julie.

Afraid of her crazed former lover, Christy moved out of her Arlington, Virginia, apartment and in with a colleague in Maryland. She did not want to go back to her apartment, for Dennis had keys to it.

The last time Dennis called her was July 3, while Christy was at work. It was a long conversation. Again, Christy asked where he was. Again, Dennis refused to tell her.

Then, suddenly, Dennis interrupted. "It's up," he said in horror.

"They've got me."

Nineteen

Hotel California

May 11–July 3, 1986

Rose Garon was a free spirit. A tall tan blonde, she looked like an aging surfer girl, yet was quite attractive. She camped up and down the California coast, sleeping in her tent during the day, working the graveyard shift at chain restaurants at night. Well into her thirties, she now wanted more stability, to come home every night to her own apartment, to go to the same job every morning. She began saving money for the rent deposit.

The afternoon of May 14, 1986, Rose was picking out a site from the map of the Sycamore Cove Campground off Highway One in Ventura County, north of Malibu, when a tall, dark-bearded stranger walked up.

He said his name was Jonathan Dennis—his friends called him Dennis—and that he, too, was looking for a campsite. He seemed to be trembling with fear. He carried a full-sized, eighty-five- to ninety-pound backpack, which experienced hikers find too clumsy. Thought Rose, He's really a novice. His only food was tins of tuna and he had forgotten to bring a can opener. He said he was hitchhiking. But Rose had noticed that a bus had dropped him off at the campground.

Because Jonathan seemed weak, "wimpy," and therefore safe,

143

Rose struck a deal with him. They would camp together. He would sleep in her tent while she worked at night at the Denny's in Thousand Oaks, and when she returned at dawn, he would leave. He would pay most expenses. Indeed, Jonathan always seemed to have money; he would leave and return with several hundred dollars, saying he had to call to Missouri for a judge to release his funds. Rose called him Jonathan, never Dennis.

The arrangement worked well and over their weeks together Jonathan confided in Rose: He had come to California to "get his head together" and "start a new life" after a rough divorce. Six weeks into his marriage, his wife had betrayed him. Towards the end of their marriage, his wife had gone on an alleged business trip. Jonathan, ever the romantic, flew off to surprise her. Instead, he got the surprise of his life—she was in *flagrante delicto* with yet another man.

"I've been an even bigger fool," Jonathan told Rose. "I put all of my property in joint names. Now, I want to kill my ex-wife."

That was not the first time Jonathan admitted to Rose that he wanted to murder his wife. Before their break-up, his wife had wanted to go drinking with the guys and did not roll in until two-thirty the next morning.

She was "reeking of sex and we got into a big fight," Jonathan said.

"Didn't you want to kill her?" Rose asked in amazement at all this adultery.

"Yes, I did," Jonathan answered. "I wanted to strangle her, but instead I forgave her."

Rose sensed Jonathan's confessions were less than true. Why did he dye his hair, eyebrows, and beard to dark brown? Why in the world did he shave all the dark blond hair off his chest?

"When I look into the mirror I want to see someone else," Jonathan explained.

Why did he make such a strange comment about her copy of serial killer Ted Bundy's *The Stranger Beside Me*? "Makes you wonder," he said. "You never know, do you, Rose?"

Rose asked him why he needed his roll of wide tape. Jonathan smiled. "You never know when you may need it," he said.

He discussed sexual bondage and asked what Rose thought

about it. "That's sick," she answered. He did not intimidate her, though he appeared to be trying. After dinner one night at the Crows Nest Restaurant in Santa Cruz, Jonathan made a pass. Rose refused and he felt rejected. She was not worried.

"Jonathan Dennis whateverhisname," she later told Lt. Niere, "is a real wuss," which rhymes with "puss" and colloquially means a wimp or worse, a pussy. "He even had to buy the *Boy Scout Field Book* to learn how to camp," she said.

After several weeks, Dennis had become a depressing companion. Indeed, he told her before they had hooked up that he had been drinking a lot of Jack Daniels and going crazy. He was obsessed with the news, reading the newspapers or watching the news on his AC-DC portable television set. Rose became frightened when she saw the TV sales receipt. It had been sold on May 11 at a California K-Mart to a Jonathan Block.

On June 20, Rose ordered Dennis out. He moved to a youth hostel (using an ID card with his alias and a fake home address) near Christian Life Center in Santa Cruz, and two days later took a short-term lease on an apartment at 350 Soquel Avenue in Santa Cruz from a nurse's aide.

When the nurse's aide returned to her apartment July 6, Jonathan Dennis was gone, but his things were scattered all over. She found an appraisal slip for a one-carat diamond engagement ring estimated at more than $4,000. The receipt was made out to Mr. and Mrs. Dennis Bulloch.

The nurse became frightened. She called the hospital where Jonathan had told her he worked. The personnel office had never heard of a Jonathan Dennis.

There was a knock on her door. Two agents from the FBI wanted to talk with her. About a Dennis Bulloch.

Dennis enjoyed using the nurse's aide's typewriter to compose his letters and his reflections for his diary. He wrote in the guise of an amnesiac, but there is no record he was ever treated for this disorder.

A health professional knowledgeable about the case says Dennis may have been thinking ahead for his trial. Murder defendants often recite this familiar litany: "I wasn't there, I couldn't have done it. If I was there, I didn't do it. If I did it, I don't remember. I don't remember, I have amnesia/was on drugs/was drunk. If I have amnesia/was on drugs/was drunk, it wasn't my fault."

With or without memory, Dennis was enterprising. He mailed a former date, the one he confided in about his orgies, an anonymous letter which she received June 4. Enclosed was an envelope addressed to "Resident, XXXX Judy Dr., Arnold, MO 63010." His parents' address.

Despite his precautions, this packet was turned over to the postal authorities, who had a federal search warrant to open it. Inside was a detailed letter about his finances, which Dennis wanted his mother to manage. He also sent his parents his chit for a complimentary lunch at the Café Des Beaux Arts at the St. Louis Art Museum for joining its Friends Association.

Fearful that more mail would be intercepted, Dennis frequently called his parents about his business affairs. To keep calls to them and Christy Meiers short and include everything he wanted, he would type up notes beforehand. He added such precautions as telling his mother to show no emotion so that no one would know they were talking; to take twenty dollars in change, go to a pay phone, and call him back. When she did, he asked if there were any problems with his insurance, cars, clothes, furniture, houses? Any trouble with his five checking accounts, including the joint ones with his late wife?

The one time he mentioned Julie by name since he killed her, Dennis ordered his parents to transfer her extensive jewelry collection—which he had put in his safe deposit box—into their safe deposit box.

With his mother taking care of business and so much free time in California, Dennis turned pensively to his diary: He wondered what wonderful things he would accomplish. How would he be remembered in history? He planned to write his memoirs.

Some of his writing was less philosophical. He listed acquaintances' names and their hometown addresses and social security numbers. His search appeared to be a transformation process. He had already picked up an application for a new passport under an alias.

In the interim, Dennis wrote ads to sell Karen's engagement ring and work as a freelance interior decorator.

Obsessed with self-improvement, he studied his paperbook copy of *Born to Win*. In his diary, he recorded how many bench presses he did, the instructions for bodylocks, karate chokes, and full nelsons. For some unknown reason, he also itemized in his diary his various internal organs.

Long letters to Christy continued to flow. His memory was rekindled about past pleasures in bed, complete with overhead mirrors.

Only once in all his letters and diaries did Dennis reveal self-knowledge:

> [Paraphrased] *I thought I could become all those dazzling creatures on television. I could perform each wonderful role. But I failed.*

Rudy Escalante came on duty at three P.M., July 3, 1986. Young and handsome in his uniform, he had been an officer with the Santa Cruz Police a little over a year. He climbed into his patrol car and began his rounds. At four-fifty P.M., he was parked along the beach when a call went out:

"Go to the corner of Ocean Street and Sokel. Subject is on the phone in an outdoor booth. He's wanted by the FBI for a homicide out of St. Louis."

A minute later Officer Escalante arrived. He recognized the gas station and remembered that the phone booth was on the north side of the building. Escalante pulled over. There was the suspect as described—white male with beard, wearing a green-sleeved white T-shirt and jeans, talking on the phone.

Escalante stepped out of his car and aimed his shotgun on the man's back.

"Santa Cruz Police!" he shouted. "Turn around and put your hands up!"

Twenty

Admissible Evidence

July 3, 1986–May 26, 1987

Dennis put his hand on the backpack lying on the change stand in the phone booth.

"Don't do it or I'll waste you," yelled Escalante.

Dennis took his hand off the backpack, turned around, and faced the cop. "What do you want me to do?" he asked politely.

Lt. Denny Niere twisted his long legs in his cramped airline seat. He tried to relax but kept looking at his watch, counting the minutes until it was time to land in Santa Cruz. For two months he had been working on the Bulloch murder case, first with the Major Case Squad, and then, after its disbandment, helping DePriest assemble evidence for the trial. The day Dennis had been arrested in Santa Cruz, July 3, back home he had been indicted by the St. Louis County Grand Jury for first-degree murder, in cold blood. St. Louis County uses the grand jury system as a prelude to criminal trials.

It had made Niere's Fourth of July holiday that Dennis was in a California jail facing Missouri's gas chamber or life in prison without probation or parole. Those sentences are mandatory for murder first degree convictions.

Niere believed Dennis might have committed the perfect crime had he acted like a proper widower and not assumed the police were so dimwitted. That was Dennis's core problem. If he were not so arrogant, Niere had said, Dennis might be living rich and free in the Caribbean.

Instead Dennis, who had waived extradition, was to be sent back to St. Louis in the custody of Lt. Niere, Ballwin Detective Steven Schicker, and their chief. When Niere saw Dennis on July 9, he was surprised. Instead of the blond, clean-shaven, and preppy Price Waterhouse consultant, Dennis was dark, furry, and unkempt, the stereotype of poor white trash from rural Missouri.

The officers found Dennis smug and condescending. He refused to talk about the case when he was arrested, during the long trip home, and when he was booked into the county jail, no bond allowed. The case of his lifetime and Lt. Niere never was able to question the criminal.

Dennis Bulloch did not want to talk to the people who had nabbed him. During his last call to Christy Meiers in Washington, D.C., July 3, Dennis had complained he was running out of money. Christy had told him to give her the number and she would call him back. She did, after first telling an FBI agent, who traced the call.

Good witnesses for the prosecution were popping up. People who could answer major questions, such as how Dennis got from 251 White Tree Lane back to Lambert St. Louis Airport on May 6. Considering that his car was found burned in the garage, the obvious conclusion was that somebody had driven him.

"Now things are falling together," DePriest said cheerfully to Niere. A housepainter named Gary Matzenbacher had come forward after seeing Dennis's picture in the news. Matzenbacher said he had picked up a hitchhiker looking like Dennis Bulloch on May 6, at five-fifteen A.M., at the intersection of Holloway and Manchester Roads, about a mile and a half from 251 White Tree Lane.

"I don't normally pick up hitchhikers, but I had a feeling this one desperately needed a ride," Matzenbacher told police. Oddly enough, considering it was cool that morning, "big beads of perspiration were running down both sides of his face and forehead," Matzenbacher said.

Matzenbacher was a very important witness for the prosecution. So far, he was the only person who could prove to a jury that Dennis Bulloch had been in the Ballwin area at the time his wife was murdered. He was the only one who could disprove Dennis's airtight alibi that he had spent the night of May 5, 1986, in St. Paul.

Prosecutor DePriest arranged a police lineup to see if Matzenbacher could identify Dennis. DePriest called Dennis's defense attorney, Arthur Margulis, to be present for the lineup. When Margulis walked into the warrant office, a funny look came over his face. He needed no introduction to this witness. Matzenbacher had painted Margulis's house in Ladue.

DePriest, Niere, and DePriest's investigators—Jack Patty, Bob Gates, and the others—now could place Dennis at the airport but could not prove how he got back to St. Paul. (What flight Dennis arrived on in St. Louis the night of May 5 was a mystery, for his alias was unknown until he admitted it at the trial. And no cabbie has ever been found who drove Dennis from Lambert Airport to his house.) There had been no tickets issued to Dennis under his own name or any of the aliases he favored on any of the flights the morning of May 6. Then, a lot of legwork brought a lead.

On May 13, a police officer went to a ticket agent, laid three photographs of Dennis on the counter, and asked the agent if he had ever seen this man. Yes, said the agent, on May 6. A man who was nervous, disheveled with wet, matted hair, and sweating, had appeared at six-thirty A.M., that day, asking if Northwest Orient [now Northwest Airlines] had any seats left on its next flight out to Minneapolis. The agent sold a one-way ticket to this man, who paid in cash and called himself David Johnson. Mr. Johnson had carried no luggage.

The agent also picked out Dennis during the police lineup.

Dennis, who had been married to two executives at Southwestern Bell, did not know how calls are traced. He had made his "cover for me" call to Jim Macke from a pay phone at the airport; he might just as well have called Macke from the crime scene.

The receiver of a phone near the gate where Dennis/aka David

Johnson departed had been left dangling. Someone reported it to the investigators, who called Bell's security department. Every pay telephone has a magnetic tape that records the times and numbers of all calls, along with whether the caller or an operator dialed the number. These tapes are permanently stored at Bell. The computer printout of this particular pay phone showed an operator-assisted call made for fifty-five seconds at six-forty-nine A.M., May 6, to the Holiday Inn Town Square where Macke and Dennis were staying in St. Paul. That matched the time Macke had given police and his recollection of the operator's voice. The call cost $1.80.

Investigators could now map out Dennis's chronology May 5 and 6:

May 5

6:14 p.m.	Dennis calls Julie from the Holiday Inn Town Square and talks for seven minutes.
7:20 p.m.	Dennis signs out of Farm Credit Building nearby.
7:30 p.m.	Dennis is last seen by Jim Macke and another co-worker walking near the Holiday Inn.
8:50 p.m.	Republic Air Flight #88 departs St. Paul.
10:11 p.m.	Republic Air #88 arrives St. Louis Lambert (the last flight to St. Louis that night).

May 6

4:00 a.m.	Neighbor two blocks away hears argument and woman screaming on White Tree Lane.
5:10 a.m.	Ballwin dispatcher receives fire call from neighbor.
5:15 a.m.	Gary Matzenbacher picks up Dennis hitchhiking.
6:30 a.m.	Dennis buys ticket from Northwest Orient Flight #421 from Lambert to St. Paul.
6:45 a.m.	Jim Macke receives long-distance call from Lambert, Dennis asks him to "cover for me."
7:00 a.m.	Northwest Flight #421 departs Lambert.
8:25 a.m.	Northwest Flight #421 arrives Minneapolis-St. Paul.

| 8:30 a.m. | Macke tries to contact Dennis in his room #901 at the Holiday Inn for half-an-hour. No answer. |
| 9:15 a.m. | Manager opens the door. Macke finds Dennis in shower. Dennis says, "Did I tell you I was married?" |

DePriest's main problem with the trial was finding friends and associates of Dennis who would testify. "No one wants to be embarrassed by the sordidness of this murder," he complained to Niere. "And a lot of people are afraid he'll come after them." Dennis's ex-wife Karen was so fearful of him, she balked at talking with detectives.

St. Louis County prosecutors found out about Dennis's ski trip with Nina Honeywell and her socialite set through the courthouse grapevine and through another prosecutor, Tom Mehan. Of the five members of the group, only Luke Jackson was cooperative with the prosecutors.

"After Dennis's fake suicide, I broke rank," said Luke Jackson. "It was a bad topic of conversation in the crowd. For a long time Nina and Muffy thought it [the murder] was accidental. I'd tell them there was no way this wouldn't come out, what with the ski trip and his being seen publicly with Nina. I wanted to make certain that the record was straight."

When DePriest called them in, Nina and Muffy arrived after first seeing an attorney and Art Margulis, Dennis's defense attorney. "To see what he planned to do with them on cross-examination," DePriest said ruefully to Niere. Except for Luke, they reeked of rank and smugness, the investigators thought.

"A snotty little twit," one investigator called Nina. She acted as though the untimely demise of Dennis's wife were a mere solecism.

But Nina et al. were not protecting Dennis because he was one of their own. Indeed, they were angered that they had deigned to allow an outsider into their exalted circle and he had betrayed their generosity, Mehan thought. Dennis was a traitor to the class he had aspired to. Nina needed to protect her reputation. Her friends needed to protect their images.

Nina said she knew nothing about any of Dennis's alleged earlier marriages, which Niere was checking.

Lt. Niere was unable to trace the persistent rumor that Dennis had been briefly married while he was in college. Then, an anonymous woman from Georgia called, saying she had been married to Dennis and he was the father of several children. She said she did not see much of him, what with his traveling and all. She had met him through a correspondence course when he was in Georgia. Now she was afraid for her life.

The dates she gave of the course checked out with when Dennis had been in Georgia. But the woman never gave her name, never called back. There were no marital records of a Dennis Bulloch being married in Georgia. Niere wondered, Did he use another name?

The Ballwin police lieutenant also tried to find links between two other bondage murders, one in Wyoming and one in Wisconsin. Both occurred while Dennis had been in the areas. Both women were found dead and burnt, strapped to their chairs.

Lt. Niere and Detective Schicker laboriously talked with every known acquaintance of Dennis Bulloch to track down the nude teenaged girl with the bound ankles in the Polaroid.

Niere took Karen Toksvig to the safe deposit box to read her ex-husband's diaries. She was heartsick and horrified by some of his entries: his affair with the live-in student and ramblings on how to kill someone and not get caught.

The mass of papers found at 251 White Tree Lane provided a possible motive for murder: greed. In Julie's handwriting there was a list of some of her valuables: Boxes of gold and silver coins; stock certificates for 200 shares of Kellogg, 428 of Exxon, 166 of AT&T, 200 Emerson Electric, 67 General Tire, and 459 May Co.; and a listing of her better pieces of jewelry appraised at $44,000. The most lavish pieces were a diamond bracelet worth $11,000 in 1983; an aquamarine and diamond dinner ring for $4,500; a gold charm bracelet with thirteen charms for nearly $7,000; and twenty-two other fancy rings, brooches, bracelets and encrusted crosses. How this golden horde must have whetted Dennis's appetite for riches.

Some evidence police found was ironic. Dennis Bulloch may have been the only person in America arrested for murder carrying in his wallet a $50 gift certificate to Saks Fifth Avenue. Some evidence made no sense, such as the receipt to Vivid One Hour Photos in Galtier Plaza in St. Paul.

Ballwin Detective Steve Schicker asked the St. Paul police to take the stub to One Hour Photo and mail him the results. When Schicker opened the envelope containing the photographs, he expected more kinky sex pictures.

These pictures were actually more tantalizing: color photographs of the household furnishings at 251 White Tree Lane. That last weekend he spent with Julie—whom he never found time to name as his insurance beneficiary or as co-owner of his stocks and real estate—Dennis photographed her silver, china, furniture, and paintings. And the day before the fire, the day he arrived in St. Paul for business, Dennis dropped off the film in a place he thought no St. Louis cop could track down.

To the prosecutors, this evidence showed Dennis committed cold-blooded, premeditated murder and arson. Tom DePriest decided he would seek the death penalty. Dennis Bulloch could become the first M.B.A. on Missouri's Death Row, maybe the nation's, thus joining the privileged confraternity of celebrity wife killers and would-be killers, including Dr. Jeffrey MacDonald and Claus von Bülow, who had not yet been acquitted in his second trial.

It was past five P.M. on a spring evening, 1987, and prosecutor DePriest was packing depositions into his briefcase to read at home. "That's about the only place where I can work on the trial in peace and quiet," he told Lt. Niere as he locked his office. It was almost impossible to work on this intricate case in the midst of running the warrant office. There were at least forty witnesses for the prosecution, compared to the handful in the average murder case. DePriest needed to interview them all, plus other people for background.

Every night, DePriest would unpack the accordion files and lay them out on the wooden table in his spare study at home. Methodically, he would sift through admissible evidence. As DePriest reread the material, he found it so fascinating that he did not feel he was missing any fun by coming home every night to work.

While DePriest usually did not take cases to trial, he wanted to prosecute the Bulloch case from the arrest warrant to conviction. His boss, St. Louis County Prosecuting Attorney George "Buzz" Westfall, agreed. No one else knew all the complexities.

To help DePriest, another prosecutor was assigned to second chair him. Tom Mehan, in his early thirties, bespectacled and preppy, the son of a respected St. Louis circuit judge, would second him in the trial. Mehan was a good friend of Margulis's partner, Bill Grant, who teased the prosecutors by calling them "the two Toms." Mehan developed his own theory of what happened that night, May 5, just before Julie Bulloch's body had been discovered at dawn on May 6, 1986.

A tall lanky man, Mehan liked to demonstrate in the office how easily Dennis could have killed Julie. Mehan would grab a small woman, who had agreed to the demonstration, by the arm, push her into a chair and tie one arm to the chair arm. Fighting her off, he would tie the other arm. "After that it would be a cinch to tie Julie up with tape," Mehan pointed out, even without using a stun gun.

Mehan hypothesized, "Dennis was outraged his wife had transferred her $64,000 from their joint account, outraged that she argued with him while he was in St. Paul. He was losing control of her. He flew home in a tirade. As he was tying her up with more than seventy-six yards of tape, Dennis was shrieking, 'Fuck you, fuck you.' "

Had Julie and Dennis engaged in sexual bondage before the night of May 5? DePriest interviewed Dr. Meagher, Julie Bulloch's psychiatrist. Under normal circumstances, a doctor cannot reveal information patients provide unless the patient approves.

But murder victims have no privacy rights. The most intimate physical, emotional, and spiritual secrets of a human life are ripped open, often out of context, during a trial. Julie's were, in late May, 1987.

In the case of *State of Missouri vs. Dennis N. Bulloch*, both sides hoped there would be some psychological evidence to boost their argument and some explanation of the three sex manuals and what the police found in Julie's bedroom: a Prelude brand vibrator, which looks like a hairdryer for a miniature Schnauzer. Attached to it was a "pleasure nubbin," the size of the tip of a child's thumb.

But Julie had not described her marital bed to her doctor. Or to anyone else—with one exception. That was her friend Terri Sacher.

Twenty-One

Inadmissible Evidence

July 1986–May 1987

At their last lunch, Monday, May 5, Julie had told Terri Sacher that over the weekend "He hurt me inside." Crying, she had asked her husband to stop, but Dennis continued. Julie pulled away, threw on a robe, and went into the kitchen where she sat at the table and smoked a cigarette. And cried. Dennis walked in. She smiled to herself, now he would apologize. Instead, he said, "You are just going to have to learn how to like that." He was more upset that his wife was smoking than that he had hurt her feelings.

"It hurt her terribly; it was important to her that he was so insensitive to her," Terri told Lt. Niere. But this testimony was not admissible. It was hearsay. What Terri knew was what a dead woman had told her. Julie could not be cross-examined.

Similarly, Julie's diaries and her audiotape could not be entered into evidence by the prosecutors. The diary in which she said on August 14, "Today, I met a really nice guy," could not be used to show Dennis had met Julie *after* he and Christy Meiers had begun bondage. Her tape in which she said Dennis had been so supportive of her during her breakdowns could not be used to demonstrate that Dennis had preyed upon an unstable,

156

naïve woman. The defendant could not exercise his Constitutional right to cross-examine his accuser.

There were legal problems, too, with testimony from Barbara Villiers about Dennis beating her during oral sex, in January, 1986. It would have been admissible, as a distinguished jurist, Judge Theodore McMillian, of the Eighth Circuit U.S. Court of Appeals explained, if the trial judge gave limited instructions that this testimony was not being used to prove the murder charges but only to show Dennis's modus operandi—his physical abuse of women. However, and this was a big however, many state trial judges are reluctant to admit such testimony, McMillian said, because it is so highly prejudicial and inflammatory. And the first thing the defense attorney would do is ask the appellate courts to order another expensive trial.

Basically, say some judges, defense attorneys can get away with murder because the government cannot appeal in state criminal cases. Barbara Villiers's evidence was also tricky because hitting her was a felony assault and Dennis had never been charged for it. Had Barbara or Karen gone to the police and had Dennis been arrested and charged with beating them, such evidence would have been admissible. If Dennis's trial judge would not allow Barbara to testify (or Karen because she had been married to him at the time and therefore technically under marital privilege), the prosecution could ask Dennis about the incidents during cross-examination.

Having never met her, DePriest set up an interview with Barbara Villiers. As she walked into his office, DePriest realized she might not be a good witness anyway. Her skirt was slit thigh-high on one side and she was chomping on chewing gum. Barb explained what Dennis had done to her and said to her, that for women, sex and violence went together. DePriest asked her if it were true what she had said to a detective from the Major Case Squad who had interviewed her in May, 1986. Barbara said it was.

"Tell Dennis," she had said, cracking her gum, "if he gets off to give me a call. He was cute." DePriest and Mehan agreed not to call Barbara Villiers to the stand.

Dennis's lawyer, Margulis, made a motion anyway to exclude Barbara's testimony on Dennis's propensity toward violence because it had to do with his reputation and his reputation was not on trial. Initially, Margulis also objected to Carter Miller's testifying.

Yet, during the trial, Carter's testimony would be twisted into that of one of his key defense witnesses.

None of the evidence would become a courtroom surprise to Margulis. State rules of discovery require that the prosecution turn over all evidence they have discovered to the defense.

The defense does not have to reveal its hand to the state. All it must provide to the prosecution is a list of the witnesses it will call at the trial. That is because the burden of proving the crime lies with the government.

The evidence in the Bulloch case consisted of three large packing boxes of physical evidence plus a one-foot thick file of the Major Case Squad, the supplemental Ballwin Police and FBI files, and the depositions. Every time the defense wanted to see any physical evidence—the defense had its own copy of the humungous police report—DePriest's investigators hauled the packing boxes from a storage vault into a private, locked room where Dennis and his lawyers could peruse them. (The pathetic charred chair in which Julie died remained in the storage vault until the trial.)

Dennis often was most interested in reviewing the lurid color photographs of his burnt-to-a-crisp wife and his sex manuals, investigators said. The Major Case Squad detectives had found in the garage on White Tree Lane a copy of *Making Love Better* in one of Dennis's moving boxes from his house in University City. The manual is profusely illustrated with photographs of unusual positions, such as a *menage á trois*, two women and a man. "Chapter Seven: The Love Boutique" displays a smorgasbord of dildos and other devices.

The Joy of Sex, discovered in the house, has a seven-page section on what the French call *ligottage* and we bondage. Author Alex Comfort specifically points out under "gagging," that it is "irresistible to some men's rape instincts" and that it is "hard to gag anyone one hundred percent safely." Comfort also says "adhesive tape is torture to take off."

And he warns that using gags on a person after he or she has been drinking is not only dangerous, it is "psychopathological."

Twenty-two

Pen Pals

July 9, 1986–May 25, 1987

After years of upward mobility, Dennis was living a life of leisure in affluent Clayton. Albeit in the county jail, there after Lt. Niere brought him back from California. Dennis was unique among inmates for his high-class mail, notices from the Young Republicans and Friends of the Art Museum and the Zoo.

Dennis was busy in his cell preparing his defense. While DePriest had the warrant office to run and Margulis had other cases to try, Dennis methodically reread the voluminous police reports. By the time his courtroom psychiatrist came to interview him in December, 1986, Dennis had spent five months recreating what had happened the night of May 5.

Feeling persecuted by the prosecutors, as Dennis wrote friends, he began a petition drive for support. Dennis wrote Dinah Moltke for help. It was his first contact with his former finacée since he had dropped her for Karen Toksvig six years earlier.

His letter oddly ignores his circumstances. St. Louis County Jail is well-run, but it is not the place one goes for the amenities:

[Paraphrased] *My life has been successful (until a few months ago). With an M.B.A. in hand, I began at Price Waterhouse and quickly climbed the corporate ladder.*

I've been very successful in real estate [which Dennis spells with capital letters]. *In just days, I'll clear nearly $15,000 on one building alone.*

You'd still have an easy time recognizing me from the way I looked years ago when we were together. That is, in one way! Everyone tells me I still look like I'm only in my late twenties [Dennis was then 33]. *I've been taking very good care of myself. I eat well—avoiding red meats and feasting on fruits and vegetables along with other high fiber foods—and I exercise daily, like I always did. Swim, tennis, ski, dance, pumping iron.*

No matter how busy I am, I join the activities at the zoo and museum and symphony. I also love going to the theatre, I've always been big in community activities—you know, charity dances.

No matter how busy I've been, I still see your picture. In fact, I have it here on my desk! And I have more, you on my Corvette, you in other poses! Call me sentimental! I like to look at them. You sure were pretty. Guess I didn't ever tell you enough. I like to look at your photos and think back. Like the time we were fooling around in the woods as the sun splattered its speckled pattern of light on the forest leaves and our idyll was interrupted only by some fat park ranger who wanted to safeguard the woods from sex. Remember the poetry I wrote you that day?

I daydream sometimes what would have happened to us if we hadn't broken up. [Dennis had been fooling around with Karen Toksvig, lying to Dinah about where he'd been.] *I know in my heart it's been sensless to think about what might have been. I, myself, look to the future.*

You've been swell to join my campaign to combat this ridiculous parody of the criminal justice system. My lawyers won't let me discuss it, but sometimes I can't imagine how this could happen to me. Many, many friends and relatives are joining me in my fight. The battle may be to do a letter-to-the editor routine in the papers and TV to balance the coverage from Westfall.

You know, something about how much I've already given to society in the way of what I've done for charities and church.

I'll keep you posted on what we will do.

Later, Dennis wrote Dinah again. This time, he said he was praying for her. That she would let go of bad feelings, which he believed, might hurt her relationships with other men. He suggested she see the God inside her. He closed with a blessing and a citation, Galatians, 5:22-23

Dennis not only found religion, religion found him. His minister, the one who had admonished Karen for provoking Dennis into beating her, had embarked on a letter-writing crusade to save Dennis.

The clergy can be poor character witnesses. A murderer convicted of the most loathsome crime—raping an eighty-five-year-old woman, stabbing her twenty-six times and leaving her naked and dying with the knife in her eye—will have some man of the cloth testify that while in jail the defendant has seen the Light. Most epiphanies occur en route to Death Row. And the number of conversions increases proportionately with the length of the prison sentences.

The most notorious inmates go to services on Sundays and to Sunday school. Even General Manuel Noreiga became devout.

The former devotee of orgies, golden showers, and sexual bondage now marched in step with the Moral Majority. When Dennis saw *9½ Weeks* on TV in jail, he complained that the S&M movie was sick and demoralizing.

Dennis's minister called on Cal Porterfield. "Dennis, that very private person, is now in a cell with other people," the minister said. "He has to wear an orange jumpsuit instead of his own clothes. The worst part is that Den, such a private person, must use a toilet in the middle of the room, in front of all those other people. Imagine how difficult that is for a man such as Dennis Bulloch. Den needs his friends to rally behind him in his hour of need. Many are sending cards and letters in support of his cause."

"Poor Julie," Cal said later, "she was a private person, too, and now she's dead and everyone is spreading rumors about her. So, Dennis has to go to the john in front of other men. Beats being murdered." Cal was disgusted with the minister. After talking with prosecutors DePriest and Mehan, Cal decided to testify against his former friend.

Dennis had better luck with his high school buddy Ed Schollmeyer and his society passcard Jas Kossuthski. They wrote frequently. Jas, in a South American jungle for the Peace Corps, was unable to visit, while Ed, who worked for the railroads as a train engineer, dropped by Clayton several times.

But Dennis did not give up on the Porterfields. They received a torrent of mail from him, clippings from *Reader's Digest* and "weirdo" health magazines with a lot of tips on child rearing. At Easter, 1987, weeks before the trial, Dennis wrote them that they were like his real family.

Dennis told Cal, Ed, and Jas that he would write the story of his legal harassments. He had always wanted to write a book, and now he had the time. Instead, he marinated in self-misery and adopted yet another role.

Dennis became Model Prisoner. In the county jail, as he did later in the state penitentiaries, Dennis taught computer classes and put himself through the jailhouse law school. (Prison libraries are required to stock legal textbooks.)

A professional familiar with the case said that this is typical behavior of narcissists and psychopaths. "Lacking a solid identity, Dennis finds it easy to go through life taking on new roles, preferably ones with clear-cut rules," the expert explained. "It's as though Dennis thinks, 'Whoops, Julie's dead, now I play Fugitive. Now, I'm caught and I'll play Model Prisoner. In the courtroom, I'll play another role yet.' "

Dennis's future appearance would be a dramatic shift away from his prior roles of Romantic Outlaw, New Sensitive Man, Price Waterhouse Man. This new image would be nourished by Dennis's well of self-pity.

Twenty-three

The Best Defense
Is a Good Offense

July 1986–May 1987

It was about two in the morning, which did not matter to Art Margulis, who needed only a few hours of sleep every night. Margulis, Dennis Bulloch's defense attorney, was meticulously rereading his copy of the police report of the case and taking notes on a legal pad. The trial was to start in a few weeks. At home, this spring night, on the screened porch with its green and white chintz-covered chairs, he was sitting back straight up, befitting a former FBI agent, which he was.

In his early fifties, Margulis was one of the leading criminal defense lawyers in Missouri. His looks were no handicap with juries. His perpetually tanned skin and silver hair accented powder blue eyes, which he further emphasized with a collection of light blue shirts. In addition, he had slanting cheekbones that added a touch of the Tartar.

Not only did he look sleek, he acted with dignity and courtly manners. When television reporters he knew came to interview him with their cameramen, Margulis surreptitiously would ask the names of the photographers so that he could greet them properly. Said one newspaper reporter, "Art thinks he's the best, but he doesn't act like he's any better than you are. He's just controlling."

Margulis had remained friends with his buddies from University City High School. He was still married to his high school sweetheart, and he was very close to his parents and four sons.

The only things Margulis had in common with his client were that he, too, had lost a little sister while he was young and that he had worked out long before it became fashionable. But he jogged more to stay in shape to endure long trials than to keep his Gucci belt taut.

As Margulis reread some of the police interviews, he was astonished. "I've been in criminal law nearly thirty years and I've never seen anything like this police report," he told his wife Joyce the next morning. "I can't believe what I read. The photographs of Julie Bulloch's body are the worst crime scene pictures I've ever seen."

Margulis received good cooperation from prosecutors and police. DePriest's investigators, St. Louis homicide sergeants, assistant United States Attorneys, all said in chorus: "Art's ethical and a gentleman." A federal prosecutor added, "Art doesn't pull rabbits out of hats in the middle of the trial. You know where he's going."

Ironically, in light of the later verdict, Margulis was not first choice as defense attorney. Dennis's parents had contacted the noted colorful criminal defense attorney Charles "Charlie" Shaw. Tall, dark, and handsome, Shaw raised horses on his huge spread of a farm and wore cowboy boots and hats into the courthouses, all belying his background as the son of a former Clayton mayor. Appealing and fun-loving, Shaw was also open and helpful. He was famous for walking clients. A few years earlier, he had won the acquittal of a trendy West County restaurateur who killed a friend in a parking lot after they argued over a woman.

After Dennis was returned to St. Louis in shackles, his parents went to Margulis's Clayton office after normal working hours on July 20, 1986. That night, Margulis called his partner William Grant at home.

"There are only two reasons to take a case," another prominent criminal defense attorney says: "It's interesting or it pays well." Margulis and Grant both had been intrigued by this case. "We were figuring it out before we were offered it," said Bill Grant. They agreed to take it after lawyer and client checked each other out. Previously, Margulis had refused to defend sex crime cases.

It was under the worst of circumstances, that first meeting with their infamous new client. Dennis was sitting in the dingy jail in his orange jumpsuit and tennis shoes. Hostile to the criminal justice system, he had not yet been given access to the police reports; he had only read the newspapers about what had happened. Margulis was impressed with how articulate and prepared his client appeared to be. Dennis already had voluminous notes to go over with his proposed advocate. "Dennis was very controlled, very organized, very self-possessed," said Margulis, who is too. Margulis agreed to take the case.

"Bad choice on Bulloch's part," said a prosecutor, schmoozing with a courthouse reporter. "Dennis should have gone with Charlie Shaw."

"Why?" she asked. "Art's very cerebral. He always wins on appeal."

"Charlie Shaw doesn't need to. He wins at trial level," countered the prosecutor.

Dennis later tried to play off one attorney in Margulis's office against another. He would call one lawyer and cite a second one if the first did not agree with him. Or, he would say to the second lawyer that the first had said such and such and would ask was that really true? With so much free time on his hands, Dennis became a jail-house lawyer, a breed known more for its second-guessing than for its judicial savvy.

Good defense work does not come cheap, even though St. Louis rates are low compared to charges on either coast. Margulis's fee, about which he refused to comment, was said to be $58,000, for what appeared to be a short trial. This seems too low. Shaw said he asked Dennis's parents for about $100,000 in fees. It is not known if money was the reason the Bullochs called Margulis.

It is not clear how much Dennis contributed toward his legal fees. It is said that his parents plundered their retirement fund to keep their sole surviving child from the gas chamber in addition to mortgaging their house.

Their son's incarceration and trials caused further economic hardship on Ginny and Bob Bulloch. Ginny had to quit her job at National Food Stores, some say to manage her son's financial dealings; a friend says because she was too overwrought to work. Even Dennis's grandmother, Gram, was pressed to raise money for his later bonds.

All this upset court workers, who saw how poorly Dennis treated his parents. "They were just hard-working plain folk," said one woman. "He was ashamed by their lack of education and refinement." Dennis seemed resentful that his mother dominated the family.

For a couple who had worked so hard to instill traditional values in their children, and then had to bury one of them and see the other in jail for murder, the year from May, 1986, through May, 1987, was emotionally and spiritually grueling. No matter what, the Bullochs continued to make the long drive from Arnold into Clayton to see their son every visiting period.

It was a typical cold, dark December evening, five months after Margulis's first meeting with Dennis. Margulis and Grant were walking to the St. Louis County Jail a few blocks away. Their last clients had left, as had most office workers in Clayton. The streets were empty; it was quiet and an easy time to think as they walked. The two partners regularly visited Dennis after hours, when the jail interview rooms were less crowded.

Grant, in his mid-thirties, had been with Margulis since he had graduated from Washington University Law School, Margulis's alma mater. A tall slender man with refined features and a mass of wavy dark hair, Grant looked like the lead in *Philadelphia Story*. He was of Wasp New England stock and had grown up summering on Cape Cod and in Maine. He collected Native American art. He led the life Dennis wished he had led. Grant and Margulis each carried brown legal files, accordion-pleated to hold the reams of papers stuffed into them.

Dennis was waiting. Grant said, "He'd come out with both arms filled with books, notebooks, and pads. Sometimes he'd be so loaded up, he'd have to turn sideways to get through the door. Dennis was ready for four-hour sessions. He had kept track of each and every paper we filed." His lawyers, in turn, got to know Dennis very well. And Julie, too.

One of the first things Margulis did was call his investigators, a man and a woman team. "I want no surprises in the courtroom," he ordered. Should his client take the stand, Margulis could not afford not to know what DePriest and Mehan could ask Dennis on cross-examination.

Explained Margulis, "This was an extraordinarily complicated case, the psychological aspects of the bondage and tangential problems." He met with a retired New York City homicide detective he had heard about through his friends in St. Louis Homicide and the FBI.

Margulis recalled, "The former cop had investigated more than a thousand homicides. He flew in to meet with me. He and I met for an entire afternoon and I didn't do anything in that meeting but listen. I got an education on homicide, particularly homicides under the most bizarre of circumstances. He thought the case was very strange—Dennis's flying here under an assumed name, an incredible amount of suspicious circumstances, which made the case so complicated, accounting for all that. He gave me a lot of very valuable information, how to have my own investigators approach these unusual circumstances.

"He finally rose to leave, shook my hand and said, 'Good luck, counselor. You are in very deep Bronze Age shit.' "

Margulis's detectives became obsessed and exhausted by the case. The low point came when they listened to the long, painful audiotape Julie had made for her husband.

She was forever asking, if not pleading with Dennis, to please discuss their problems. To entice him to do so, Julie agreed to suffer his anger. She would "atone" for her snooping into his Day-Timer address book and putting her money back in her name alone.

Then, in tears, she would describe her thoughts and pain as "babbling."

It was hard for the investigators on both sides, male or female, to maintain professional stoicism.

Such a tape could crucify Dennis in court. DePriest could not introduce it because the tape fell within the hearsay rule. The defense could have introduced it, saying that it rebutted the prosecution's charges that Dennis did nothing for his wife. On the tape, Julie acknowledges his support during her breakdowns.

If Margulis introduced it, however, the tape could ruin his defense. It could cause the jurors to feel sympathy for Julie's plight instead of seeing her as a partner in deviant sex; it could establish money as Dennis's motive for murder; and Julie's implying Dennis wanted her to have an abortion would weaken the defense.

Meanwhile, Margulis had more exciting evidence he planned to use. About Carter Miller. That worried DePriest.

Margulis also argued that the following evidence was unconstitutional: everything taken from 251 White Tree Lane and in Dennis's briefcase when he was interviewed by the Major Case Squad as well as items seized from his California backpack. The latter included a passport application as well as notes about an alias. There had been no proper search warrants, Margulis said. The judge who would hear the case beginning May 26, 1987, had overruled the defense. The evidence would not be thrown out just because the Major Case Squad had not secured search warrants. The police did have probable cause.

Judge Milton Saitz, who was presiding over the Bulloch trial, did rule in Margulis's favor on another motion: Margulis could use what Carter Miller said during his lie detector test on May 6, 1986. It would be the foundation for his defense, along with what Terri Sacher had told police.

Terri repeated the tale she had told police in early May, 1986, about Julie's alleged sex partner. This time under oath during Margulis's deposition. That meant if she changed her story appreciably while sitting in the witness chair testifying during the trial, she could be charged with perjury.

Terri did not say much. One sentence in her deposition about an unnatural sexual relationship. It destroyed the dead woman's reputation.

Part Five

The Murder Trial:
The Delusion
of Appearances

May–July, 1987

Twenty-four

The Trial

May 26–30, 1987

It is amazing how complete is the delusion that beauty is goodness.

—Count Leo Tolstoy
Quote copied in Dennis Bulloch's diary, 1980–1985

*Alfred the Great, when he invented trial by jury . . . was not aware
. . . the condition of things would be so changed . . . it would prove
the most ingenious and infallible agency for defeating justice that
human wisdom could contrive . . . in our day . . . [we] swear in
juries composed of fools and rascals, because the system rigidly
excludes honest men and men of brains.*

—Mark Twain, *Roughing It*

Art Margulis walked into the courtroom early, Tuesday, May 26,
1987. It was not yet eight-thirty in the morning when he laid his
files on the defense table. He was early so that he could talk to
Dennis, now in a holdover cell en route from the county jail to
the courtroom. Margulis sat and thought for a minute: Anything
less than the death penalty would be a major victory.

This courtroom was no stage set for high drama. It was unlike
the federal courts downtown, where Margulis often practiced,

with their high mahogany-paneled walls crowned with egg-and-dart moldings from which hung larger-than-life portraits of bearded judges. St. Louis County courtrooms were the last word in bland government modern: low ceilings, light woods, and bright swivel chairs. At least, the counsel tables were not kidney-shaped. This room was more appropriate for a yuppie divorce. Divorces had once been the bread and butter for Margulis. Now he defended the children of federal judges and university chancellors. (He also had represented Dr. Dale Cavaness, who had murdered his son, as told in the book *Murder in Little Egypt*.) The Bulloch trial promised to be the most spectacular of Margulis's career.

Margulis walked down the back corridor to meet with his client in his cell. At least I don't have to teach this defendant how to dress, thought Margulis approvingly. His client was wearing a conservative dark suit, white shirt, and rep tie. Indeed, Dennis insisted that his parents bring him a fresh change every day of the eight-day trial.

As Dennis emerged with Margulis from his cell, the television cameras began rolling. Whenever Dennis was taken in shackles along the corridor behind the courtroom by the guards, his attorney walked beside him.

When they arrived inside the courtroom, Margulis insisted that his client be unbound before the media and jurors could see him.

The trial began with proceedings in the judge's chambers. Margulis, Grant, DePriest, and Mehan all gathered around Judge Saitz's desk with the door closed. The defense team argued that Terri Sacher should be allowed to testify as to what Julie had told her. Terri had told police, and had repeated under oath during her deposition, a cryptic comment from Julie.

Terri had never said when their conversation took place or whether Julie was on heavy medication then or what Julie really meant. All Terri had stated was, "Just that they [Julie and her brother Carter] had had sex. The way she [Julie] worded it was that they were very close and that they had sex." Terri had added she did not remember when or where this act allegedly took place.

The tale seems, at best, a terrible distortion. Carter Miller emphatically denied it and there was no psychiatric evidence that any such incest ever took place. What may have occurred was that when Julie was heavily drugged, during or after her two hospitalizations, she told Terri she and Carter had slept together, meaning in the same room, perhaps for comfort the night they had buried their mother. Did Julie mutter this story to Terri while she was psychotic and hallucinating, in the fall of 1985? The idea of incest does not seem true. None of the prosecutors or police involved in the investigation believed it.

The real question was why did Terri tell this story when it had nothing to do with the case? Alone of Julie's friends and neighbors contacted for this book, and in general by the media, she has refused to talk.

The prosecutors argued that Terri's testimony would be hearsay, for she was quoting a dead woman. Grant pointed out that the tale was admissible under federal rules of evidence because Julie's statement was self-incriminating. Julie's incest remark should be considered truthful because why would she say something terrible about herself if it were not true? But this was state court, said Judge Saitz as he barred the comment from the trial before him.

Terri was one of the three key witnesses pivotal to the defense. Another was Carter Miller. As Bill Grant argued to the judged, Dennis's defense was that Julie Bulloch was no helpless victim in sexual bondage, but the initiator and instructor. Julie was not only "sexually promiscuous," she also was sexually abnormal, Grant said. "A jury could reasonably infer that the deceased was a willing participant in the sexual bondage activity that led to her accidental death."

The rest of May 26 and May 27 were spent picking a jury, slow for Missouri courts, where impaneling a jury usually takes at most half or a whole day. While the Bulloch jury took longer to select because of the complexity of the issues involved, the *voir dire* was faster than in other states. No-nonsense judges in the Show-Me state laugh at California trials in which three months are spent picking a jury.

After lunch on Thursday, May 28, the prosecutor and defense attorney presented their opening statements, summaries of what evidence they would offer. From this, one basic theme emerged: Who was the victim on May 6, 1986? The dead bride or the defendant?

DePriest emphasized how Dennis Bulloch was a decadent, philandering, lying, social-climbing sadist who coveted Julie Miller's estate. Dennis secretly wed the unstable woman for her money, and after ten weeks, when he could no longer control it or her, he tied her up and watched her slowly suffocate, DePriest said. Bulloch had committed the perfect crime. Until he failed to behave as a grieving widower. His suicide jump was as big a fraud as he was. Dennis fled to California, where he was preparing to leave the country, DePriest said. Instead he was caught.

Margulis described Julie as a femme fatale who lured Dennis into bizarre sexual rituals to satisfy her unnatural cravings. As a result, she died accidentally. So depressed was he over the break-up of his first marriage, Dennis failed to sense Julie's insanity. A successful investor and Price Waterhouse consultant, Dennis did not need his wife's money. Dennis, said Margulis, thought Julie burned to death in the garage fire. He ran away, blaming himself. He was too bright to have committed a crime with so many mistakes. Margulis repeated what would become the defense refrain, "It was all an accident."

DePriest and Mehan called forty-one witnesses to testify, five to ten times the number in the average murder trial and thirty-two more than the defense used. Most of the witnesses were called in chronological order to simplify the case. The first were the police, firefighters, and fire marshals on the scene May 6, 1986.

They explained how arson had incinerated most of Julie Bulloch's car and the garage in less than an hour. The fire had been started in the back seat of her Buick Regal. And a rag had been wrapped around and stuffed into the exhaust pipe and secured with blue tape. The gas cap had been removed. An accelerant must have been used, the fire marshal said, otherwise the fire in the backseat would have died out. But specifically which accelerant had never been determined. And Dennis never admitted using one.

Dennis sat impassively when his former superior at Price

Waterhouse took the stand. He did not flinch as Jim Macke described Dennis's long-distance phone call early the morning of May 6. Dennis had asked Macke, "Cover for me."

Macke had asked Dennis if he had had a long night. Dennis said, "Yes."

Macke testified that when he heard that Dennis's wife had been killed, he assumed the woman was Karen Toksvig, whom Dennis was divorced from six months earlier. Macke and another man went to Dennis's hotel room and knocked; there was no response. Afraid Dennis had hurt himself, the two men had the hotel manager unlock the door. As Macke walked in, Dennis came out of the shower.

"Did I tell you I'd gotten married?" Dennis asked. "I'm not sure if I should have done it, but I'm happy about the marriage."

Macke went over and cleared a part of the hotel bed for Dennis, wrapped in a towel, to sit down. Macke moved to the other side. The other man said, "Dennis, your wife died in a fire."

Flushed and looking stunned, Dennis asked, "Are you joking?"

"I'm sorry, but it's not a joke," the man said.

"Dennis began to cry, and he sat on the bed and he continued to cry, and then he kind of fell to the floor on his knees, kind of hunched over, and asked us to leave him alone for a few minutes," Macke told the hushed courtroom.

He told Dennis he would take him back to St. Louis, adding he would be back in ten minutes to help pack. But when Macke returned and knocked on Dennis's door, there was no answer. When Macke had the door opened, again, there was no one there.

Anxious, Macke and his associate began combing the skyways linking the hotel to other buildings. A police officer joined the search. In the midst of this frenzy, a hotel employee spotted Dennis in the lounge.

Macke and his associate joined Dennis there. It was nine in the morning. After a few rounds of drinks, Macke took Dennis for a drive. They stopped at the Sheraton Hotel on Highway 94 for another drink.

Dennis complained to Macke how unfair life was. He said his wife had emotional problems she hid from him until their marriage. She had considered suicide and he felt responsible for her death because he had been gone when it happened. Macke added that Dennis seemed drunk.

Macke took Dennis to the airport and helped him into the men's room, where he vomited. A Sky Cap wheeled Dennis into the plane where he promptly fell asleep. Upon arrival in St. Louis, Macke rented a car and drove Dennis straight to the Ballwin Police Department. Dennis slept until they pulled up.

Macke said, "Dennis asked, 'Why do we have to stop here now?' And then he grabbed my arm and told me, 'Don't let them take me away.' "

After the police interview, Macke took Dennis to dinner at Andre's Swiss Restaurant, near Clayton, a patisserie long appreciated for its serious chocolate desserts, and then to Macke's house in Glen Carbon, Illinois, where Dennis spent the night at Macke's house. Dennis refused to talk about what had happened to his wife of ten weeks. The next morning, May 7, Macke drove Dennis to his parents' home in Arnold and flew back to St. Paul.

Macke was surprised to hear from Dennis the following morning, Thursday, May 8. Dennis said he was flying up in an hour to see him and emphasized that this was a secret trip.

Over lunch in the St. Paul airport, Dennis had made it clear to Macke he wanted to talk about anything but his wife's death. He complained for the hour and a half he was there that his relatives were "babying" him and he had no time alone.

Macke told him to get back and take care of the funeral plans. As they waited early that afternoon at the flight gate, Dennis complained that the police suspected him of killing his wife. Macke replied they were just doing their job.

"The last I saw of Dennis Bulloch was when he walked through the doorway of the walkway to the aircraft." Macke never saw his former colleague again until he took the stand against him.

Carter Miller was eager to begin his testimony. He waited in the room reserved for witnesses so that they cannot hear what others testify and then alter their own testimony. Carter's wife, Judy, who was five months pregnant with their first child, sat with him. They believed that within hours Carter would restore

Julie's good name, and within days the jurors would convict Dennis of murder and Carter's long ordeal would be over.

"No one can imagine what it's like to have to live with the knowledge your sister was murdered," he told his wife. "Well-meaning people come up to me and say, 'I just know how you feel.' They have no idea. That makes it worse.

"But everyone says it's bound to get better," he sighed.

Sometimes it seemed the only thing that kept him going was that justice would be served. Carter admired DePriest, sensing that the prosecutor believed in what he did, that he was out to avenge Julie's murder. DePriest was not like some prosecutors, who seek flashy trials to enhance their own careers. Carter felt protected by DePriest, that DePriest was defending the Millers the way Margulis was defending the Bullochs.

His sister would be vindicated and her killer punished, thought Carter. People would realize how proud he was of his big sister: When the story came out, they too would appreciate what a wonderful thing she had done, taking care of their dying parents. Then, he could concentrate on his wife, now pregnant with their first child. So preoccupied was he with justice for Julie, Carter was unconcerned about what could happen to him on the witness stand.

Suddenly, the bailiff came. It was Carter's turn.

DePriest was nervous. Yet, in court, like Margulis, he wore the blank mask of a television network anchor. DePriest worried that Carter's words would reverberate long after he left the witness stand.

At first, Carter's testimony went well. He told how his sister had married Dennis Bulloch on February 22, 1986, after a brief courtship and even briefer engagement. Other than the minister and the bridal couple, Carter and his wife were the only members of the wedding. Dennis invited no family or friends. Only Julie took a wedding ring. Dennis refused to wear one.

After his sister's murder ten weeks later, Carter never saw Dennis again. Carter was forced to identify the body, make arrangements for and attend its burial, and have the house on White Tree Lane boarded up.

Margulis rose for his cross-examination. Again, he and De-Priest argued before Judge Saitz outside the jurors' hearing. While DePriest agreed to allow Margulis to question Carter beyond the scope of his testimony, the prosecutor did not want Margulis grilling Carter about his own sexual practices. DePriest argued that what Carter had done had nothing to do with what happened to his sister. Judge Saitz, a former police officer, again overruled the state's motion to prohibit such testimony.

Margulis could ask Carter what he had wanted.

Carter Miller's words would give Margulis the material he needed to build an image of his client. The murder trial was not over right or wrong. The adversarial system used to be compared to a medieval jousting tournament in which a knight/ lawyer represents each side and the two battle it out. Not necessarily so anymore. Defense lawyers go one step beyond Abe Lincoln's dictum, "If you have law, argue the law; if you have facts, argue the facts; if you have neither, scream for mercy." Today the defense can be a public relations campaign of carefully calibrated images. Which is not to say prosecutors do not do this too.

Margulis, who with clients or anyone needing his protection placed "an invisible arm" around the person's shoulder, also possessed a tongue like a surgical laser. There was not a lot of bleeding, but the witness he cross-examined would be exposed to the bone.

Margulis opened with, "Mr. Miller, with all due respect to you and your deceased sister and the situation in which we are unfortunately involved, you were very unhappy about the fact that your sister was engaged in sexual activity with married men, weren't you?"

Various forms of the question were repeated seven times, a good courtroom technique for revealing Julie's sexual behavior. If any of the jurors had been daydreaming or dozing, he or she would have realized eventually that Julie Bulloch had had "an affair or two" with married men.

Then Margulis asked Carter how long he had lived at 251 White Tree Lane after his mother died. Carter replied he moved out soon after his mother's death. Margulis repeated that there had been some time between Mary Jane's death and Carter's departure and marriage, that Carter and Julie had lived alone together. That point won, Margulis aimed his laser at the soft spot and struck.

"Do you remember some time after your marriage engaging in sexual bondage with a woman at the Lake of the Ozarks?"

Carter admitted under questioning that he had initiated bondage on numerous occasions with three women. He said he used clothing or tape, maybe even microphone cables, as bindings to tie himself or his lover to a bedpost or chair. He had also used gags. "Not to the extent of anything with my sister, what happened to her . . . a small piece of tape, something like that."

"Now, I have not named these girls," Margulis said, "and I am not going to, and I am not asking you to. So, when I ask you where did it occur, you don't have to give me an address. It occurred at her parents' home, didn't it? . . . Where else did it occur?"

MILLER: . . . it may have happened at 251 White Tree . . .
MARGULIS: So there may have been bondage at 251 White Tree?
MILLER: There's a chance.
MARGULIS: Julie lived at 251 White Tree during that entire period, didn't she?
MILLER: Yes.

Carter's pregnant wife sat immobile. She looked as though she had been slapped across the face in public. All around her people whispered as they rose for a trial recess.

In the hall, Ginny Bulloch was friendly and chatting with reporters. With her was her husband and their minister.

As the recess ended, Margulis did not accompany Dennis when he was taken through the corridor in shackles. Accustomed to his attorney's presence, Dennis refused to walk alone with the guards. Busy with a legal point, Margulis exploded with, "Oh, for God's sake, Dennis, just go sit down."

After the recess, DePriest called eight witnesses to demonstrate the motive for murder: avarice.

Dennis stood to inherit more than $300,000 from Julie's estate, which in 1986 would have bought him a fully paid house in the best suburbs. As primary beneficiary, he would gain $18,472 from his wife's savings plan at Southwestern Bell; $40,000 from her life insurance there; $1,577 in employee stock ownership;

$3,227 in unpaid wages; $39,310 in sickness-death benefits, for a total of more than $100,000 from Bell alone.

Julie had kept a $10,000 life insurance policy from her first employer, Prudential Insurance Company, and a week before she died, Dennis called the company to have himself named as beneficiary. That was in addition to her house worth about $90,000, jewelry now totaling close to $50,000, stocks and bank accounts of more than $70,000.

Julie had a $63,000 time deposit open account at Boatmen's Bank in Ballwin and a $4,000 account. On March 8, 1986, a week before his ski trip with the country clubbers and two weeks before he told Nina Honeywell his marriage was to be annulled, Dennis went to Boatmen's with his bride to change her surname and to add his name to her accounts. (On those signature cards, Dennis lied about his age, lowering it two years.) The newlyweds also consolidated the two accounts into a funds management account.

On March 17, while Dennis was out skiing with Nina Honeywell, his wife returned to Boatmen's to open an IRA with Dennis as beneficiary. On March 22, while Dennis made plans to take Nina to the Young Republicans party, Julie closed their joint account and transferred her $63,000 to a new account in her name only. On April 25, Julie returned to her personal banker again to check her balance before she closed the account.

The next day, she and Dennis opened a joint money market account and a joint checking account at Mercantile National Bank in Chesterfield. Julie put $63,000 and Dennis $21,000 into the money market account. She also deposited a total of $3,300 into the now account. On May 5, Dennis deposited $1,000. The couple also opened a joint safe deposit box.

One witness after another was asked, "If anything would have happened to Julie Bulloch, who would have gotten all this money?" Dennis Bulloch was the unanimous answer.

A teller at Boatmen's Bank in Manchester told jurors of an ugly incident. On Monday, March 24, Dennis drove through the drive-up window alone about eight A.M. He wanted to withdraw a large chunk of money, but was told for such a sum he must come inside. At nine A.M. as the doors opened, Dennis approached the teller. He asked for a cashier's check for about

$60,000. The woman told him there was no balance, his wife had withdrawn her money.

Dennis lied and told her, "Oh, my wife is out of town." This was about the time Jane Muster and the vanpoolers noticed Julie had what appeared to be cigarette burns on her face.

What would Julie have inherited had she survived Dennis? Not much, according to his bankers and insurance brokers, about $22,000. A vice-president at Roosevelt Federal Savings & Loan in Chesterfield testified that none of Dennis's five accounts there named his wife as joint tenant or beneficiary. One was a checking account that Dennis closed May 8 by withdrawing $1,000 just before he fled to California. Julie probably did not know about Dennis's accounts, for he had had the statements sent to his three post office boxes.

Dennis had not listed Julie as beneficiary for his John Hancock Life Insurance policy of $63,000 through Price Waterhouse. Nor did he name her on his $200,000 accidental death policy with Connecticut General Life Insurance. His Price Waterhouse 401K plan and group travel accidental policy named his parents or the Porterfield twins as the beneficiaries.

The Price Waterhouse personnel spokesman said Dennis took out their group health plan in February, 1986, but did not list a wife for coverage. Nothing in his personal file showed he had remarried, although it noted his divorce from Karen, December 20, 1985. No one at Price knew he had a new wife.

One of the state's key witnesses was Dr. George Gantner, Medical Examiner of St. Louis City and County, member and former president of the American Academy of Forensic Science. Dr. Gantner explained how Julie died of asphyxia from the gags and why it was a homicide. He had determined she died before the fire was started. Liquor and drugs were not involved in the murder. Indeed, Julie had had nothing to drink; her blood alcohol was zero. She did not die from the chair tipping over. There were no bruises on the back of her head. She had died from the gags.

DePriest asked him if it were unusual that so much hair was on the sticky adhesive tape removed from Julie's head. "Yes," answered the medical examiner, "because an individual who gets into bondage has the intention of coming out of bondage and being able to return to their normal life pattern . . . They certainly want to survive. Anyone experienced in bondage would protect his or her hair," he said. "Usually with a cloth put between the hair and the tape." Skin and hair were found on the tapes, Dr. Gantner said. The fire had not increased the adhesion, he pointed out.

Dr. Gantner said the taping was so extensive, his assistants were forced to cut the corpse of Julie Bulloch from her rocking chair. There had been forty-seven feet of adhesive tape on her arms: twenty-nine feet of white one-and-a-half-inch fabric tape with adhesive on Julie's right arm along with three feet of vinyl-coated blue tape. Her left arm had been bound with fourteen feet of the white tape and three and a half feet of the blue tape. There was more than thirty feet of white adhesive tape wrapped around her face and hair. There was a total of seventy-six feet of tape around her head and arms alone.

More tape, unmeasured, criss-crossed her breasts, binding Julie to the back of the chair.

Showing a photograph, DePriest asked Dr. Gantner if there was anything unusual about Julie's hands. They were so swollen from the tight taping, the pathologist said, that the skin had blanched white from lack of circulation. The swelling indicated that Julie had been bound five to ten minutes before she died. Swelling cannot occur after death. But Julie had died from the gags, not the bindings, the medical examiner repeated.

The terry cloth gags had been jammed in, forcing back her tongue and blocking her airway, he said. Bits of material had been found between her teeth. "Julie must have attempted to struggle against those bonds," said the medical examiner. She must have made noises for help. After she was deprived of oxygen for eight minutes, Julie became so brain damaged, she could not have been resuscitated or revived to live a normal life. "Eight minutes from the point of lack of oxygen to the point of no return," as the expert put it.

There had been no attempt to remove those bindings, Dr. Gantner said, nor any evidence of trying to resuscitate Julie. (Julie's housekeeper had told Lt. Niere that Julie kept about five pairs of scissors in the master bedroom and its attached bathroom.)

Julie died needlessly. There was a fail-safe mechanism, Dr. Gantner testified. "If a bondage situation gets beyond the control of the individual, then they rely on the other partner." Gantner was knowledgeable about erotic fatalities from attending seminars and reading forensic literature of the American Academy of Forensic Scientists.

This was the first bondage death on record in the metropolitan area, even the state.

"It was a homicide," Dr. Gantner repeated.

"Could her death have been accidental?" Margulis asked during cross-examination.

"Yes," the medical examiner admitted. Dr. Gantner, who died two years later, went to his grave angry that he had not been called back to the stand to explain why he had said that. (Yet, Dr. Gantner later told Westfall that DePriest did a fine job. "Was there something else DePriest should have asked?" said Westfall. "Nope," said Gantner.)

During the lengthy medical description of the burnt remains of his bride, during the display of the hideous evidence pictures of her, Dennis showed no emotion. No remorse. Nor was there any flicker of reaction in his eyes at the next string of witnesses, five of his former friends and lovers.

Twenty-five

Friends and Lovers

May 30, 1987

Nina Honeywell, Muffy Spencer, and Luke Jackson sat smoking at the table in the witness room. The women were dressed in dark colors and pearls. Luke wore the collar of his black Lacoste shirt turned up like Snow White's.

Nina and Muffy were hostile witnesses, forced by subpoena to testify. They had met with Margulis, so he knew what they would say. The defense lawyer had seemed worried about Luke.

Luke said later that some men from Margulis's office came to the witness waiting room, a small anteroom between the courtroom and the public hall, and asked Luke to come out for a brief question. Luke said the man maneuvered him into the hall, saying, "You want a lot of publicity? Here's your publicity."

As he spoke, a television camera was rolling with lights blazing away. But the tape was never broadcast.

Luke and the women almost lost their precious anonymity. They had made a deal with Mehan: they would testify only if the prosecutor would not ask them to state their names and occupations in open court, as all witnesses traditionally do. The socialites' names would be noted only in the trial transcript, but without addresses and jobs.

Not giving one's name and occupation before testifying is unheard of in the annals of fair trial. The battered victims of gang rape and child abuse are not granted such privileges. The only exceptions are Mafia witnesses in federal protection programs who wear hoods and whose voices are altered through synthesizers to escape detection and revenge from the mob hit men. (Margulis said the defense had no problem with this. "Dennis knew who they were," he said.)

Margulis not only called Luke by his name during questioning, but he also asked how to pronounce his real first name and then repeated his whole name. Similarly, the lawyer called the women by their first names.

Luke had not been embarrassed to talk to the prosecution when they called him. But the women were humiliated. (Investigators and prosecutors never even got close to talking with socialite Becky Cabot, who had also dated Dennis. Her family whisked her off to Cairo, Nairobi, and Kathmandu after Dennis was charged.) Mehan had made call after call to Nina Honeywell and Muffy Spencer, at home and office. None were returned. Fed up, Mehan called Nina one more time at home. Her mother answered.

"Look," Mehan threatened, "your daughter has a choice. She can take my calls. Or, would she rather be served with a subpoena by the sheriff when she's lunching at Busch's [Grove] or when she's coming out of Pillar [Our Lady of the Pillar Church]?"

Nina and Muffy agreed to talk. Before and after they saw Mehan, they conferred with Margulis. "To protect themselves," Mehan explained. "They had let an outsider into the club and he had embarrassed them. They were closing ranks not out of loyalty to Dennis but because he made them look bad.

"I kept telling Nina, 'Look, I don't care if you were sleeping with him. Just tell me, did he ever suggest anything kinky to you?' Nina denied any sex. She and most of her group didn't care that Dennis had killed somebody. All they cared about was their own image, except for Luke."

Dennis was no different. "He was into propriety and appearances," Mehan said. "On the witness stand, he never admitted to any sex, kinky, premarital, extramarital, anything, except with Julie and that was all perverted at her direction. *He* says."

Why did Luke testify? "I vehemently believe he did it," Luke explained years later. "Nothing made sense. Why didn't Dennis call 911? Why did he shower, clean the house, and put all the physical evidence into the trunk of his car? When Dennis said he tried to commit suicide by putting a hose on the exhaust pipe but he couldn't keep the engine running, he lied. No garage is airtight enough to put it out. It happens all the time, someone leaves the car running in the garage and the guy in the apartment overhead dies. And the day before the murder he takes pictures of the house to be developed. He presumes arson ahead of time. And he claims that Julie shoved a gag into her mouth and taped her mouth. It's physically impossible. She would have convulsed before she taped her face. It's like gagging when you put your finger down your throat.

"He married her with the intention of using her. Later he decided to kill her. The murder was premeditated, but I have no idea if he planned it before he picked up his wedding license."

Muffy was the first of the group to testify. Tom Mehan asked her if Dennis told the group why he had married Julie Miller. "Yes," said Muffy, "because she was threatening to commit suicide. . . . Just calls, and pounding it over and over again . . . 'If you don't marry me, I'll kill myself.'"

Mehan wondered aloud why Dennis had succumbed to such pressure. Muffy explained he had been under a lot of stress from his recent divorce. Margulis, during his cross-examination, asked Muffy if she would describe Dennis as "a perfect gentlemen." "Yes," she said. This became a refrain sung by sympathetic witnesses at Margulis's request.

Nina Honeywell testified she had no idea Dennis had married Julie Miller until the day after the group returned from the ski trip. The couple went to a party, and later that evening, when he took her home, Dennis turned to Nina.

"I have something to tell you," he said. "I'm married."He then gave her the impression he was trying to get an annulment. But he never said that directly, Nina emphasized.

Dennis was clear that he did not love his wife, Nina testified. He said he had only married her because she would kill herself otherwise. He was used to discussing his feelings with Nina, how distraught he had been by his divorce, how he felt he had failed, how he wanted a family.

Margulis, during his cross, asked Nina if Dennis had tried to have sex with her?

"No," she said.

"Would it be fair to say that at all times Dennis was the perfect gentleman?"

"Yes."

When Mehan questioned Nina about the oddity of Dennis marrying out of mercy but then abandoning his bride, her answer came as comic relief.

MEHAN: Mr. Bulloch told you that he married a woman because she would commit suicide if he didn't. Did you consider that a kind gesture on his part?

NINA: Well, I don't know if you call it—he was a very kind man and I think he did it at a point when he was depressed, and he helped her out . . .

MEHAN: His marriage to her was helping her out?

NINA: Yes.

MEHAN: With that in mind, you think leaving her for ten days when she was in this state was helpful to her?

NINA: Do I think?

MEHAN: Yes, ma'am, do you think?

NINA: I don't know.

MEHAN: Well, you said it was a kind gesture on his part to marry her because of her state.

NINA: Yes.

MEHAN: As a follow-up, leaving her for ten days, would that help her?

NINA: I'm not—I don't know. I never met her.

Luke Jackson's testimony revealed irony. He recalled asking Dennis, while they were in Jackson Hole, if he were "interested" in Nina.

"Dennis answered, 'I don't want to date anyone seriously. I just want to play the field.' "

During a recess, Ginny Bulloch beguiled the media. "Why we just loved Julie," she told reporters. "We didn't have her long to love, but we loved her." The Bullochs had met their daughter-in-law of ten weeks exactly once, according to what Ginny had told a friend. "Is he really married to that little girl or just pulling my leg?" Ginny had said.

Next to testify was the man Dennis had called his best friend, Calvin Porterfield. Cal characterized Dennis's moods during his separation and divorce as ranging from despondent to self-pity to normal. Between Karen's exit in May, 1985, and Dennis's flight to California a year later, Cal and his wife entertained Dennis at least once or twice a week. That was in addition to Cal's lunching with Dennis and working on his house with him.

On February 7 or 8, 1986, two weeks before he married Julie, Dennis complained to Cal that he had no relationships. "He wished he could find someone very similar to Karen but a little older," Cal testified. Ten weeks later, April 14, over lunch in the Central West End, Cal asked Dennis where he would go after he sold the house on Stanford. Dennis said he most likely would move in with his Gram. On April 22, the evening Dennis was moving out of Stanford, he called Cal, saying he was depressed and wanted to come over. Dennis stayed more than half an hour, saying he probably would move in with his best friend from high school. Who lived out in Ballwin.

Cal did not know Dennis had remarried until he read in the newspaper that Dennis was the widower of the woman who died in the fire.

Under cross-examination, Cal said Dennis had opened a $100 account at Roosevelt Federal as a gift for the twins before he remarried. And he had a number of smaller accounts for them. Cal and Tina had given all the money back.

Finished, Cal sat in back of the courtroom to watch the trial. Upon seeing him, Dennis's mother waved and blew kisses to him.

The state's last witness is traditionally its strongest. That burden of responsibility can be intimidating. All of which can make the prosecutors very nervous. Their star witness in the Bulloch trial had flown into St. Louis the night before, Friday night. After meeting with DePriest, she had gone to her Clayton hotel room. Worried she might panic and leave, DePriest had asked that a police officer be stationed secretly outside her door.

Alone in her hotel room, the government's chief witness worried about telling a packed courtroom the most intimate details of her sex life. She would be betraying the man she had once loved. Had he not betrayed her?

Looking straight ahead at DePriest who had coached her the evening before, Dennis's lover Christy Meiers walked calmly to the witness stand. Looking like Miss Middle America in a cornflower blue suit and fresh white blouse, she softly told a tale of sexual bondage and adultery.

It all began before her birthday on August 9, 1985. Dennis had been dating Christy for several months, just after his first wife, Karen Toksvig, had left in early May, 1985. For Christy's birthday, Dennis sent her a gift of some books on car repair and a woman's tie with the note they could use the tie later for other things. If they had not engaged in bondage before August 9, she would not have known what the card meant, Christy said.

It was crucial to DePriest's case to prove that Dennis was a devoté of bondage before he met Julie Miller on August 14. Christy testified that sometime in July, 1985, Dennis used his necktie to tie her arms together over her head and then to her bedpost.

Dennis tied her up about four times after that. She never tied him up.

There had been a frightening incident in March, 1986, over Easter weekend, Christy explained quietly. "He tied my wrists, my left wrist to my left ankle and my right wrist to my right ankle. . . . He tried to cover my eyes with something. I don't know what it was. And I didn't want him to do that. He tried a couple of times. I said, no. So, he got upset and left the room."

That incident had occurred in Dennis's bedroom. He had invited her to spend Easter with him, as she had Thanksgiving. On the Monday morning after Easter, Christy was packed and ready to fly back to Washington. But "Dennis became really upset and told me he did not want me to leave. He was crying, so I called my supervisor and told her I wouldn't be in for another day."

The woman Dennis told his mother he was going to marry the coming August—despite the fact he had just married Julie Miller February 22—did not hear from him again until she called him in mid-April. Christy hoped to get together with him during her upcoming business trip to St. Louis on May 5. Dennis was noncommittal about seeing her.

Christy heard nothing for ten days, until Dennis's parents called her looking for their son, who was now a federal fugitive wanted for his new wife's death. New wife? thought Christy, who had no idea her beau had married Julie Miller on February 22, just weeks before their Easter tryst. DePriest asked Christy what she did after that phone call.

"I was afraid to live at my house by myself," she answered. "I moved in with friends."

A few days later, Dennis called Christy's office. "I asked if he were okay. He said he was. He told me he didn't do anything, that his life was a mess, and something had happened, and somebody was trying to set him up for something." Dennis refused to tell Christy where he was, but asked about extradition laws in Canada. Dennis called seven more times. On July 3, as they were talking, Dennis exclaimed, "They found me."

Dennis had taken to calling her again recently, Christy added.

After her testimony, Cal Porterfield, who had never heard of Christy before, called his wife and said, "Dennis was born under a warped star." He walked out of the courthouse, telling a reporter that morally he had no choice but to testify against his former friend.

Cal added it was incredible that Dennis thought he could get away with a secret marriage. Julie's friend, Jane Muster reiterated: "Everything here in St. Louis is connected. You can't escape the past."

Twenty-six

Eros Thanatos

June 1, 1987

Arthur Margulis rose for the defense, impeccable in his khaki-colored suit and powder-blue oxford-cloth shirt. Defense lawyers do not usually wear dark suits in trial. The lighter colors make them appear as the White Knight. Attorneys from the Deep South even wear cream-colored linen suits, as if to say their client is equally unsullied.

Margulis, in calm, cool tones built a stone bulwark out of airy images. It was not like DePriest constructing his case, for the prosecution had the facts and the burden of proving the murder. Margulis's images gave the appearance that the Dennis Bulloch who sat before them now could not have committed such a crime.

The hallmark of Margulis's style was subtlety. It was like waking up one morning and realizing that you've been in love with the boy or girl next door all along.

Margulis brought forth an account executive for *The Riverfront Times* as his first witness. The man read Julie Miller's ad in the eligibles column. To conservative St. Louis, this ad implied Julie was soliciting for sex. She had asked for it. That impression

was amplified by the first piece of evidence for the defense.
Margulis read into the court record portions of Julie's psychiatric records during her stay at St. John's Mercy, September 23
until November 14, 1985, the time when she was dating Dennis.

These doctors' notes demonstrated to the members of the
jury how demented Julie was. The psychiatric comments also
hinted at depravity. There are sizable numbers of educated St.
Louisans who believe that having a fatal disease is preferable to
seeing a psychiatrist.

Julie's problems were diagnosed as "effective disorder/major
depression and, secondarily, a borderline personality disorder
with intense depression, mood swings, self-destructive behavior, poor relationships, problems with closeness and bound-
aries, mistrustful, suicidal, inappropriate behavior, delusions,
psychotic regression, paranoid thinking, bizarre hallucinations,
histrionic behavior, and hostility." If the diagnosis did not shock
the jurors, her sexuality did. It was more than titillating.

Julie's answers to a standard psychological personality test
were: "My sexual behavior has caused trouble . . . I have indulged in unusual sex practices . . . I sometimes feel I must
injure myself or another . . . I have had 'strange' thoughts." The
most damaging evidence was that her doctors noted three epi-
sodes of "sexual acting out." Those unfamiliar with severe depression would not know that such behavior was common
during the mania stage of bi-polar depression. No doctors testified.

An uncertified activity therapist, who formerly worked in the
psychiatric ward at St. John's Mercy Medical Center, named
Patrick Stack, testified against former patient, Julie Miller. Most
of his work was with teenagers, Stack had to admit.

Julie took a fancy to Stack during her worst period, asking him
to date her after her discharge: "She indicated that I was a good-
looking guy and that she was a fairly good-looking young woman, we could get it on together." Then Stack began receiving late
night anonymous phone calls from a woman who he suspected
was Julie. Around this time Julie became psychotic and dressed
inappropriately. Nurses commented, "Her blouses, she would
sometimes have her stomach bare." Other outfits of Julie's were
"unusually revealing under the circumstances."

Stack admitted during cross-examination that Julie was quite ill at that time. (Her records show she was suffering from delusions.)

> DePriest: Was her condition any better when she left than when she got here?
> Stack: I have no idea.
> DePriest: Do you think they would have let her out if she had not been?
> Stack: Well, St. John's is an outstanding hospital. I have been a very fortunate young man, having lived in various parts of this country as well as in Europe, and all I can say is the care . . . is just outstanding. . . .
> DePriest: And so she was making . . . an honest effort to cure her problems?
> Stack: I don't know about that.

As a character witness, Dennis's old chum Ed Schollmeyer, Jr., testified in his behalf. Under Margulis's questioning, Ed explained how despondent Dennis had been when his first marriage broke up. More interesting was Dennis's reaction to his sister Cindy's death in 1979. He had blamed himself, Ed said. Dennis withdrew from everyone and even disappeared right after she died. No one knew where he was, Ed testified. He refused to contact anyone. Dennis acted similarly when Julie died. While he was in hiding in California, Dennis called Ed in St. Louis. Ed told Dennis then that an FBI agent had wanted Ed to be the go-between. "I could help Dennis work things out, to return back home from California," Ed testified.

Dennis told Ed, " 'That would be great.' He said that would help him out a lot." Dennis was to call Ed back in three hours about details. But he was arrested.

DePriest, during cross-examination, showed Ed a passport application with a photograph of Dennis inside. Ed said he knew nothing about Dennis trying to flee. When asked, Ed admitted he did not know Dennis had remarried until May 6, 1986.

Margulis called his star witness, an eminent forensic psychiatrist. With intense, piercing eyes under dark arched eyebrows, he looked like a healthy vampire. He had been the chief government witness against John Hinkley, the man who attempted to assassinate President Reagan. An international authority on erotic deaths, Park Elliot Dietz, M.D., was a highly credentialed expert witness. He had been chairman of the American Psychiatric Association committee on misuse and use of psychiatry in the U. S., a member of the U.S. Attorney General's Commission on Pornography and author of chapters in a dozen professional books and of three dozen professional articles. Dietz himself was a consultant to the FBI's behavioral sciences unit, the National Center for the Analysis of Violent Crime. He said that half the time he was an expert witness for the prosecution and half the time for the defense.

Dr. Dietz currently was studying 150 cases of bondage deaths for the National Institute of Justice. That included, he said, determining whether a death was suicide, homicide, or an accident.

Dr. Dietz said he had reviewed all the police reports, the interviews of the fifty-plus friends and neighbors and colleagues of Julie and Dennis, the defense investigative report, Dennis's suicide notes, the photographs of Julie in the chair, and her hospital records, and he had interviewed Dennis for eight hours on December 18, 1986. The psychiatrist began the interview by asking Dennis his sexual history.

Dennis, Dr. Dietz said, knew nothing about sexual bondage until September, 1985. Then Julie Miller instructed him in bondage along with the use of vibrators and dirty talk during sex. Dennis told his expert witness that he assumed Julie had done these things before. Dr. Dietz apparently never wondered why Margulis could not find her former partners in bondage.

And apparently, the psychiatrist did not know Dennis had tied up Dinah Moltke in the late 1970s. Nor did Dennis tell him he had wanted to give his first wife golden showers, had asked her to use obscene language in bed, and that he had said he enjoyed orgies. No mention was made of Dennis in his mid-twenties sleeping with underage girls such as Dinah.

Bondage is prevalent in our society, the psychiatrist said. Bondage chic is in *Vogue* fashion layouts: a pair of lingerie models with their ankles tied together by stockings, a third model in a corset blindfolded with a stocking. Sexual bondage is a joke in *Playboy* cartoons and on television shows such as

"Saturday Night Live" and "Night Court." "Bondage chic is an effort to incorporate this subtly threatening image from another sexual world into mainstream culture," testified Dr. Dietz. It is a staple of stag movies and a feature in serious films such as 9½ *Weeks*, the movie Dennis said he found so disgusting. Bondage appears in every type of pornography, Dietz said. It is common knowledge that pornography is usually degrading to women.

The purpose of bondage restraints, whether silk scarves, leather harnesses, or mounds of adhesive tape, was to immobilize one partner while the other performs sexual acts on that person, Dietz said. In addition, some bondage advocates like to restrain their senses. They add blindfolds and gags. Such practices are called sensory bondage. Commercially prepared gags have rubber or leather straps that go around the face and neck. Attached to this harness is a red ball that fits into the mouth and cannot come loose. The real aficionados use handcuffs, harnesses, velvet restraints with Velcro closings, and the gags with rubber balls, all sold in pornography shops catering to the bondage subculture.

Margulis asked if there were a risk to tying someone up. Yes, said Dr. Dietz, in addition to bruises and cuts or circulation loss from the various restraints, the major risk is that a partner could die. Every year, about 250 Americans are found dead from bondage. But, said the expert, those represent only one-quarter to one-half of the real total. Often the crime scene is changed by relatives who find the bodies, or the deaths are misdiagnosed. Dietz said he had a different estimate:

Five hundred to a thousand Americans die each year from sexual bondage. Most bondage deaths occur alone by men engaged in autoeroticism. Many are homosexual in nature. Only one out of thirty bondage deaths involved a partner. Almost all involved casual sex partners. Of the cases in which a husband dies and his wife finds him, it seems he was alone and she was not involved. Few women have suffered bondage deaths.

Could Julie's death have been accidental? Margulis asked.

"This certainly could have been an accidental death," replied the expert. Dr. Dietz said he based that on the fact it was obviously sexual, as opposed to criminal—such as a cashier being tied up during a robbery—because of three criteria:

"It's neat, which is the first thing we look for. In fact, the

phrase we use in our research is 'wrapped as neatly as a Christmas package' because people go to some effort . . . to make sure
that the corners are straight or that there is some design to it or
that it's not slipshod, because it's the visual image of it that may
matter."

Two, the bindings on Julie's body were excessive. Remarked
Dietz, "There was far more restraining material there than is
necessary to immobilize a person."

Three, it was symmetrical. Even the blue tape was even on
both sides. Sexual bondage, the psychiatrist said in summary, is
neat, excessive, and symmetrical.

The big difference between murder and accidental death in
sexual bondage is the use of gags, Dietz explained. He had
studied sexual homicides. When a person was murdered sexually, he or she usually was strangled or smothered. "But what is
very rare in sexual homicide is the use of a gag as the means of
committing murder, because one risks getting one's fingers
bitten in trying to put something into a partner's mouth if they
are struggling, and because there is no particular pleasure for
the offender in trying to insert a gag in the mouth. Offenders
who enjoy creating asphyxiation like to strangle their victims. . . . I am even more skeptical of it being a murder when I
see that there is all this tape over the top of the gag. It doesn't
make sense for someone who means to be killing a victim to go
to the trouble of this very elaborate symmetrical, neat bondage,
then to insert something in the airway in the mouth, and then
to tape over it in such a exaggerated manner when there's
simpler ways to produce death."

Dietz said he had asked himself why Dennis did not do
anything when his wife began to choke on the gags. "You should
be able to see that. Because the first rule of safety for bondage, as
mentioned in the *Joy of Sex* and every other book that tells you
how to do safe bondage, is to make sure that you never leave
your partner alone and that you do not put things in their
mouth that can slip loose. Those are two different rules that
seem to have been broken. Well, without telling him that was my
concern, I asked him what had happened."

Dr. Dietz said it was impossible to know whether a gag would
dislodge and choke someone.

"Purely chance?" asked Margulis.

"Yes," replied Dr. Dietz.

Then, Margulis asked the question everyone was wondering. Was this kind of behavior normal?

Said Dietz: "People who are normal do experiment with such things. People who make a habit of this have got a problem. It's a sexual perversion. . . . Doing this, whether one is normal or not, carries with it risk of serious injury or death."

And, speaking of perversions and problems, Margulis asked what Julie's psychiatric records suggested about her sexual behavior. Dietz said he thought the most significant comment "was a suspicion of sexual abuse in her family." While Julie's behavior in the psychiatric hospitals may not have been typical of her actions because she was so depressed, Dietz said, he did note all her sexual actings out. Next, he noted, that Julie had taken "a variety of sexual partners, including married men, but didn't know why she had done that."

Apparently the psychiatrist did not consider significant Dennis's far greater number of sexual partners and adulteries.

Margulis asked the doctor about Dennis's aberrant behavior. Was it suspicious that Dennis flew to St. Louis under an assumed name on May 5? Yes, said Dietz, that implied he had something to hide. What if Dennis were having a rendezvous with another woman? asked Margulis. "That's probably the most common reason for using an assumed name," Dr. Dietz said.

According to the standard manual for psychiatric diagnosis, the DSMI IV, a criterion for sociopathy, that is, criminal behavior, is the use of aliases. Checking into a motel with one's mistress as John Doe is not the same as two airline tickets issued to two different aliases. There was no reason for Dennis to think his bosses would see tickets he paid for himself. Did Dr. Dietz read the comments in the police reports about Dennis's list of aliases?

Dennis told his expert witness that when he discovered his wife had died accidentally, he panicked. Margulis asked, "Would you consider panic a normal response under those circumstances?"

Dietz answered, "Certainly, one of the several normal kinds of responses." Margulis repeated this back to him twice more. The word "normal" was used three times in regard to Dennis's conduct. The use of repetition was necessary to fix the image Margulis wanted.

"What effect would it have on his mental state if the next morning he [Dennis] were advised by friends, 'Your wife died in a fire?' " Margulis asked.

"Devastating," answered the psychiatrist. To hear she had been alive and he could have saved her was a terrible blow. Margulis asked if Dietz were aware that from May 6 until July 3, Dennis thought his wife had died in the fire.

Then, Margulis switched from implying sympathy for his client to the real defense: "Doctor, I have no further questions except to ask you by way of repetition, you do believe Julie's death could have been accidental, don't you?"

"Yes," said Dr. Dietz, "it could have been."

Dennis was curiously impassive while Dietz testified, as he had been when Christy described their sex life and the medical examiner gave his gruesome evidence.

DePriest rose. He could not wait to begin the cross-examination. Direct, as always, his first question was, "Could it have been murder?"

Dietz responded, "It could have been murder."

Who did the thirty feet of taping over the gag? the prosecutor asked. "I think he [Dennis] wrapped it [the tape] all around her head," Dietz said.

When the medical examiner pried open Julie's mouth, the gags flew out, DePriest pointed out. If Julie had put in the gags herself then how did they get from outside her teeth to inside her teeth? DePriest inquired, using photographs to show bits of material hanging from the teeth before the mouth was opened.

Dietz, who had said he was not a pathologist, answered, "Well, there is no reason that her jaw wouldn't be able to open its full range while she's taped that way."

"With thirty feet of tape?" DePriest asked incredulously.

"He didn't tape from the bottom of her chin to the top of her head, so she should still be able to move her jaw," Dietz said.

"I'd have you look at this exhibit closely. . . . Dr. Gantner explained the tape went from right under her nares [nostrils] to the end of her chin. Thirty feet. You think she'd be able to possibly get that inside?"

"Well, I can—we may need a better expert than I—I tell you, sitting right here, I can hold my lips together while moving my jaws apart," Dietz proclaimed.

"Can you hold your teeth together and do that?"

Dietz did not respond, saying instead, "I can move my teeth up and down while my mouth is closed."

"What about the pulse?" DePriest asked. Dennis had said he tried to check his wife's wrists for her pulse.

"Yes, but he couldn't feel there," Dr. Dietz said.

"Right," DePriest said. "Would it seem reasonable he could . . . seeing her arms bound as they were, Doctor, and taped to the chair?"

"But if she was dead, there wouldn't be any pulse," Dr. Dietz replied, adding that Dennis said he had felt Julie's neck for a pulse and put his ear to her nose to see if she were breathing.

The prosecutor pressed on. "Doctor Gantner . . . said her tongue had been pressed back to close off the airway and the rags were in front of it, so that jamming of the rags in the mouth transported the tongue back, which closed the airway . . . from nose to mouth. Are you saying it could have been possible Dennis could have blown hard enough to make her stomach expand, even though Dr. Gantner says her airway was blocked by the fact that her tongue was jammed back in her throat?"

"I don't see why not," the psychiatrist said.

When asked, Dr. Dietz said he thought it likely that Dennis had read all the evidence against him before the psychiatrist interviewed him December 18, 1986.

Returning to the gags, DePriest quoted Dr. Dietz as having said earlier that the main purpose of gags is to prevent speaking. The doctor agreed, adding that sometimes gags are used to enliven a fantasy. How could Dennis testify that Julie had orchestrated the whole bondage routine, DePriest asked, when the gag prevented her from speaking?

Dietz said, "She had told him even on prior occasions that what she wants is to be bound tightly. 'Snugly' is the term he said she used. She was already bound to the chair. So all he had to do after she puts these things in her mouth, which by the way, I wouldn't call gags, I'd call the adhesive tape over her mouth a gag. These, I don't know what I'd call."

Julie was tied up with more than seventy-six feet of adhesive tape, the prosecutor said. "At some point wouldn't common sense dictate that there is something wrong here?"

"There is something wrong?" asked Dietz.

"You know, that's my opinion. But I mean, at some point in time, maybe after ten feet of tape or twelve . . . wouldn't common sense dictate that's enough?"

"For what? If the purpose is sexual, then the specific image and whoever is asking for this, that determines how much is enough. Doing this at all is more than enough."

"Let me ask you this. Julie Bulloch was five foot two, weighed about a hundred pounds. Are you telling me and the jury it's reasonable that it's going to take seventy some feet of tape to satisfy this woman?" DePriest asked incredulously.

DePriest pointed out there was skin and hair all over the tapes. "This girl worked every day, she caught her van pool about seven o'clock in the morning. Would a reasonable person expect that his wife was going to get up the next morning and go to work with half the skin off her face and hair off her head?"

"On this occasion, too," Dr. Dietz said, "he told me she had asked him to, and he thought he had put terry cloth behind her head to protect [her hair]. . . . He thought he had and he was surprised when it [the autopsy report] didn't say anything about it." Dennis realized then he had forgotten to put the cloth between his wife's hair and the tape.

"Do you think everything Dennis told you is the truth?" De-Priest asked.

"No," said Dietz, "Even when I assumed everything he told me was a lie, I still reached the conclusion that this could have been an accident because of the use of these things inside the mouth. It's such an unpredictable way to kill someone." The fire was explainable, Dr. Dietz said, because Dennis was panicked and disorganized.

"After you hear something like this you would still say what he told you is probably true?" DePriest asked.

"I'm not sure," Dietz said. While he believed Dennis had panicked and was confused, he was not certain how serious his suicide attempts were.

Returning to the bondage, DePriest suggested, "It's a crazy way to see someone die, but do you think if you wanted to talk and torture somebody, it doesn't sound like a bad idea to me"

But, said Dietz, sadists do not go in for neatness, symmetry, and excessive restraint. They like simple stuff.

Regarding the date Dennis and Julie began bondage, Dietz said, "I always take the defendant with a grain of salt. Even if everything he told me is untrue, the way in which she died, as revealed by the autopsy and the investigation, leads me to conclude it could have been an accident. The dates [July or August or September] don't leave much time for him to have done it with Julie first and then Christy, but it's possible, depending on how soon after August 9 he had had that first encounter with Christy."

On the rarity of sexual bondage deaths, DePriest asked again about the statistics—of the 250 substantiated cases each year, how many involved partners?

"Most of the deaths are among people acting alone," Dietz said, "and it's thought that the presence of another party usually protects against these kinds of accidents, because you are supposed to have signals worked out with the partner so you can get free, and a certain set of safety rules," said Dietz. His study found that one out of thirty bondage death cases included a partner.

"Have you got any cases where spouses have been engaged in this and a death has occurred?" DePriest asked.

"One or two," said the doctor. Most were casual sex partners. There was only one other case involving a married couple that Dietz could recall: A wife who went downstairs to answer the telephone, leaving her husband tied upstairs in bed and smoking a cigar. While she was on the phone her husband burned to death.

"That is lousy luck," agreed the prosecutor.

"That is the only married one I can think of," replied the psychiatrist.

Julie Bulloch was the first reported case in America of a wife dying by bondage.

On the rarity of sexual bondage deaths, especially those involving a married couple, DePriest asked if there were any others in which on the night of the death the other partner used an alias to fly home. Dietz replied, just this one.

Any other bondage deaths in which the dead partner has signed over all her death benefits along with her property during a ten-week marriage? the prosecutor asked.

"I agree these are all suspicious," the expert said.

And then, DePriest continued, the partner flees the authorities and is caught living under another alias in another state?

"Yes. There's many suspicious facts here."

And after the death of the spouse, the partner sets his own home on fire, burning his wife's corpse, leaving her looking "like a big piece of charcoal?"

"They are suspicious. They don't prove murder."

Margulis asked Dr. Dietz if he had finished his answer.

"I said they are suspicious but they don't prove murder."

DePriest asked Dr. Dietz what he was getting paid for his testimony. His answer was $2,000 to testify and a total bill of $6,000.

It was now nearly four P.M. The judge ordered the court in recess until the next morning. The twelve jurors and two alternates filed out, with the defense's refrain sounding over and over in their heads—accidental, accidental, it could have been accidental. Along with the portrayal of Julie as the warped vamp.

The first thing next morning, June 2, Dennis was to take the stand.

This would be the first time he would talk—outside his friends and family—since the day after Julie's body had been found in the fire. That had been nearly thirteen months ago. It was with more than professional interest that Lt. Niere awaited his testimony. As for Carter Miller, he could not stay away. No one could.

Twenty-seven

What Happened That Night?

June 2, 1987

Outside the locked courtroom, crowds were lined up by nine o'clock on the morning of June 2, 1987. These were not the typical trial watchers, middle-class retirees who flock to watch the theatrics of the more celebrated trial lawyers. One perfectly coiffed socialite clutched her navy quilted Chanel shoulderbag to her pink Adolpho suit as a reporter raced past her. Teenagers in Guess? jeans popped their gum and waited giggling, as though the murder trial were a rock concert. The bailiff had to evict a dowager in a floral frock from the front row media bench.

All the other witnesses had been heard but one, all the evidence presented. All along, Margulis had caught himself thinking, "I've got to ask Julie about that. What does Julie say happened?" It bothered Margulis that there were only two people who knew what occurred on May 6, 1986, and one of them was dead. He would never know the whole truth. It bothered De-Priest that the survivor of that night had enjoyed more than a year to rewrite history.

Dennis Neal Bulloch was called to the stand at ten minutes after nine. He strolled up as though he were going into a job interview he knew he could cinch. He looked straight at his lawyer. Margulis had positioned himself in front of the jury box so that his client would be talking directly to the dozen people who would decide if he was to be sent to the gas chamber. If the jury convicted Dennis of first-degree murder, the cold-blooded killing of his bride of ten weeks, the state would ask for the death penalty.

The charred chair in which Julie had died sat directly before the judge's bench. The prosecution had brought this macabre piece up from its evidence locker and entered it into the record. This reminder of his wife's death did not faze Dennis. But reporters on the media bench were forced to look past the chair to follow the testimony in the witness box.

Under Margulis's careful line of questioning, Dennis discussed his degrees, his career, his close family, his attachment to the Porterfield twins and the bank accounts he had set up for them. Few criminal defense attorneys emphasize their client's background, but Margulis knew that Dennis's illustrated the proper image. This man is one of us, and deserves to live in society, not in a prison. This man was unfortunately involved in an accident.

Dennis calmly discussed the death of his little sister and the end of his first marriage. He showed no emotion. He kept people and his feelings for them separated, as sectioned meal trays on airlines keep the peas from mixing with the chicken.

His relationship with Christy Meiers was merely one of convenience, Dennis said. "Christy came in at the right time," in June, 1985, asked him to dinner, and was "very helpful." Dennis explained that he had been "devastated" over his separation from his first wife, Karen Toksvig, a month earlier, May 9, 1985.

After Karen filed for divorce, Dennis answered four or five personal ads in *The Riverfront Times*, in mid-July, 1985. Julie responded to his letter the third week in July. Sometime in late July or early August, he met her for lunch at the Branded Bagel downtown. A few days later, he recalled, they went out on their first date.

"It was a typical date, just a show, and I think we had Mandarin food, Chinese food. She suggested a drink over at her house. We got over to her house, and, you know, we went into her house, we went into the family room, sat on the couch a little bit, touched, you know.

"She was very relaxed about touching and, you know, being close, and that made me feel real relaxed. Normally, I am not, you know, real touchy right away, so, you know, we kissed and that, and had a couple glasses of wine. She excused herself. When she came back into the room she had a black negligee on.

"It kind of boosted my ego, you know. It was the first time anything like that had happened to me. So, anyway, you know, I was obviously giving her signals that I was interested, and I guess that was her way of taking the initiative. So, we started petting and, you know, getting into foreplay, and we actually moved to the floor. The couch was a little bit too thick to lay down on, you know, or move around very much. And when she unbuttoned my shirt she said she liked running her fingers up and down my chest, trying to, attempting to give me goose-bumps or tickle me. And eventually she got me undressed.

"And she kept wanting to entice me or rise my interest, I guess. And then, you know, during her time of doing that I would kind of grab her, want to roll around. To tell you the truth, I was kind of anxious to just get into the sexual part of the evening. Well, I'd grabbed her a couple of times and pulled her close and she told me I wasn't following the rules, you know, that I had to keep my hands behind my back. When I wouldn't do that, she took my silk tie and tied my hands behind my back." After she untied him, Dennis said they had conventional sex.

Dennis said he did not notice that Julie was unstable, only that she waited on and for him. He had no idea about her hospitalizations until after he had married her. Julie explained away her absences with out-of-town training programs. Dennis testified that he did not know she had been institutionalized at St. Luke's until his attorney subpoenaed Julie's records there.

Prosecutor DePriest was irate over this egregious lie. But there was nothing he could legally do to refute Dennis. DePriest could not call one of Julie's friends or her former housekeeper to testify that he drove her to St. John's Mercy Medical Center or that he called and visited her there and at St. Luke's. Such testimony would be hearsay, what the dead woman had told a witness. Nor could DePriest read Julie's diary entry about Dennis coming over to her house September 19, 1985, the night she threatened to throw acid on her face, and calming her down. Nor could the prosecutor play Julie's audiotape in which she thanks Dennis for being "so supportive" during her breakdowns. All these things were hearsay, the words of a dead woman who could not be cross-examined. Under the U. S. Constitution, Dennis had the right to confront any witnesses against him.

Although he was still seeing Christy sporadically that fall, Dennis said he was losing interest. "Christy had trouble expressing herself. If I wasn't talking there was little or no communication." Around October, 1985, Christy asked Dennis to join her in La Crosse, Wisconsin, for her family's Christmas. Dennis hesitated until Julie invited him to her aunt's and uncle's Christmas dinner, which he accepted with alacrity.

By mid-January, 1986, Dennis said he decided to cool things with Christy. "I realized after I met Julie that [Christy] was a dependency relationship. I told Christy I needed time to myself to decide what I wanted to do."

Dennis did not mention to Christy that there was someone else. After Christmas, he had begun seeing Julie "regularly, weekly . . . a steady date basis, even though I had no commitment to her."

But Julie wanted more, Dennis said. She aggressively pursued him to the altar, he said, much as his first wife had done.

Margulis asked, "You were interested, too, weren't you?"

(From here on, Dennis's comments have been edited to eliminate his repetitive speech patterns.)

"Yes, I was," Dennis said. "It was very satisfying to have somebody so attentive and want to take care of me. My first wife was always too busy. Not enough time at home to spend with me. Julie was very attentive, she'd want to caress and touch me. She volunteer[ed] to drop my clothes at the cleaners, do errands for me. That boosted my ego. That's exactly what I needed."

What Julie needed, Dennis testified, was light bondage. Neckties and blindfolds. They took turns covering each other's eyes, five to eight times, as they took turns tying each other up with the ties.

In February, Julie proposed, Dennis said.

Before they were wed, Dennis was well aware of Julie's healthy financial condition. He said she had asked him to review her investments after she had cashed out $25,000 in the stock market. But, Dennis said, he did not know the details of her inheritance until they were married.

A week after the wedding, Dennis said, he told his mother he had remarried. Margulis pointed out that the marriage was no deep dark secret.

Dennis said he never told Karen and their friends he had remarried for fear his ex-wife would become "more vindictive about the settlement when she found out." (Karen said Dennis and she used the same attorney, so there was no financial battle.)

The first three weeks, the marriage was "normal," Dennis continued. "I was very comfortable, content, very satisfied. It seemed Julie was, too. I was getting over my rebound, which Julie and I discussed. I still felt like my boat was rocking. She assured me that there wasn't any problem. The confidence from her helped me."

Three weeks into the marriage, Dennis went skiing with Nina and her crowd. "I am a ski nut, an avid skier, and I love to go skiing. I am sure I talked about that with Julie. I had talked about going in January, February, sometime when I could afford to take off. A friend called, she wanted to go skiing. I told her, well, I wasn't sure—I had not heard from them in quite a while.

"I talked with Julie, [who] was very attentive and caring for my needs. I think she was aware of what I was going through with my depression, and she said, if I really wanted to go that bad, go. In transferring to a new department, she wanted to make a good impression on her boss, jump in there and hit the books and the learning curve real quickly, so we agreed until she felt comfortable with that job [no honeymoon]."

When Dennis returned from Wyoming with Nina and her group, he said he went by his house in U. City to move some things to Julie's. He called his wife from his house. They fought because she thought he had been home all week, staying there with Karen.

Soured by their fight, Dennis decided to spend the weekend at his house. Muffy phoned and asked him to take Nina to a Young Republicans party, he said. "I was planning on going in order to promote Price Waterhouse anyway." He agreed to pick up Nina.

He voluntarily told Nina he was married. "I thought Nina and Muffy had found out from Julie when she called to check on my trip." The following day, Sunday, Dennis said he drove to 251 White Tree, apologized, and made up with his wife.

Monday morning, Dennis went to Boatmen's Bank to withdraw $60,000. "The money wasn't there. I just felt like crawling inside my shoes." Then, he said, Julie told him she had been institutionalized.

As a culmination of the money transfer and the psychiatric problems, the newlyweds decided to separate, he said.

Dennis moved back to his house on Stanford in U. City. And Christy popped up again. "I don't recall if she had actually called me or if I called her, but again I was in need of a counselor. When Julie and I broke up, I didn't realize it was Easter, but I did invite her [Christy] for the weekend."

After which "I realized just what I had with Julie" and returned home two days after Christy had left. Julie greeted him "with open arms. I think we both came to the same conclusion that it was better to work together than on an individual basis."

But what he had with Julie was not love, Dennis explained.

However, he did look for a job with less traveling so the bridal couple could be together. Dennis was out of town seventy percent of the time for Price Waterhouse in 1985. Because he expected to change positions soon, Dennis said he did not list his wife as beneficiary on his Price benefits. "I anticipated getting a job much quicker than I really got one. When I started looking in February, I was used to having people grab me up pretty quickly."

Dennis testified he did not list Julie on his four bank accounts at Roosevelt Federal Savings & Loan, which totaled about $1,000. "Those accounts were closing out. An insignificant amount of money." Dennis said he did deposit money in his and Julie's joint $83,000 account at Mercantile; one of the defense exhibits was his paycheck of $1,900 deposited there Friday, May 2, 1986.

Dennis said he nagged his wife to bring home insurance forms from Southwestern Bell so he could be added to her policies. His benefits at Price were not as comprehensive. He said he was paying $125 a week for therapy and wanted her coverage. In fact, Dennis said he had told Julie again to change her policy when he left for St. Paul, May 5, 1986.

Dennis said he knew Christy would be in St. Louis that week. She had called him in mid-April about a business trip there and wanted to see him. "I had decided to break it off with her. I was in a quandary on whether to do it the coward's way with a letter, or just quit seeing her, and I had planned on doing it that way. But when she called I . . . thought I could do it face-to-face." Yet, Dennis admitted he "left it up in the air" about getting together.

When Dennis arrived in St. Paul, he was told he would be there four to six weeks instead of the one week originally planned. Calling Julie from his hotel room to tell her, Dennis said she interrupted him in one of her "fits." They fought. Dennis said he felt badly that she was so upset and called her back to soothe her feelings.

Afterward Dennis returned to work and flipped open his Daytimer calendar. He discovered a note to himself about Christy's trip to St. Louis. (Police never found the alleged note.)

"I decided that it was best to break it off, or let her know what was going on in my life, so she wouldn't come in in a vindictive manner or carrying any animosity," Dennis testified. He said he feared Christy would seek revenge.

Instead of calling Christy, Dennis said he flew back to St. Louis from St. Paul to tell her in person. He used the alias John Jackson, he said, because Julie had been known to check his flight schedule and she would be furious that he was meeting another woman in St. Louis. (It is not clear what flight schedule he meant. The average citizen cannot obtain passenger information from the airlines.)

Dennis said when he landed at St. Louis Lambert Airport, he called the Sheraton Hotel where Christy usually stayed. She was not registered there. He tried other hotels, he said, but he could not find her. Dennis did not phone the Clarion Hotel where Christy had stayed before and was staying now.

Not knowing what to do, Dennis called his wife to tell her to pick him up. Julie said she had already undressed for bed and to take a cab home. To explain why no cabdriver for this fare had been found, Dennis said he may not have given the cabbie his exact address. Just directions to the area.

Margulis interjected with a question about the three sex manuals found on the nighttable—*Joy of Sex, More Joy of Sex,* and *Making Love Better.* His client said he presumed those belonged to his wife. He had never read them. He said he had seen them in a box with her vibrators.

Julie hugged and kissed Dennis when he walked in the door. He said she was ecstatic he was home. They went to bed, talking about where to go for their wedding trip. "What I wanted to do, I wanted to go skiing. I suggested a ski trip for a honeymoon. She wanted to go someplace warm. She suggested the Caribbean or Hawaii, which I was very receptive to because, you know, I love the beach."

Julie hopped up to get some champagne. They both drank, he said. " 'Well,' " she said. " 'The lady has a request.' "

That meant she wanted to perform a fantasy, Dennis explained. From prior experience, he said he knew Julie wanted bondage with tape and gags. That night, he said, was the third time since their marriage that the couple used tape as bindings and gags. In the past, Julie had protected her hair from the adhesive tape by either wetting it or placing a rag in front of the tape.

The defense reiterated that tape and gags were part of the nuptial package. Dennis testified, "I remember when she introduced me to it, she made the statement, 'Now that you're part of the family, I want to show you something.' "

Margulis asked his client, "And the remark was again, please?"

"Something like 'Now that you're part of the family,' or 'in the family,' " Dennis replied. This was the root of the defense.

Dennis said he thought Julie's penchant for bondage and taping odd. But he dutifully followed her fantasies. He said after she bound his legs and arms with non-adhesive athletic tape, she sat on his lap outlining what he was to do. Julie helped him sip a screwdriver, having run out of the champagne. Dennis was naked; Julie was wearing a robe.

"She did the goosebump treatment. She was kind of a dictator-type, control-type situation. *I* think the fantasy was that we were in a cabin alone, and she had found me in the snow, and brought me in, and she was kind of nursing me back to health, and 'drink this' position-thing."

Margulis interjected, "She is reciting these things?"
Dennis, "Yeah."

"What are you doing?"

"Just sitting there."

"Did you ever think it was nuts?"

Dennis did not respond.

Dennis said he was tied up about forty-five minutes while Julie recited her fantasy. Nothing sexual was going on. "I was becoming really hot, and I really told her I wanted to stop," Dennis said. "I was feeling real good. She unwrapped the athletic tape and said, 'Well, now it's the lady's turn.' "

She wanted her Knight in Shining Armor fantasy. Julie enjoyed medieval characterizations and liked to refer to herself as "the lady," Dennis said. She wanted to be rescued. By her husband.

They went into their adjoining master bathroom where Julie directed Dennis to tear a terry cloth washcloth into gags. He said she inserted them into her cheeks, one on each side. She began wrapping her jaw with adhesive tape, having exhausted their supply of athletic tape on Dennis. Sitting on the bed now, Dennis said he watched Julie wrap her mouth and chin. As she wound the tape about her head, she called him into the bathroom.

"She was standing there with a roll of tape in her hand and indicated what I was to do. I assumed she had the rag [on her hair to protect it]," he testified. Dennis wound her head twenty-six times with the tape. "That's just the way she had me do it before. What she was very much into is the pressure, of the tape, the restraint. She told me to make sure and get everything even on both sides. She told me she wanted to see the final thing."

"I was supposed to take a picture of her, but I couldn't find my Polaroid," Dennis said.

Dennis said he just knew that night, May 5, that his bride wanted to be wrapped snugly against the back of the chair and her arms taped tightly to the chair arms. He taped Julie's nude body in a figure eight about her breasts, more tape on her shoulders and arms. Dennis ran out of white tape and added blue for shackles. He said he learned all this from his bride. Her feet were unbound. Dennis said the strips of tape found hanging from the chair legs were left over from his bondage.

Julie indicated that she wanted Dennis to use the vibrator by moving her legs, he said. "During this sexual stimulation she would either pull me towards her or push me away or direct me right or left. I was supposed to move the vibrator in that direction."

With his wife tightly trussed, Dennis began foreplay. "I was bending down, kissing her leg and I started getting nauseated, the room was spinning," he testified.

"I felt nauseous, and I went into the bathroom to get sick. A couple of times. I was there five or more minutes, it seems forever when you're sick, five or ten minutes maybe. I laid down to the toilet and I fell asleep." Dennis said he heard no noises from the bedroom about ten feet away. When he felt better, he said he returned to his wife.

"Julie was laying on her back. I thought she fell over. She might have tried to get up to come see where I was. I went over and picked up the chair. I thought she'd wake up and open her eyes. She didn't. I shook her. She just didn't wake up. I assumed something was wrong.

"I tipped the chair back so she'd be laying down. I tried to blow air in through her nose. In Boy Scouts, we had training about resuscitation." Dennis did not try to unwrap the tape, thinking there was not time for that. Nor did he cut away the tape, claiming no access to scissors. "With my free hand, I tried to check for a pulse. When I blew in her nose, it was very difficult. And when I went to listen for the air to return, I noticed that the stomach had come up a little bit, it looked odd, so I pressed on the stomach. . . .

"It occurred to me [to call 911], but I didn't think I had time . . . she wasn't breathing. I couldn't get a pulse. When I realized she was dead, I threw a tantrum, pounding on the floor, saying 'Oh God, oh God,' just self-pity. I decided my life was ruined. It had gone through my mind—I don't know if this was right or wrong—to hide the body. I laid there for a while trying to think of what to do. . . .

"I decided to move Julie into the garage. I was fluctuating between taking her someplace else or hiding her." He dragged her body tied to the chair into the garage. He placed her between their two cars in the tight space at the back wall. He covered Julie with an afghan and tucked her favorite teddy bear on her lap. Police found the afghan near the body, but not the stuffed animal.

Dennis said he vacuumed the house twice, straightened up and showered and dressed for the office. "I decided that I didn't want to live any more. . . .I had seen a movie with Jimmy Stewart where he and his wife asphyxiated themselves in a car. I took an old rubber hose and taped it to the exhaust pipe and pushed it into the window of [her] car."

After he started the engine of Julie's Buick, Dennis said he curled up with his dead wife and waited to die. But the Buick died instead. Dennis tried five or six times; the car refused to run. Angry, Dennis pulled the hose out and threw it into the trunk. He admitted he turned to arson.

"I wanted to be close to Julie. I went in [the house] and searched for one of her diaries, just to read. I thought somehow that would make me closer to her." Reading Julie's descriptions of her emotional agony, of which Dennis said he had been unaware, "I went into a rage and started the fire with it [the diary]. Because I needed to take out my anger on something.

"I had collected all the paraphernalia, the tape, little cardboard rolls from the tape, some body paint, and thrown them in a bag and put them in a car." He picked up a lighter in the kitchen, lit Julie's diary and "stuffed" the burning paper into the bag of sexual paraphernalia. Dennis said he threw this torch into the backseat of Julie's Buick. That ignited the garage, he said.

Dennis's attorney interjected, "Don't you understand you're making a judicial admission to a Class C felony?"

"Yes," Dennis answered.

"I walked around the car and sat with Julie. I pulled her down to be close to me. Then I just decided to leave. I don't remember consciously deciding to leave, but that's what I did. I just started wandering around. I remember walking down the side street and I ended up out on Manchester. A police car almost ran me down. It came down with lights and a siren. I didn't think about what I was doing. I was just walking. I remember trying to get a ride."

Dennis admitted he flew to St. Paul under an alias. He described how ill he felt that morning.

He had no intention of murdering his bride, he said. In fact, he had planned to take Karen's engagement ring, which was in his safe deposit box, and trade it in for something nice for Julie.

After Dennis's colleague told him that his wife had died in the fire, Dennis thought he had burned her alive and could not face her wake. Days later, thoughts of suicide returned. "I had a lot of problems in the past with mortality and death. I just felt like I couldn't take the pain anymore. I was going to try suicide again. I drove down to the river.

"I got out and stopped there. I just couldn't contemplate the jumping. The only thing that really stopped me was the question of whether I would burn in hell forever. That's my belief. I drove around for a little bit, and then I went home."

Dennis said that on Thursday, May 8, he left his parents' house to go to the funeral home. But "I just couldn't do it." Dennis flew to St. Paul instead, to talk with his colleague, Jim Macke. "I needed to talk. I was having a lot of trouble dealing with what needed to be done, financial, what was required."

Before he left, Dennis had gone to his safe deposit box, which was filled with his diaries. "When I have a problem and I don't have anybody to talk to, I will review the diary."

The next morning, May 9, Dennis found himself down by the river again. "All the pain, and I didn't see any other way out. I am drawn to water anyway, waterfalls, the ocean, and I needed to reflect or take some action.

"I went out on the bridge and had my argument with myself on the choice between suicide and life again. Then I just walked back into town and just started walking down the highway and got a ride to the airport." He flew under another alias to California, where he wanted to "find himself."

The whole time, the two months he was there, Dennis said, he suffered horribly, believing he had burned his wife to death.

As his testimony was reported on the evening news, a group of Dennis's former friends laughed. "After a year in jail, all he can come up with is, 'She made me do it'?"

The next morning, Karen read what her ex-husband had said in the *Post-Dispatch*. She told Tina Porterfield, "Dennis had a dream to become a writer. He said he wanted to write things that 'moved' people. This stuff is a joke. Who'd believe it?"

Twenty-eight

"A Piece of Charcoal"

June 2, 1987

DePriest had fumed silently during Dennis's testimony. That son-of-a-bitch, he thought; he had taunted her as she was dying in that chair. The prosecutor had contained his fury by making notes to catch Dennis on cross-examination. He had been waiting for a year for this opportunity.

The prosecutor began by asking when Dennis had been brought back to St. Louis to stand trial. Dennis said he could not remember. He thought it was July 10 or so, 1986. DePriest asked when he first read the police reports. Dennis said he did not know, for he was quite depressed when he arrived in jail.

Dennis had testified that during the ten weeks of his marriage, he stayed over at his house in U. City no more than ten times and Julie was with him four of those nights. Margulis had pointed out that prior to their marriage, Dennis had lived with Julie at her home on White Tree Lane. Since living together is frowned upon among conservative St. Louisans, this added to the defense's carefully contrived image of Julie as the promiscuous vamp.

(Indeed, the wealthiest city in the metro area, Ladue, won a lawsuit in 1985 against a middle-aged unmarried couple who lived together with their children from prior marriages. The state appellate court upheld Ladue, saying the couple violated the city ordinance by having an excessive number of unrelated people cohabiting. The couple later married and Joan Kelly Horn went onto become the first U. S. Congresswoman from Missouri's Second District, in 1990.)

DePriest asked if Dennis knew his neighbor on White Tree who was also his colleague at Price Waterhouse? Dennis said yes.

> DePriest: He says that the maximum number of times he saw you over at White Tree from January 20, until May 6, 1986 was half a dozen.
> Dennis: Yes.
> DePriest: Is that a lie?
> Dennis: No.
> DePriest: Now, you say in 1985 you were with Price Waterhouse and you worked out of town approximately seventy percent of the time.
> Dennis: I really don't know the percentage.
> DePriest: Well, did you work out of town more than half the time?
> Dennis: Probably.
> DePriest: At the time of your marriage were you working in town or out of town?
> Dennis: In town.
> DePriest: Isn't it true that this trip that you went on May 5 was the first time you had been out of town that year?
> Dennis: Correct.
> DePriest: Isn't it true that you stayed at your old house when you told your wife you were out-of-town [on business]?"
> Dennis: Correct.

When cross-examined about his early phone call to Jim Macke, Dennis said he was upset at the time.

> DePriest: You had the presence of mind to ask Jim Macke to give you an alibi about the night before.
> Dennis: (no response)
> DePriest: Did you do that?
> Dennis: Yes.
> DePriest: So, something up here is ticking, right, in your head?

DENNIS: Yes.

DEPRIEST: You knew at that time you were in trouble, didn't you?

DENNIS: I was. Yes.

DEPRIEST: Jim came to your [hotel] room. You got out of the shower. Do you recall telling him, "Did I tell you I got married a few weeks ago?"

DENNIS: That was a clarifying statement. I told him I needed to talk to him. . . . I did not have the opportunity.

DEPRIEST: Didn't you know that when Jim Macke came in the room he was going to tell you that your wife was dead?

DENNIS: I didn't know that was his specific reason to be there.

DEPRIEST: Why else would he come to your room? You knew she was dead.

DENNIS: Any number of reasons.

DEPRIEST: Why did you start crying when he told you your wife had died?

DENNIS: Because he told me.

DEPRIEST: Isn't it true that you had to give this kind of reaction to conceal your involvement?. . . Who did you feel sorry for? Did you feel sorry for Julie Bulloch or Dennis Bulloch?

DePriest pulled out an exhibit, asking Dennis to identify a photograph of the master bedroom. The picture was from the roll of film Dennis had dropped off in Minneapolis–St. Paul on May 5, the day before the fire. But Dennis could not recall the photograph he later had to admit he had taken. DePriest flashed more of Dennis's photos of the interior of 251 White Tree Lane. The prosecutor repeated to the jury that Dennis had taken these pictures to St. Paul, May 5, to be developed.

Then DePriest turned to a police photograph of the master bedroom after the fire, May 6. Why were there a pair of women's Levi's on the foot of the bed when Dennis had testified that Julie was in her nightgown when he returned home May 5? DePriest asked. Dennis said he did not know.

Dennis had said the three sex manuals were Julie's, which she kept on her nightstand. But DePriest pointed out that at least one of them was found in Dennis's boxes in the garage. Indeed, *Making Love Better* was stiff from being waterlogged. Dennis denied it was his.

DePriest turned to the suicide attempt. He asked why, if Dennis had wanted to kill himself, he never let either of the cars run in the closed garage. Dennis admitted he never bothered to try.

The prosecutor questioned why Dennis showered and attired himself in slacks, dress shirt, tie, and jacket before going into the garage.

DePRIEST: Did you get dressed because you knew you were going to leave?

DENNIS: I got dressed because I thought I was going to die.

DePRIEST: Well, let me ask you something. Weren't you concerned what Julie would look like when she was found dead in there?

DENNIS: I didn't think about it.

DePRIEST: You didn't think about anyone but yourself, did you?

DENNIS: (no response)

DePRIEST: But you went into the house and got dressed? While she is lying out there nude in this chair with over seventy feet of tape on her?

DENNIS: Yes.

DePRIEST: After you believed she was dead, and she is in the master bedroom, did you clean up the house in any way?

DENNIS: Just arranging things. I recollect vacuuming the family room.

DePRIEST: How did you get Julie from the master bedroom to the garage?

DENNIS: I carried her out.

DePRIEST: You picked up that chair with her body in it and carried it out? [A dead weight in a chair is extremely heavy and cumbersome.]

DENNIS: I don't recollect.

DePRIEST: Did you carry it or drag it?

DENNIS: I don't remember.

DePRIEST: You can remember cleaning the house, vacuuming the family room, but you can't remember how you got your wife into the garage?. . . Did you consider maybe taking some of the tape off before you carried her out?

DENNIS: No, sir.

DePRIEST: You really didn't care what she looked like then?

DENNIS: I didn't think about it.

DePRIEST: Isn't it true you were hoping that the whole garage would explode and when the police and firemen got there all they'd find is a big piece of charcoal and we'd never know she died tied to that chair?

DENNIS: (no response.)

DEPRIEST: Isn't it true that you destroyed all the evidence of bondage except for your wife's body?

DENNIS: As far as I can see.

What about the secret wedding? DePriest asked. Dennis said he did not invite his parents because, at age thirty-two, he wanted to do it on his own.

He did not remember what he was doing the morning of his marriage, February 22, when he had been working on his house in U. City with Karen. The prosecutor said he was amazed a man could not recall what he did right before his wedding. Dennis said he stayed with his bride at 251 White Tree Lane on their wedding night. As far as he could remember.

While Julie was upset about his alleged traveling so much, Dennis maintained she was not unhappy about his ski trip. Of course, she did not know it was a singles group, he admitted. Dennis said they separated the week after he returned. He could not recall the dates.

DePriest, exasperated, said, "I don't know if I am unreasonable or what, but was it a coincidence every time you had an argument with her you ended up with a date?" Dennis did not answer. He said later he did not consider himself Nina's date to the Young Republicans party or on the ski trip. Dennis never admitted to sex with anyone other than his wives. And he indulged in perversion only at Julie's command.

Was Nina, as well as Christy, lying then? "My remembrance is just different," Dennis said.

Was it coincidental, DePriest demanded, that Dennis left Julie after he went to withdraw the $60,000 and found she had beat him to it? Dennis replied, "She told me she was under a lot of pressure. The issue of hospitalization came out and it was a great shock to me." Dennis admitted he had not discussed withdrawing her money with Julie.

How could it be, DePriest asked, that Dennis did not know about Julie's psychiatric stays when they had dated just before and after she was institutionalized? "That's true," Dennis said in a *non sequitur.* DePriest asked whether he had ever noticed anything strange about her. Dennis said no.

DePriest repeated the facts: Dennis's ski jaunt, fight with Julie, staying over at his house, date with Nina, reconciliation with Julie, attempted withdrawal of funds and, upon that failure, separation from his bride. And days after that, his Easter with Christy Meiers.

While Margulis used repetition to build his image of Dennis as victim, the prosecutor repeated evidence to remind the jury of his guilt. Where the defense repeated the questions over and over, the prosecution would jump back and forth to goad the defendant into exposing his cover-up of the murder.

DePriest asked Dennis to describe a police evidence photo of the inside of the refrigerator. Dennis said there was a bottle of wine. "Cold Duck or something to that effect. It's not in the same class [as the champagne Carter Miller had given], but it's liquor." Dennis could not explain why it was there when he had testified they had run out of wine. Nor could he say why no orange juice had been found, if he was drinking screwdrivers.

DePriest asked how much did Julie drink, when her blood alcohol test during the autopsy showed zero-point-zero? Dennis said he did not know.

DePriest repeated his earlier line of questioning.

"When you realized she was dead, did you consider maybe taking some of the tape off?"

"I didn't think about it."

Regarding the fire, DePriest asked, "Weren't you concerned what Julie would look like after the fire?"

"I didn't think about it."

"You really didn't care what she looked like?"

"I didn't think about it."

"You didn't think about anyone but yourself, did you?"

Dennis did not answer.

DePriest harangued again: "Isn't it true you hoped the whole structure would burn and that would leave her a big piece of charcoal and no one would ever know how she died?"

Dennis made no response. He was that self-controlled.

DePriest grilled him about his suicide attempts. On cross-examination, Dennis said he did not intend to die when he started the garage fire and lay down next to Julie's body. He said he did not intend to die the two times he went down to the river. He really did not attempt suicide, he just thought about it.

Apparently there was no intent to put out the fire although the means was easily at hand. DePriest showed Dennis a photograph of the basement stairs at 251 White Tree Lane. At the top of the steps was a fire extinguisher.

Although he said he had lived in the house since January and had stored his things in the basement, Dennis said sometimes one can see something, but it does not "click."

Asked his prosecutor: "After it got too hot for you in the garage, did you ever consider going in and attempting to put out the fire so your wife wouldn't look like she does in the photograph?"

"No," Dennis said. Nor he did not know how far the Ballwin fire department was from his house. (It is several blocks away.)

Although DePriest could not enter Julie's diary into evidence, legally he could question Dennis about portions of it during cross-examination. He led up to it by asking Dennis about his birthday gift card August 9, 1985, to Christy. Dennis staunchly maintained he had not begun bondage with Christy until he had learned it from Julie. Indeed, Dennis testified that the reason he had tried to blindfold Christy at Easter was because his wife enjoyed it so much he thought his girlfriend would, too.

Had he read the unburned portion of Julie's diary? DePriest asked. Dennis said he thought so. DePriest quoted one entry, "I met this really nice guy on August 14."

Dennis was at a loss to explain how Julie could have introduced him to bondage before August 9.

The really nice guy then was led to reveal all the aliases he had employed in the case—Jonathan Dennis, John Jackson, Jonathan Block, John Mason, Dennis Bender, David Johnson. He used the last, to fly back to St. Paul, because he had "panicked" after Julie died.

When Margulis objected, on grounds of hearsay, to DePriest's asking Dennis whether he had listened to his wife's audiotape, the prosecutor tried another tack. He switched to asking Dennis if various things Julie had said on the tape were true. Margulis objected to using hearsay on cross-examination. The judge sustained him. The two lawyers approached the bench.

Margulis tried one last time to bring in Terri Sacher's allegation that Julie had slept with her brother. His argument was that if the state could bring up the diary and the tape, what about Julie's statement to Terri? DePriest argued that while the tape was in Julie's voice and the diary in her handwriting, what Terri claimed was strictly hearsay. It did not matter. Judge Saitz again ruled that the audiotape, diary, and Terri's tale of incest were all inadmissible.

DePriest brought into evidence the wills Dennis had concocted, leaving the bulk of Julie's furnishings to Christy and his former wife's sister, before his wife was even buried. As DePriest itemized Julie's house, stocks, jewelry, and insurance, Dennis agreed it totaled about $300,000, even correcting DePriest who said one insurance policy was worth $10,000. "It was $13,000," Dennis pointed out.

Angry because his wife had died, Dennis again explained, he had destroyed all evidence of her death—the rags for the gags, the spools from the tape.

It was hard for him to answer some of the prosecutor's questions. "My reference for time went kilter. I can't even estimate," Dennis said when asked how long did he clean up the house, how long after he found Julie dead did he drag her body into the garage, how long was he in the bathroom while she lay dying. He agreed he had said during direct questioning that he was sick in the bathroom for five to ten minutes.

"Isn't it true that Dr. Gantner stated the other day when you were here that your wife could have survived eight minutes without air to her lungs?" DePriest said.

"I was in there actually much longer than that after I passed out."

"When did you pass out? We haven't heard this before."

"After I got sick, I lay down next to the toilet and fell asleep, passed out, whatever you want to, what term you want to use."

"Could you have been in there a half an hour?"

"Yes, sir."

"An hour"

"Yes, sir."

"You got into the bathroom and you get sick and your wife is sitting in the bedroom with an excess of seventy feet of tape on her and a gag in her mouth and you leave her alone for an hour?"

"Not purposely."

"Well, when you got sick, why didn't you unbind her before you went into the bathroom?" DePriest asked again.

"It's not something you think about when you're ready to heave."

"You don't think about the safety of your wife?" DePriest repeated for emphasis.

Once again, there was no response from the witness chair.

DePriest said, "You state you are an 'avid reader.' "

"I try to be."

"These books, *The Joy of Sex, More Joy of Sex*, and others, did you ever read these books?"

"Not until after the case started. Art flipped through them and I saw some pages."

"Did you even consider reading these and seeing the rules about how you should act when engaged in bondage?"

"I hadn't thought of it."

In fleeing the murder scene, why did he go to California? "You said you left to visit California," DePriest asked. "Who were you going to visit in California that was going to help you solve your problems?"

Dennis swallowed and said, "God."

Twenty-nine

Who Was the Victim?

June 2–3, 1987

Margulis resumed questioning Dennis to reaffirm two images in the jury's mind: Julie as the decadent vamp and Dennis as the victim. She had led Dennis into the sexual bondage ritual, she had been the writer, director, producer, and star of their fantasy shows. Dennis was a bright man, too bright to have deliberately murdered his wife with so many glaring errors. He just had panicked. Wouldn't anyone, thinking he had killed his wife in a fire? Perfectly normal human reactions.

Closing arguments were set for the next morning, June 3, at nine-thirty.

DePriest pointed out in his closing argument that "the law does not require proof that overcomes every possibility." Dennis had an excuse for every fact and piece of evidence against him because he had spent a year in jail fabricating these lies. But Dennis never could explain away the passport application he picked up in California with his photograph showing him with dyed hair and beard, DePriest said. Nor the photographs of the house Dennis had taken before the fire.

The prosecutor hammered on Dennis's August 9 bondage birthday gift to Christy *before* he met Julie August 14: "A tie.

How many guys send girls ties through the mail?" Julie told her doctors she had performed unusual sex acts. "Who was she dating when she answered these questions? Dennis Bulloch . . .

"He married Julie for her money, he had nothing but a thousand dollars in the bank and a book of car payments when he walked down the aisle."

DePriest quoted Park Dietz, who was paid $6,000 to tell the jury Julie's killing might have been an accident, that this was only the second case of spouse death from bondage. And Julie Bulloch was the first American woman to die in bondage. At the hands of her husband, who planned her murder.

Margulis, who had the energy and intelligence to obsessively work through every detail in a case, had spent the previous night and early dawn working and reworking his closing argument. This was his second death penalty case, and if he lost it, his young client would spend the next seven or eight years appealing the case before taking that pathetic walk to the gas chamber.

Margulis pointed out that Julie had not been a bad person, indeed she had been a nice person who did not deserve the death she had. She had been ill, she had suffered from bizarre delusions. She had told therapists when she was institutionalized that she had indulged in unusual sexual behavior.

Immediately, Margulis turned to discussing Julie's brother. He had testified to sexual bondage with tapes and gags over the last four to five years. "He told you that he lived at 251 White Tree with Julie for some period of time. And then when Julie introduces after marriage sexual bondage of this heavier kind to Dennis, for the first time after they are married with tapes and gags, she says to him: 'You are one of the family now.'. . .

"And you can use your logic to figure out where she found out about it."

The jury was instructed to find Dennis guilty or not guilty of murder in the first degree (premeditated), murder in the second degree (in the heat of passion), or involuntary manslaughter (recklessly and consciously ignoring a substantial risk. "A gross deviation from what a normal person in similar circumstances would do.")

The case of *State of Missouri vs. Dennis Neal Bulloch* went to the jury at eleven-forty, the morning of June 3, 1987.

Reporters and court watchers stuck around. They assumed the jury would reach its verdict by one, two o'clock tops. Then the court would hear the death penalty arguments and the jurors would go out again to deliberate. Dennis probably would be sentenced to the gas chamber before six, in time for the local news broadcasts.

One and two o'clock came and went. The crowds were afraid to leave. It could be any minute now. The television and radio reporters set up for live shots the minute the jury came back.

Three and four P.M. came and went. By five o'clock, only the people to be affected directly by the verdict were left: Bob and Ginny Bulloch, with their minister consoling them, pregnant Judy Miller trying to calm her husband Carter, and the omnipresent reporters and cameramen who cajoled the Bullochs and Millers for interviews after the verdict.

There was talk of a hung jury.

While arguing behind their closed door, the jurors called to re-examine pieces of evidence or to ask questions. The judge did not mind.

Six hours after they went out, at five-forty P.M., the jury sent a message to the judge: They had finally reached a verdict.

Art Margulis was about to dive into his long-awaited steak at Candici's, an Italian restaurant around the corner from the courthouse. It was his first meal of the day, as his stomach always knotted up during trials. His wife Joyce was with him; they were semi-relaxed, total relaxation being impossible while a jury is out. A waiter hurried over to their table. He said the judge's secretary was on the phone. They had a verdict.

DePriest had gone back to the warrant office to process charges. As soon as he put down the phone, he raced to the elevator bank to go to the courtroom.

Reporters called their editors before they ran into the courtroom to get their seats. As soon as all were assembled, at six-fifteen, the bailiff locked the double doors to the courtroom to maintain silence while the verdict was being read.

The two brothers-in-law, Dennis Bulloch and Carter Miller, each held the same feelings about the case. Each believed he would be vindicated. Ginny and Bob Bulloch were praying with their minister for the release of their only remaining child. Margulis and Grant and the two Toms—DePriest and Mehan—

were numb. Mehan's wife and Grant's future wife sat among the media and watchers, as did Joyce Margulis and her husband's parents, then well into their late seventies. (Margulis's father died several years later.)

Way in the back was Lt. Denny Niere, who hoped that all his year-long labors would come to fruition.

Everyone stood as the jury and judge entered. The jury foreman handed back the verdict forms. The room was still. The clerk opened the verdict and read it aloud.

Thirty

Blinded Justice

June 3–July 10, 1987

"We, the jury, find the defendant, Dennis Neal Bulloch, guilty of involuntary manslaughter."

There was a buzz in the courtroom. People were uncertain of what they had heard. A deputy sheriff repeated the verdict. Margulis looked up toward the ceiling and closed his eyes as if in gratitude. DePriest seemed stunned by disbelief. Lt. Niere and Carter Miller each felt ill.

"They may be a jury of Dennis Bulloch's peers," said one courtroom watcher, "but thank God, they're not peers of mine."

Dennis showed no overt emotion. Only relief by relaxing the muscles in his clenched jaw. His parents were jubilant. Their boy had suffered enough.

That Dennis's life was already ruined was Margulis's argument for the minimum sentence. DePriest argued, his life might be ruined, but Julie's was over. Looking at her widower, DePriest pointed out that not once had Dennis shown any remorse. Not once had he said he was sorry.

Quickly the jury returned with its sentence. The maximum of seven years. Judge Saitz set a date for the formal sentencing after he received a pre-sentence investigation report from the probation and parole board.

When questioned, several jurors and their foreman said a majority, eleven jurors, had found Dennis guilty of murder in the first degree on early ballots. But jury decisions in criminal cases must be unanimous. The jury foreman kept pushing for first degree. A sixty-seven-year-old widower allegedly held out, saying he would deadlock the jury until they agreed with him. He felt that Dennis had suffered enough. He did not believe "in an eye for an eye," he allegedly said. His fellow jurors believed he was opposed to the death penalty, although, during jury selection, he had given his oath he was not opposed to it.

The eleven other jurors gave in to this man.

The hold-out juror told the *Post-Dispatch* newspaper that he had received a barrage of crank calls within days of the verdict, and had been forced to change his home phone number. He grew depressed, he said.

Cal Porterfield worked with one of the jurors. A meek, demure woman, she was so distraught by the verdict that she took several days off before returning to the office. She told her boss, "Never again will I let someone change my mind. I'll have to live with this the rest of my life."

Carter Miller was crushed. "Others go through their lives blessed, yet they criticize my sister. Aren't they aware what it must have been like being twenty years old and uprooted to St. Louis with Dad dying and Mother just diagnosed with cancer? We were never any 'Leave It to Beaver' family and now at age twenty-one Julie had to be head of it.

"I'm proud of her. She lived through things her peers couldn't comprehend. When they were worrying about where to get their M.B.A., Julie was picking out a nursing home for my father. Inside that task-oriented woman was a little girl who never got to complete her adolescence. She never got to live her own life."

Karen did not believe her ex-husband had killed his bride of ten weeks for the money itself. "That wouldn't have been enough for Dennis. No, he killed Julie over loss of control. Control of the money. The money he could invest and turn himself into a real estate and stock entrepreneur."

Jane Muster could not believe that prim, professional little Julie had been made into the Whore of Babylon. "That girl did

not even truly know how to flirt. She kept her reserved façade of
little navy suit, little closed toe pumps, little bowtie. There were
no sensual aromas, no sexual vibes. No aura. She didn't want
anyone to take her wrong.

"All she ever wanted was to make a life with a partner and a
family. Her goals were good red-blooded American goals."

In nearly all jury verdicts in which there is a conviction, the
defense says it plans to appeal. Margulis told some reporters
privately that night of the verdict he would not do so.

The next day, all day, June 4, the telephone lines were
jammed with irate callers to the county prosecutor and the
Ballwin police. The public was outraged by the jury verdict.
There were even death threats against Dennis Bulloch.

DePriest learned not to open his mail, there were so many
hate letters blaming him. In sympathy, Cal Porterfield wrote a
long letter to him, saying how good and decent DePriest was.
Cal had been impressed that the prosecutor cared about fair-
ness and was above using the death of a bright young woman to
build his career.

The juror who allegedly had turned the verdict around ran
into DePriest one afternoon weeks later outside the courthouse.
"How come you didn't put on all that evidence I read about in
the *Post-Dispatch*'s trial coverage?" he asked. "I'd a voted for
murder first if you had."

DePriest walked away, speechless.

Two days after his verdict, Dennis was released on $50,000
dollars bond until his July sentencing. He said at a news conference, "I want to give thanks to my Christian friends." The
attorney who had freed him was Jewish.

Julie's neighbors on White Tree Lane tied black ribbons
around their trees. Molly Flowers and her husband wrapped
black crepe around a stake they placed in their lawn that flowed
onto 251 White Tree. The Flowers felt Julie had been betrayed
once again.

Julie Miller Bulloch suffered the final betrayal. She may have
been betrayed as a child when she was sexually abused. She
had been betrayed by a husband who feigned love and who
married her for her money and then denied he had wed her.

She had been betrayed when she trusted him enough to let him take her into bondage. She had been betrayed when he stood by and let her die.

The ultimate in this sordid history was her husband's portrait of her as an S&M Eve who led him to perdition and died as a result of her sins.

DePriest's and Mehan's boss, St. Louis County Prosecuting Attorney George "Buzz" Westfall, moved swiftly. "Dennis Bulloch," Westfall said, "is getting away with murder." But he was not going to get away with other felonies, the prosecutor promised. Outraged, Westfall called the first verdict "a terrible mistake." In Missouri, when a defendant is tried on a capital crime, murder first degree, he or she cannot be tried for lesser crimes at the same trial. Westfall, known as an aggressive and tough prosecutor, announced Dennis would face additional charges.

Fifteen days after the jury verdict, June 18, Westfall asked DePriest to issue two more warrants against Dennis. He was charged with tampering with evidence (burning Julie's diary and other paraphernalia) and armed criminal action (using a weapon to commit a felony, that is, using tape to suffocate his wife).

A week later, June 25, the St. Louis County Grand Jury indicted Dennis Bulloch on those charges. And later, on September 11, the grand jury indicted Dennis for second-degree arson, the burning of the garage. First-degree arson is "knowingly" starting a damage fire that endangers a human. Second-degree is "knowingly" damaging property alone. Large urban areas in Missouri use grand jury indictments as a basis for trial. Prosecutors expected the three charges to be joined together in Dennis's second trial.

Dennis was rearrested on June 18 at his Gram's house in South St. Louis. His bond was raised to $500,000, which Margulis had reduced to $300,000. Dennis's parents could not come up with that much money, so their son remained in jail.

Margulis protested that Westfall was being vindictive. The president of the American Civil Liberties Union of Eastern Missouri, Lawrence Katzenstein, said the new charges raised the specter of double jeopardy: trying a defendant twice for the same crime, which is prohibited by the Fifth Amendment. A prominent criminal defense lawyer, Donald Wolff, called the armed criminal action charge "frivolous." Wolff said Westfall was overreacting to public pressure.

Another Fifth Amendment issue would be raised in Dennis's second trial.

Under the statute providing that a criminal cannot profit from his or her crime, Westfall froze Dennis's inheritance from Julie's estate. Investigators seized $75,000 in cash and $50,000 in jewelry. Her insurance companies sued her widower so they would not have to pay death benefits. Carter Miller sued his former brother-in-law for the return of his sister's property.

Julie's neighbors added white ribbons to their black drapings along White Tree Lane. White signifying that Dennis would not go unpunished.

Dennis Neal Bulloch was sentenced on July 10, 1987, to seven years in prison and a $5,000 fine. After he was hauled out in manacles like any other criminal, Ginny Bulloch turned on the media.

"It's all your fault," she hissed at a reporter. "The media has turned this into a circus."

"Lady," the reporter said under her breath, "I've been at this ten years and I've never seen anything like it. Your son did it. We didn't."

That day, Tina Porter became irate reading in the *Post-Dispatch* about a case in adjacent St. Charles County where a fifteen-year-old youth was sentenced for possession of marijuana. It was his first offense, which in St. Louis City and County would bring a suspended sentence. But St. Charles was more conservative. The teenager was sentenced to sixteen years in prison. "Nine more than Dennis, who killed his wife," Tina said bitterly.

But Westfall vowed to change that.

Part Six

"Remember Julie Miller"

1987–1991

Thirty-one

"Sparky"

Autumn, 1987–Spring, 1988

Maybe I'm not destined to be a great man. Maybe it's beyond me.
But I can't accept the fact I'm an ordinary person.
—From the diary of Dennis Bulloch
(paraphrased)

On top of a hill overlooking the greensward of its golf course sits the Bogey Club. The white-pillared, red-brick building, the sanctuary of St. Louis's corporate power elite, looks as though it were built by slave labor, which some of its members might prefer to dealing with labor unions. Bogey is one of the most exclusive and one of the richest clubs for several states around. It's sixty-three members, all white males, are CEOs of major corporations. To join the elect one must be patient until death or retirement opens the ranks. And then one must be "invited to join." Apart from its golf course, Bogey is renowned for its chef. Every Saturday, the members lunch together.

For years, the alumni of Price Waterhouse gathered every autumn for a black-tie dinner at Bogey. Price encouraged the parties, for its alumni were a network of business referrals. All former employees were eligible to enter the sanctum sanctorum of St. Louis business for the reunion in October, 1987. That would have technically included Price Waterhouse's most famous alumnus, Dennis Neal Bulloch.

235

But, of course, he could not join Jim Macke, Leslie Jefferson, and his other former colleagues. Dennis was elsewhere.

The Maximum Security Penitentiary sits on a barren flatland surmounted by guard towers, high walls, and barbed wire. MSP, as it is known, is Missouri's toughest prison. Dennis was an inmate here, in the state capital, Jefferson City.

While his old friends dipped into *paté* and *petits fours* that fall evening, Dennis was trying to swallow the pallid prison food he slopped onto his metal plate. Dennis's dining companions were mostly born and bred in derelict trailer camps and slums, the out-of-sight poor as Paul Fussell described them in *Class*. They were the most vicious convicts in the state.

One wonders how Dennis, who could not disrobe in front of another man, managed with these creatures. At least twice he allegedly was the object of their amorous advances.

The cons had a pet name for Dennis Neal Bulloch. "Sparky."

While Dennis's former colleagues were sipping good Burgundies, his former socialite pals were tossing down bloody marys and gin and tonics in the crowded, dark bar at Busch's Grove Restaurant in Ladue.

Nina Honeywell and friends also drank at a trendier place, a spot in Clayton that opened after Dennis was taken away in shackles from the county courthouse. So popular did Cardwell's Restaurant become that its bar became known as the place to meet upscale members of the opposite sex.

Indeed, a few years later, Nina was introduced there to a dark handsome lawyer with a mustache. Both were embarrassed. The attorney was John Ross, who would prosecute Dennis his third time around.

As the chief trial assistant to the county prosecuting attorney, Ross was aware how much Westfall, DePriest, and Mehan wanted Dennis permanently esconced in prison. Their next shot came in July, 1988, when Dennis would be tried on arson, tampering with evidence (destroying Julie's body and her diary in the fire), and, possibly, armed criminal action.

DePriest believed he now had new evidence that could put Dennis away for decades.

In March, 1988, Ballwin Detective Steven Shicker took the photograph of the nude teenage girl to Karen Toksvig. He hoped that Dennis's first wife might know her ex-husband's old flame. She did. It was the girl Dennis had left her for. Dinah Moltke.

Two Ballwin officers flew to San Francisco to interview Dinah Moltke, now a marketing manager there. Dinah said she would not only cooperate by providing information, she would return to Missouri to testify against her ex-fianceé when he was tried for armed criminal action, using tape to murder his wife.

Dinah's testimony would prove that Dennis had been experienced in sexual bondage long before he met Julie Miller. And with an underaged girl.

Thirty-two

The First Arson Trial

July 1988–August 1990

Dennis Bulloch betrayed no emotion when he was found guilty a second time, a year after his first conviction for Julie's death. In this trial, the jury found him guilty as charged, of tampering with evidence and second-degree arson in the fire he set May 6, 1986, to cover up the killing of his wife. The jury in the arson trial had not taken long, always a bad sign for the defense. The seven women and five men had deliberated only three hours, compared to the seven spent behind locked doors in the first trial.

Dennis's second trial was held in the picturesque one-hundred-thirty-five-year-old Greek Revival courthouse in Cape Girardeau, in Missouri's Bootheel, where cotton is still grown. It had been moved to Cape Girardeau, about two hundred miles from St. Louis, to escape the notoriety of the banner headlines of the first trial thirteen months earlier, in June, 1987. In comparison to the lurid and complicated murder trial, this one was like reading the federal tax code.

The arson trial lasted less than two days, July 12 and 13, 1988, in contrast to Dennis's eight-day first trial in which he was convicted of involuntary manslaughter in the death of his wife. Dennis would stretch the definition, saying it was accidental death. It was not. Involuntary manslaughter meant he "recklessly caused" the death of Julie Bulloch.

In this trial, the defense called no witnesses, not even Dennis. When asked by the judge if it was his decision not to testify, Dennis said he was following his lawyer's instructions. When asked if he was satisfied with his lawyer, Art Margulis, who had saved his life a year earlier, Dennis replied, "I am not qualified to say yes or no."

In his closing argument, Tom Mehan, who was prosecuting this case again with Tom DePriest, characterized Dennis as an opportunist. Dennis had admitted arson in his first trial to get away with murder, Mehan said. The prosecutor pointed out that Dennis was not testifying this time.

Margulis appealed this second trial of his client on grounds of prosecutorial misconduct by DePriest's and Mehan's boss, St. Louis County Prosecuting Attorney George "Buzz" Westfall, and of double jeopardy. Margulis argued that Westfall was being vengeful by trying Dennis for lesser crimes after losing the murder trial. The Fifth Amendment to the U. S. Constitution prohibits double jeopardy, trying a person twice for the same crime. The Fifth Amendment also gives defendants the right to remain silent at trial.

After convicting Dennis of arson and tampering, The Cape Girardeau jury recommended he be sentenced to eleven years. Ironically, Dennis could have received only probation. Dennis had been a model prisoner, making "outstanding institutional adjustment," said his report. Dennis was a hard worker with various self-help organizations. He posed no threat of violence.

According to the pre-sentence investigation report in the second trial, the arson trial in 1988, Dennis Bulloch had no prior offenses beyond traffic violations except one. If that crime had not resulted in the death of his thirty-one-year-old bride, his parole officer would have recommended probation. He wrote that Dennis's assets outweighed his liabilities.

Before the August, 1988, sentencing, Cape Girardeau County Circuit Judge A. J. Seier, a former prosecutor not known to be light on his sentences, received a packet of letters. Many were from Julie's vanpool, other co-workers, and friends morally outraged that her killer was serving so little time.

Many letters were pro-Dennis. Twenty-seven friends and

neighbors from Jefferson County sent a petition to Westfall's office protesting what they called double jeopardy, his second trial. A relative wrote that Dennis, before his wife's death, had visited his grandmother every Sunday, took her out to dinner, and helped around her house. (Indeed, Dennis used to joke that Karen Toksvig was jealous of Gram because, as he proudly put it, "Gram came first.")

A lawyer who worked with Dennis in the prison found him to be "responsible . . . has outstanding social skills . . . he has expressed a deeply felt and sincere remorse over the loss of his wife." Dennis's minister back home wrote he was "a compassionate and caring person . . . trying to understand how he may best work for the benefit of society."

His former brother-in-law's latest conviction was no consolation to Carter Miller. The week of the 1988 arson trial, his wife Judy, humiliated by his testimony of adultery and kinky sex during the 1987 murder trial, filed for divorce. The night she and their baby son left, Carter opened the last of the three special bottles of champagne he and Judy had brought back from their honeymoon in France. Remembering how he and Judy had given a bottle to Julie and Dennis as a wedding gift, Carter poured the last of the wine down the drain.

Judge Seier sentenced Dennis to the eleven years recommended by the jury. Just before Dennis was led away again in leg irons and handcuffs, his old prosecutor and, to him, persecutor, was getting himself into trouble.

St. Louis County Prosecuting Attorney Westfall was angry the Missouri Court of Appeals had thrown out the armed criminal action charge against Bulloch, ruling that a second trial on the same issue as the first—killing his wife—would be double jeopardy. (Armed criminal action is committing a felony with a weapon. Westfall had argued that the adhesive tape which bound Julie Bulloch constituted a weapon.)

During a television interview on KSDK-TV, the NBC-TV affiliate, in early August, 1988, Westfall criticized the appellate judges for dismissing the armed criminal action charge against Dennis. Westfall said on camera that the judge who wrote the opinion was "a little bit less than honest."

That comment was perceived as a personal attack on the judge's integrity by a committee of the Missouri Bar which investigates possible violations of ethics rules. Westfall claimed he was referring to the opinion, not the judge. But the bar group said Westfall broke the Missouri Supreme Court rule: No lawyer shall unfairly impugn the integrity of a judge. The committee decided Westfall should be disciplined.

Westfall apologized privately to the judge, but the committee wanted the apology made public, arguing that Westfall's attack on the court was made on television. Westfall refused. The committee offered the prosecutor an informal, private reprimand, not an uncommon penalty for prosecutors. Westfall rejected the reprimand, replying that he wanted a public hearing.

In early 1990, a subdued Westfall walked into the St. Louis County courtroom in Clayton, where the hearing was held. A handful of reporters was taking notes, having been tipped off by Westfall's office. Until then, no one outside the bar committee knew about his investigation.

The special prosecutor in the case, John Oliver of Cape Girardeau, argued that prosecutors were not above the law. "He [Westfall] must be held to the same standards that the rest of us are." Prosecutor Westfall appeared contrite.

Oliver also pointed out that the Missouri Supreme Court and the U. S. Supreme Court had allowed the lower court ruling to stand prohibiting a trial on armed criminal action. Westfall should lose his law license for three years, Oliver argued, which would be a first in Missouri. No prosecutor had ever received more than a reprimand for his or her public remarks.

Westfall's lawyer attacked the disbarment proceedings with, "This is America and lawyers do have the right to criticize a judge's opinions." Six months later, the hearing judge ruled Westfall should lose his law license for one year unless he publicly apologized. The Missouri Supreme Court would set his punishment.

Politics complicated the case. Not the backroom variety, but the kind in the voting booth. Westfall had announced in early March, 1990, shortly after his hearing, that he was running for St. Louis County Executive on the November, 1990, Democratic ticket. The Missouri Supreme Court could not afford to look as though it were influencing a major election.

Would his "trial" hurt Westfall at the polls? "Most people think judges are about as exciting as a center cut of eggplant," said Cole County Circuit Judge Byron L. Kinder, himself the former prosecuting attorney there. "We're about as welcome as aluminum siding salesmen," Kinder added.

"Judge bashing will only help Buzz in the November election," the judge predicted.

Thirty-three

"Bulloch II: Coming to a Courtroom Near You"

February 13–October 9, 1990

"My wife says vote for me. I need the job," Buzz Westfall joked with the spring 1990 lunchtime audience. "If I get disbarred over the Bulloch case, I'll have nowhere to go. If my opponent loses, he can go back to the insurance business," Westfall added with his hands folded together. Cherubic-looking and chubby-faced, the career prosecutor was turning his problem into a campaign bonus. One of Westfall's platforms in running for county executive, the head of St. Louis County government, was fighting crime, and no criminal was better known in St. Louis County than Dennis Bulloch.

The county prosecutors and their public enemy number one, Dennis Neal Bulloch, were squaring off to face each other a third time.

On February 13, 1990, a panel of three appellate judges had reversed Dennis's arson and tampering convictions and ordered a new trial, which would be his third time in court. In his rebuttal closing arguments, prosecutor Tom Mehan had referred to the fact that Dennis had not testified. That violated the defendant's Fifth Amendment right to remain silent, the judges ruled.

Dennis would be freed on bond while awaiting his third trial, his second arson trial. He was eligible for parole from his first conviction, for involuntary manslaughter in the death of his bride, in 1987. Dennis had served four years of his seven-year sentence for manslaughter, which included one year in jail before his murder trial.

"Was this guy born under a lucky star or what?" DePriest's investigator Jack Patty asked, shaking his head when he heard about the reversal. "It's the case that wouldn't die."

The afternoon of June 18, 1990, Dennis wheeled a grocery cart filled with his television set and other belongings through the doors of the state penitentiary into the outside world. He was free, temporarily. Maybe forever, if his lawyer would let him tell his story.

Ginny and Bob Bulloch and Gram, Dennis's beloved grandmother, were waiting in their car. They and a friend had listed their houses as collateral to make Dennis's $150,000 bond. A local television station had promised Dennis a helicopter ride between the bond office and the prison, giving Dennis his liberty hours earlier. The reporter sought an interview in return, but Dennis was not talking. Yet.

Dennis, his parents, and Gram drove to the Ozarks for a brief vacation. Once back in Arnold, they frequently went out for dinner. "Shoney's, Bonanza. Nothing fancy, but it's a big deal after prison food," his friend Ed Schollmeyer explained. Dennis also went out with Ed and Jas Kossuthski, his two friends.

Spotting Dennis became big that summer, though not quite on the level of Elvis sightings: Working out at a South County Vic Tanny (along with the *Post-Dispatch* reporter who covered his murder trial), shopping for new clothes (bought with an International VIP credit card at South County Mall), checking out the van Goghs at the Impressionist Exhibit at the Art Museum. One evening at the Botanical Garden, Tina Porterfield was taking her twins into the Rose Garden when she felt somebody staring at her. She looked over. It was Dennis.

According to those who knew, he was getting a perverse kick out of all the attention. "He is suffering from delusions of grandeur. He thinks he's a big celebrity," said one man. Dennis loved being able to turn down all the media requests.

Shortly after he returned to Arnold for the first time in four years, Dennis was reindicted. His tampering with evidence charge now included his burning of Julie's body along with her diary. The prosecutors reasoned that because her remains were so charred, it was impossible to tell whether Julie had fought against being tied and gagged.

Margulis wanted his client to plead guilty, for there was no point in going through another arson trial when Dennis had admitted during his murder trial setting the garage fire on May 6, 1986. But Westfall was unwavering: Dennis would be retried for arson and tampering unless he pleaded guilty and accepted a sentence totaling ten years. Ten years of jail time was too much for the defense to accept.

There was no way Margulis would let Dennis be tried in St. Louis, city or county: Dennis Bulloch had better name recognition there than Mayor Schoemehl, Senator Danforth, or his *bête noir*, St. Louis Prosecuting Attorney Buzz Westfall. The second arson trial could not be held in Cape Girardeau. Westfall's personal attack on *his* prosecutor, John Oliver, would antagonize the local jurors, the Oliver family being ancient and well-regarded in Cape Girardeau. ("When the first white settlers came to the area," Judge Byron Kinder said, "they were greeted by the Indians and the Olivers. That's how long the family has been there.")

The defense hoped the third time around that the trial would be held in Kansas City or Columbia, the latter being a university town. While St. Louis County is conservative and a rough place to try a bizarre sex case, it is Greenwich Village in liberal attitudes compared to rural Missouri, which is an unholy amalgamation of staunch Catholics, Bible Belt Baptists, and Little Dixie.

The prosecutor's office alleviated the pre-trial tension with Dennis Bulloch jokes. Tacked up on their message board was *The Riverfront Times* personal ad that someone had run as a gag: A white male wrote he was "relocating in the near future" and was seeking a "short-term relationship." Nearby was a large printed button, in the style of movie ads, reading, "See Bulloch II: Now coming to a courtroom near you."

Westfall announced that this time his Chief Trial Assistant John Ross would prosecute Dennis. Open, ethical, and hard-working, but still fun-loving and witty, Ross at age thirty-six had been a career prosecutor.

Despite eleven years of studying the most gruesome evidence photographs, Ross literally could not stomach looking at the burnt remains of Julie Bulloch. A meat and potatoes man, he was so sickened, he could only eat fish for ten days afterward. Ross intended to use these horrible photos as evidence in the upcoming trial.

Right before the trial, Dennis called the police. He had bor-rowed his parents' car to go to a dinner party in Lafayette Square, a nineteenth-century enclave of mansard-topped man-sions near downtown St. Louis. When Dennis left the party, the car was missing. The man who had once kept more than thirty-four police officers plus FBI agents busy, now was turning to the authorities for help.

Meanwhile, his parents' home in Arnold was spray-painted and egged, a putrid nightmare in the sweltering August heat.

The day before the trial, Dennis the jail house lawyer called Margulis and said he wanted the case continued. Margulis refused to ask the judge for a change.

The morning of his third trial, August 28, 1990, Dennis stood outside the courthouse in Columbia, Boone County, stopping passing lawyers with, "I hear Judge Conley is a pretty easy touch for a continuance." When one would agree, Dennis would go yell at Margulis, who knew better.

Boone County Circuit Judge Frank Conley was a hardened, tough former prosecutor who was not about to appease Den-nis's whims. Lean, mean, and white-haired, Judge Conley looked and acted like the stock character in a Western movie, the judge who pounded his gavel and yells, "Get out of town by sundown." To Judge Conley, the law was the law and silliness punishable by hanging. He ran a very tight courtroom.

Dennis marched toward reporters gathered around the white Greek revival pillars flanking the WPA courthouse in Columbia, Missouri. "Do you have anything to say?" they asked, expecting a "No comment." "It would be a big shock to all of us if he talked," one said.

Dennis broke his five-year moratorium on discussing his

wife's killing. With his bright blue eyes blazing, he answered, "It's just unbelievable the feelings I've gone through."

"Do you feel you had made any mistakes?" a reporter asked.

"The main mistake," Dennis said, "was getting into the situation in the first place. The main mistake was not thinking clearly and panicking, leaving the area."

"Was the use of more than seventy feet of tape a common sexual aid in your marriage?"

"It was athletic tape. Yes, at the direction of my wife. That's what we did. I can't discuss it in detail, this is pretty emotional for me."

Dennis added he might sue Westfall for the costs of the defenses in the three trials, noting, "I have found some case law on that."

Dennis blamed Westfall. "This is purely political. Mr. Westfall is being vindictive, I believe. I'm not sure why, I can only see political motivation," Dennis said, referring to Westfall's campaign for county executive. Dennis attacked his qualifications: "Westfall's personality fits the prosecutor's office pretty well. He's not capable of leadership of the county."

Dennis's arrogance did not pay off with the jurors.

One of the first witnesses, Lt. Niere described what he saw when he discovered the remains of Julie Bulloch. Dennis, sitting at the defense table, pulled out his handkerchief and wiped his eyes and mopped his brow. But there were no tears, said a television reporter. After four years of investigating Dennis, Niere, guileless himself, was taken aback.

John Ross introduced the photographs of Julie's house that Dennis had taken and dropped off on May 5, 1986, in St. Paul for developing. These pictures, Ross said, showed that Dennis wanted a record for insurance purposes. And they illustrated Dennis's intent to burn the house and garage, Ross said. Not only was Dennis planning to murder his wife and destroy all evidence, he was also plotting to file a fraudulent insurance claim.

Initially, there were no defense witnesses. Margulis had said his client would not testify, but it was obvious Dennis was not cooperating. Indeed, Dennis seemed competitive with his own lawyer. When Margulis stood up, Dennis rose. When Margulis picked up his glass of water and sipped, Dennis did likewise.

Margulis appeared to realize that Dennis was out of control. Dennis second-guessed him throughout the trial, stopping attorneys walking into the courthouse and asking them how tough Judge Conley was and about other issues and then running back to Margulis to cite their opinions.

Suddenly, ignoring his attorney's advice, Dennis took the stand himself. He wanted to set the record straight, he said later.

Prosecutor Ross railed at Dennis, "At the time [of the murder trial], it served your purpose to admit burning the evidence, but now it doesn't serve your purpose to admit that. Isn't that what's occurring here?"

Dennis equivocated, saying he did not understand the question, which Ross rephrased several times. Dennis arrogantly assumed he could best the prosecutor.

Ross, far, far cagier, said again, "Isn't it true that you tell whatever story is necessary at the time to serve your purpose?"

Dennis bit the bait. "Are you calling me a liar?" he demanded.

"You're not a liar?" Ross asked incredulously, not believing his good luck.

"No," Dennis said defiantly.

"How would you define a liar?" Ross demanded.

"Somebody who doesn't tell the truth," Dennis said primly.

"Okay," Ross began. He was having fun. "Let's go back through the investigation and determine if in fact, Mr. Bulloch, you are a liar. Let's start from when you flew to St. Louis from Minneapolis. You did not use your name. Isn't that right?"

Before Dennis could answer, Margulis approached the bench trying to save his client from himself. He argued that the scope of the cross-examination was beyond the areas covered in the direct examination. Judge Conley overruled him.

Ross repeated the question, "You flew here under an assumed name, didn't you, Dennis?"

DENNIS: That's correct.
ROSS: So, the name you used, John Jackson, when you flew down here on the night of May the 5th, 1986, was a lie. Isn't that right?
DENNIS: Yes.
ROSS: And when you flew back to Minnesota you used a different name. Isn't that correct?
DENNIS: Yes, sir.

Ross: And that was a lie, was it not?

Dennis: Yes, sir.

Ross: And when you went out to California you used a different name. Isn't that right?

Dennis: Yes, sir.

Ross: Do you recall using the name Jonathan Dennis in California?

Dennis: Yes, sir.

Ross: And that was a lie. Isn't that right?

Dennis: Yes, sir.

Ross cited more lies: Dennis asking Jim Macke to lie for him; giving the Major Case Squad false suspects; implying to the Major Case Squad that his house had been burglarized; saying that Julie had committed suicide; telling detectives to look for Julie's diary when he had burned it (they found others); concealing his appearance in California by dyeing his hair and beard.

Dennis tried to excuse it all with, "I was in a panic. I thought that I had caused her death."

Ross: You're talking about being in a panic. You had the presence of mind to get dressed, isn't that right?

Dennis: I really don't remember getting dressed but I did get dressed. I got dressed when I thought I was going to commit suicide.

Ross: Well, in fact, you didn't commit suicide, did you?

Dennis: No, I didn't.

Ross: You had the presence of mind to get dressed in such a manner to go back and be presentable to your co-workers, isn't that right?

Dennis: I don't know if I was presentable or not.

Ross: Mr. Bulloch, you didn't go in blue jeans and an open collar shirt. You didn't just grab whatever was handy. You put on pants, a nice shirt and a tie, similar to how you're dressed here.

Dennis: Actually that's what was handy.

Ross: It's handy to put on a tie?

Ross pointed out that Dennis, who allegedly had panicked, had the "presence of mind" not only to dress himself properly, but also to run away from a burning house, hitchhike to the airport, pay cash for the ticket back to St. Paul, use a fake name, call Jim Macke to establish an alibi, and tell Macke he had remarried when he had told no one else at Price Waterhouse.

Dennis, looking wounded, said, "That's not true. Mr. DePriest and I have a mutual friend that I told [I had remarried]. He knew about it but did not give that to us in discovery." A reporter wondered, if this was true, why Dennis had not told his lawyer to call the friend as a witness.

Ross launched into a series of questions about the burning of Julie's body. He presented Dennis with a blow-up of the photograph of Julie in the chair as she was found between the two cars. The picture showed how difficult it must have been to squeeze the body into such a tight area.

Dennis, upset, averted his head: "I would rather not see that, please." Again, Margulis tried to protect Dennis. Again, the judge overruled him, implying that if Dennis was using his alleged panic as an excuse, he would have to explain himself to this courtroom and jury.

Dennis stammered that he could not recall the process of dragging Julie in her chair. Nor could he remember what he was thinking when he picked up a lighter in the kitchen. "I was just fidgeting with it in the garage at the time."

> ROSS: You just happened to start a fire in the same place that you had taken your wife's body? Isn't that right?
> DENNIS: Well, I wanted to be close to her.
> ROSS: So that's why you set her on fire?
> DENNIS: I didn't set her on fire.
> ROSS: You wanted to be close to her in the garage?

Margulis objected again that the prosecutor was going beyond the scope when Ross flashed Dennis's photographs of the furnishings at 251 White Tree Lane and asked, "Isn't it correct that you had taken a series of photos in anticipation of filing a claim with an insurance company after you set it [the house] on fire?"

Unlike Judge Saitz, who had presided over the murder trial in 1987, the judge in this third trial, Judge Conley, was unintimidated by Margulis. It is unknown if anyone has ever intimidated

Conley. Conley agreed that Ross could use the photographs during Dennis's cross-examination to illustrate his intent to set the fire.

Dennis said he had not taken the photographs to file an insurance claim. He added, "I'm not even sure I knew what was on the film." He said he could not identify the claim ticket from One Hour Photo in Minneapolis with his name on it and the date May 5, 1986, the day before the fire and killing of his wife. Ross showed him photos of the stereos, television sets, and kitchen with appliances. By arguing that anyone could have taken the pictures, Dennis set himself up to be ridiculed.

> ROSS: Would this not be the type of information that you would submit to an insurance company if you were filing a claim for a fire that burned down your house?
> DENNIS: Yes.
> ROSS: Isn't it true that you compiled a list of all the items in your residence with a value that you attached to them?
> DENNIS: That's a list of property that we had to apply for a bank loan.
> ROSS: It just so happens that you had it with you at that time and it lists all the property?

Dennis repeated that he used no accelerant, only his wife's diary, to start the fire. But the fire marshal had testified that an accelerant had to have been used: A burning cigarette makes a hole in the upholstery and smolders for hours before it starts a fire, if at all. The marshal added, "It's hard to burn car upholstery."

Dennis claimed only to have burned the roll of tape, the diary, and his bag of paraphernalia. Julie's Buick was where the evidence and fire were. Dennis's Honda sustained only heat damage.

After another set of objections by Margulis and overulings by Judge Conley, Ross showed Dennis the lists of questions Dennis wrote out to use in long-distance calls from California to Christy Meiers and his parents. The lists were taken from the knapsack he carried when he was arrested. After Dennis admitted that the notes were in his handwriting, Ross asked about one in particular. He read to Dennis, " 'Ask Ed if he knows someone to locate a new ID.' " Then Ross pointed out that Dennis was trying to create a new identity.

Dennis retorted with, "At what time? At what time? When I was really panicked and confused, that was my intent. But after I settled down and cleared my head, I changed my mind." Over and over, Dennis repeated that he only was on the "run" because he thought he had killed his wife in the fire.

"I don't know if it was just an emotional trauma or what, but I just could not get my mind together and my nerves settled down," Dennis said. He added that was why he could not bring himself to attend Julie's wake and funeral.

"That's why you used two different names—Jonathan Block and Jonathan Davis—in California?" retorted Ross.

Dennis went on about how "confused" he had been after discovering Julie was dead. But Ross led Dennis back through the chain of actions he took that caused the fire: picking up the lighter, igniting the diary, tape, and tape spools.

> ROSS: And you did that for the purpose of destroying evidence. Isn't that right?
> DENNIS: I didn't even realize it was evidence.

Dennis claimed that if he really had wanted to destroy Julie's body, he would left her in the house and doused her with fuel from the gas cans in the garage.

Ross snapped back, "Isn't it true that you knew that there were two gallon containers of gas, that you used a flammable liquid in the backseat of the Buick, that you had two cars with full gas tanks, that if the cars' gas tanks ruptured, you would have a tremendous explosion and there would be no evidence of anything?"

Dennis finally had to admit that the burning of Julie's body eliminated any trace of defensive wounds and fingerprints. That meant that he had destroyed evidence of the killing. But he persisted in saying he did not mean to do so.

Ross quoted Dennis's testimony from the first trial in which he said that reading his wife's diary caused him anger and pain. "I assume that's because she was saying things about you so clearly it [the diary] would have been evidence," Ross stated.

Dennis besmirched his dead wife's reputation: "Actually she was saying things about herself and her brother." If that was true, why had he not told his attorney, who might have used the information in cross-examining Carter Miller?

In returning to the fire, Dennis's defense was that if he intended to destroy the garage and the house, he would have removed his many valuable things that "I couldn't replace ever." None of these unique treasures had been listed in his will or alleged insurance notes.

On redirect examination, Margulis tried to ressurect the image of frightened Dennis fleeing prosecution because he mistakenly believed he had murdered his bride of ten weeks in the fire.

Ross had another barb to throw at Dennis on recross-examination, an odd fact DePriest had told him: Why had Dennis years ago ordered seven color photographs of his wife still strapped to her rocking chair lying on the morgue table before the autopsy began? And that was in addition to demanding multiple copies of other pictures of Julie's charred remains. Margulis had never requested them. What bizarre purpose did Dennis have in mind, especially when now he could not bear to look at the pictures?

When Ross again brought out photographs of Julie after the fire and flashed them ten inches from Dennis's face, Dennis protested he did not want to look at them and turned his head. Ross barked, "You've seen these several times. One you wanted several copies of."

Glaring at the prosecutor, Dennis did not respond. He appeared furious. "I thought he was going to hit me," Ross recalled later, with a chuckle.

The jury left to deliberate.

Lt. Niere was excited by Dennis's testifying. "I just know the jury will come back with guilty on the arson and tampering charges," he said, adding that he also expected the jurors to recommend the maximum sentences of twelve years. His only regret was that he had not been allowed to hear Dennis on the stand because he was being used as a possible rebuttal witness. Witnesses in trials are banned from the courtroom until they are finished testifying.

While the jurors debated what to do with him, Dennis sat

under a shade tree wearing *his* shades and talking with reporters. "I think if you sit down and get to know me as a person, you'll find me an individual good to know," he said.

Another judge, Byron Kinder, who had been following the trials, responded to Dennis's last television revelation. "Character isn't always destiny. Sometimes fate and fortune intervene. But a character disorder is destiny."

Said a television reporter, after interviewing Dennis, "I look at him and something's missing. A piece is missing. This guy showed no remorse at all. Nothing for his wife. Only for himself. I had expected a bizarre madman. Instead, all he was was your run-of-the-mill psychopath. He was ordinary in his evil."

The jury apparently did not find Mr. Bulloch "good to know," for in less than ninety minutes they found him guilty on all counts and recommended the maximum sentences of seven years on the arson charge and five years on the tampering with evidence charge for a total of twelve years in prison. Which, with overcrowding, meant Dennis, who was currently out on parole, would have to go back and spend another four to five years in prison before becoming eligible for parole again, sometime in 1995-96.

Bob and Ginny Bulloch, sitting in the front row of the courtroom, held hands as the verdict was read. Their son stared straight ahead.

Dennis emerged from the verdict smiling, carrying his briefcase, and announced, "It's disappointing, but there are certain challenges you have to live with." Then he blamed his superb attorney, who had saved his life a year earlier: "Certain facts were not brought out in the case."

The jury foreman told reporters that testifying was Dennis's fatal mistake. They thought he was lying.

When interviewed, Margulis seemed tired and embarrassed. Never before had a client of his talked to the media during trial, never had one been so out of control in what he said and how he said it.

Dennis's parents remained silent.

Awaiting his October 9 sentencing, Dennis was optimistic. He took a job making real estate referrals by telephone. He appeared fine and in control, "a little big on himself," said one acquaintance whom Dennis called for advice on "a relationship problem." Dennis began dating a woman in her early thirties said to be indulged by her affluent father. She was also said to be attractive, intelligent, a dilettante, and not particularly realistic.

In addition to dating, Dennis regularly attended St. Mark's United Church of Christ in Arnold, where "he's heavy into the Bible, going to Bible classes and everything," a fellow parishioner said. "Some members are behind him. Some are upset. Dennis shows no remorse for what he did [to his wife]. He had no remorse for his parents who have ruined themselves financially over him. He shows none of the emotions most people would show."

On October 9, 1990, Judge Frank Conley sentenced Dennis Neal Bulloch to five years for tampering and seven for arson, running them concurrently for a total of twelve years. However, the judge allowed Dennis to remain out on his $150,000 bond pending his appeal for a new trial (which would take about nine months before the appellate court would hear the case and several more before the judges would rule).

Dennis was subdued coming out of the courthouse, less loquacious than before.

To the knot of reporters, his last public remark was, "That's it."

He walked away arm-in-arm with his mother, his father trailing behind, the eternal configuration of the Bulloch family.

Thirty-Four

Conclusions: "Just Plain Evil"

May 1991

While the cameraman was carrying his gear downstairs, the researcher stayed on to schmooze about the case with Margulis, whom she had known for years. "Art, I've asked the medical examiner, some judges and prosecutors, and an eminent shrink. No one can answer," she said.

"Try me," Margulis replied.

"What in God's name can you do physically when your partner is tied up with seventy-six feet of tape?"

Margulis blushed and laughed. "Beats me." He handed her a copy of a May 23, 1988, *Time* magazine story on Dennis as she walked away.

What was Dennis's reaction when he saw himself in *Time* magazine? At the top of the page was a photograph of Dennis Bulloch along with two other sex/crime defendants above a full-page article. Dennis had pondered over and over in his diaries what his "contribution to society" would be. Now he had made one, of sorts. Dennis had originated the increasingly popular

256

"she made me do it" defense, later used in the so-called preppy murder trial of Robert Chamberlain in Manhattan.

It now seems obvious that Julie did not make Dennis "do it," that is, indulge in bondage. There are various theories of what really happened the night of May 5, 1986. One is that Julie's killing really was an accident. But it was not, as Dennis maintains, the result of a night of liquor and kinky sex.

William Lhotka, who covered the two Bulloch arson trials for the *Post-Dispatch*, proposes that Julie died accidentally because the evening's events were a dress rehearsal gone awry. Dennis planned the murder for the future. He had plenty of time, his one-week business trip to St. Paul had been changed to five or six weeks.

But on the night of May 5, 1986, during their long-distance phone calls, Julie threatened him with divorce. "It was now or never," Lhotka says. Julie had already switched a large chunk of her money and was moving further and further away from his control. Dennis flew back under a fictitious name, just as he said he did, murdered her, torched the evidence, planned for the house and garage to explode, but without working out all the details of his return trip to St. Paul.

A variation of Lhotka's theory is that Dennis had worked out a plan to kill his wife while he was out of town, but wanted a test-run first. He flew back to St. Louis under a fictitious name and surprised his wife, just as he said he did. After he tied her up, he had no intention of letting her die. Not until all the kinks in his plan were worked out, such as transportation back to the airport. But Julie died that night by mistake.

But how? Where was Dennis while she was dying?

Swooning over his own orgasm, suggested Sgt. Steven Sorocko of Bomb and Arson in St. Louis City Police. Indeed, Dennis's known acts of violence are all against women in bed or during sex. Sorocko thinks taping and gagging a woman until she was totally under his control was a big turn-on for Dennis. What is the ultimate enslavement if not tying up another person in more than nearly eighty feet of tape?

Indeed, while Dennis testified that Julie had tied him up, his former bondage partners told police they never had bound him.

"He was known to be a big kink," Sorocko emphasized, "and with time Dennis needed more and more perversions to get aroused. Maybe while Julie was dying he was masturbating. Her struggles and muffled squeals probably just heightened his pleasure." There clearly was no way for Dennis to have any kind of sex with Julie while she was bound the way she was.

Not only is there no evidence that Julie had been involved in bondage before she met Dennis, there is nothing but rumor about her wild behavior and alleged sexual relations with her brother. Today, five years after her death, many St. Louisans, like those in the Bible Belt, believe Julie must have been a little wild because she solicited her killer through a personal ad. It is obvious why Dennis would say what he did, but why did Terri Sacher, Julie's friend, tell police and Art Margulis during a deposition that Julie admitted to committing incest with her brother? Why would anyone say something so awful about a dead friend? Did Terri misinterpret what Julie said to her?

In everyone's life there is usually at least one so-called friend who is more like the bad fairy in *Sleeping Beauty*. This trouble-maker may do some nice things but basically is malevolent.

All allegations about Julie's behavior could have been eliminated from the trial in two ways. First, some states prohibit any evidence delving into the erotic past of a murder victim. What the dead did sexually before they were murdered is considered as irrelevant as how many lovers a rape victim had. While Missouri's rape laws do not allow using the victim's past against her or him, its murder laws have not been changed.

In the wake of similar problems in the Chamberlain trial, New York Attorney General Robert Abrams proposed a bill making the sexual history of murder victims inadmissible.

The whole sexual bondage issue appears bogus in the Bulloch case. "Whatever sex occurred May 6, 1986, was peripheral to the murder," said John Ross, who prosecuted the last trial against Dennis. "This hadn't much to do with sex. Bondage was an easy way to incapacitate Julie, who was so easily manipulated [perhaps into allowing Dennis initially to tie her up]. The fire burned away any traces of her fighting against being tied up—bruises, fingerprints, whatever."

"The whole sexual aspect of this case is a canard," St. Louis Homicide Sgt. Michael Guzy emphasized. "No one flies in from

St. Paul under an assumed name to satisfy his wife's alleged ongoing proclivity for kinky sex. He might have had a history of golf, too, but this wasn't golf. This was pure homicide.

"And Dennis wasn't this sensitive sharing and caring character who made a special trip to break off with Christy Meiers. Dennis didn't care about anyone else but himself. And he wasn't so impulsive by nature to come in to settle a fight with his wife or have sex with her or break off an affair," Guzy said. "It's simple premeditated murder. Money is a great traditional motive. Money always works. This murder was an open and shut case, just a poor verdict.

"Read William of Ockham. Ockham's Razor says you can't proceed to a more complicated hypothesis without ruling out the simpler one."

Why did Dennis pick bondage as a means to kill his wife? That remains unknown unless Sorocko's theory about Dennis's perversity is correct. Nor will the mystery be answered whether he married Julie solely to kill her and inherit her estate.

I believe he married her to have access to her money and build his real estate empire. He was not faring that well at Price Waterhouse and he wanted to switch into property anyway. But when Julie balked at allowing him to control her property, beginning in April, and started thinking about divorce in May, Dennis became alarmed.

The public is unaware of how much individual judges influence the outcome of trials by their admissibility of evidence. Judge Saitz, who presided over the murder trial, Dennis's first trial, in 1987, should have prohibited any mention of Julie's premarital sexual activity: There was no proof Julie had taught Dennis bondage, let alone the implication she had learned it from her brother. It was irrelevant who taught whom, because Dennis, having testified this was the third time they had performed the ritual, should have known the basic safety principles by then.

A tougher judge could have demanded that the defense prove that Julie taught Dennis bondage before allowing Margulis to cross-examine her brother on his activity. Or, the judge could have said that Carter's behavior was not on trial and, therefore, inadmissible.

But in defense of Judge Saitz, the media and courtroom

watchers who sat through the trial were not swayed by the
defense arguments. Only one juror was. "Which shows what a
crap shoot jury selection is," a federal prosecutor says. "It's
strictly a roll of the dice, despite all these psychologists who like
to talk about 'jury science.' " And this one juror may have
changed his mind after jury selection when he had said he
could vote for the death penalty, according to other jurors.

Sometimes, jurors fail to understand simple concepts, the
federal prosecutor points out. Such as if they disagree, it is a
hung jury. Sometimes, the more educated a jury, the worse their
verdict, St. Louis Homicide Sgt. Dan Nichols pointed out. "I
think jurors expect a little drama," his friend, Sgt. Guzy, added.
"They're unfamiliar with the law. Facing a heavy responsibility,
they're made to feel important," Guzy said. "Jurors can be
impressed by whoever puts on the bigger show."

There can be an unjust result in any lawsuit, cops, prosecutors, and defense lawyers say. The system is set up to protect
the defendant in case of a mistake. "Which is the way we want it
to be," Guzy pointed out. "We don't want an innocent person
swaying from a noose on a tree."

Would a different judge have made a difference in this manslaughter verdict? No, if there is one juror who is against the
death penalty and the rest are weak and irresponsible, the
assistant U. S. Attorney says. If the other jurors had gone to the
judge and complained, Judge Saitz could have fined the juror,
saying, you're entitled to your opinion, but we are entitled to
findings of the truth. That fine would have sent "a message," as
prosecutors call it, of how much Americans rely on the jury
system for justice.

And did this one hold-out juror ever wonder how Dennis—
who testified he was so drunk the night of May 5 that he passed
out—managed to tape more than sixty feet around his wife so
methodically and evenly that she was "wrapped like a Christmas
package"? How did the other eleven jurors explain that away?

Can one possibly trace Dennis's physical abuse of Julie, his
first wife Karen, and Barbara Villiers to his father's alleged
throwing of him across the room as a teenager? Social workers
love to point out that abused children often abuse their children
or spouses. Violence begets violence.

But Dennis was emphatically not an abused child, according

to teachers, family friends, his friends and his first wife. No one believes Bob Bulloch pounded on his son. An expert familiar with the family says Dennis was untouched and spoiled. Margulis flatly stated, "In no sense Dennis was abused as a kid. He was not unbalanced in any way." One teen thrashing does not a wife-killer make, or there would be a dearth instead of an abundance of women aged twenty to fifty. Not every murderer was an abused child, Sgt. Guzy emphasized. Nor does an over-protective, domineering mother create a wife-killer.

So where did Dennis learn such sociopathic behavior? To quote Judge Theodore McMillian, of the Eighth Circuit U. S. Court of Appeals, a former prosecutor and juvenile court judge: "Some folks are just plain evil, ornery and mean."

One unexamined facet of the case and the three trials is whether Dennis physically abused Julie. Not only had he beaten his first wife and girlfriend, Barbara Villiers, but Julie's friend Jane Muster suspected he pulled out Julie's hair and put out cigarettes on her face in April, 1986. Most domestic murderers have a history of violence, especially toward their wives, Sgt. Guzy stated. More and more research, in addition to U. S. Justice Department statistics, reinforces what detectives like Guzy have said for years.

Will Dennis be welcomed back into polite society when he gets out? As Judge Kinder said, "When some muckedymuck in Ladue does something passing strange, it's decadent. When some hoosier from Jeff County does it, it's degenerate."

It is a summer day, four years after Dennis Bulloch was arrested for the murder of his wife. His attorney Arthur Margulis is being interviewed. Margulis is sitting behind his mahogany desk, the sunlight streaming in from the floor-to-ceiling windows in his large corner office. The warm mellow light burnishes his silver hair, which in turn sets off his tan and powder-blue eyes. Margulis is in his blue oxford-cloth shirtsleeves, tie loosened.

It's an informal conversation. He and the writer have known each other a decade; her older male cousin is a childhood friend of Margulis's and was the best man at his wedding. She is seated in a comfortable leather club chair on the other side of the big mahogany desk, taking notes.

As he answers her questions, Margulis looks her in the eye. Occasionally, he leans back in his chair and folds his arms behind his head. When the questions are harder hitting, he sits up ramrod regulation-FBI straight.

"Art, in looking over the evidence and interviewing people, it's even more clear than at the trial that he killed her. Don't you think, late at night, in your heart of hearts, that Dennis killed her intentionally?"

Margulis creases his mouth and, without shifting his perfect posture, turns and looks at out the window to his right.

"Well, Ellen, a jury of his peers said it was an accident."

Epilogue

"Remember Julie Miller"
May 1991

While Tom DePriest and Jim Macke, who testified against his erstwhile colleague, are listed in the 1990 Price Waterhouse alumni directory, Dennis Bulloch, Price's most infamous alumnus, is not.

Luke Jackson and the other socialite men in Nina's group settled down into marriages and houses and onto civic boards.

Now well into their thirties, Nina Honeywell, Muffy Spencer, and Becky Cabot continued dating and dabbling at jobs—all part of the proper young lady's life cycle. Only they seemed stuck. The cycle was as follows: private school, fortnightly dancing school, college (majoring in "something interesting"), debut, "an interesting job," engagement parties (where silver patterns are discussed as though they are interpretations of Joyce's *Ulysses*), quitting work to plan the wedding, marriage and junior membership at the club, maybe work one more year at new job, get cleaning woman once a week, have first baby, get cleaning woman twice a week, have second child three years later, get cleaning woman three times a week, join charity boards, redecorate the house.

Becky was serious for a while with one of Nina's crowd—Jack

Laclede—but after a year or so it broke up just before Dennis was sentenced for the third time. The three women seemed like Sleeping Beauty, waiting for life to begin when the prince arrives.

Dennis's former friend, Tina Porterfield, clings to the belief that what goes around, comes around, "though in Dennis's case it may be a while." Dennis finally stopped writing her and her husband Cal while he was in prison. Similarly, Dennis quit sending clippings on child care from *The Reader's Digest* to his ex-wife Karen Toksvig, who had remarried and become a mother. By the time Dennis was being cross-examined in his third trial, Karen was reading bedtime stories to her two children, had earned her M. B. A., and, with the help of a nanny, went to her office every morning as a vice-president of American Express. Karen uses her new husband's name, O'Shaunessey, to avoid any link with Dennis. She is living the life Dennis always craved.

Gary Matzenbacher, the man who gave a sweating hitchhiker a ride in the early hours of May 6, 1986, made the news himself in 1991. He received the Southwestern Bell reward of $10,000 from Julie's employer for providing information leading to the conviction of her killer. When he realized who his hitchhiker was, Matzenbacher had called a lawyer. But the attorney had advised him against going to the authorities. "You'll spend all your time in court, it isn't worth it," the lawyer had told him. "Stay out of this." Matzenbacher had decided to be the good citizen instead.

Tom DePriest took his loss philosophically: "If I could predict what juries will do, I'd be in Las Vegas." Still fascinated, years later, he discusses pivotal details and new evidence over lunch. He remains head of the warrant office, under a new prosecuting attorney. DePriest still acts self-serving only in cafeteria line. He has won his recent murder trials.

His former boss, Buzz Westfall, was elected in November, 1990, to the office of St. Louis County Executive. He pulled considerably more votes among women than his opponent, leading to conjecture that his vigorous prosecution of Dennis Bulloch appealed to women.

In one of his first executive acts, Westfall announced plans to establish the first shelter in the county for battered women. (The

Women's Self-Help Center, where Karen Toksvig went, is in St. Louis City.) As prosecutor, Westfall was long sympathetic to abused women.

Westfall's former first trial assistant, John Ross, who tried the second Bulloch arson trial in 1990, is his county counselor, responsible for the civil laws in St. Louis County and an office the size of a small law firm.

DePriest's second chair at the murder and first arson trials, Tom Mehan, ran as the Republican candidate for County Prosecuting Attorney and lost when the Democrats won big in the November elections. Mehan is now an assistant U. S. Attorney for Eastern Missouri.

Two of the principal people in Dennis's first trial are dead: St. Louis County Medical Examiner Dr. George Gantner and St. Louis County Circuit Judge Milton Saitz.

Art Margulis spent the summer of 1987 harassed at parties with "How did you ever come up with that story of Bulloch's?" Angry, he would reply, "I don't write fiction. It's my client's story." His big win boosted his already large law practice.

Three hundred lawyers and their spouses honored Margulis at a lawyers association dinner in April, 1991. Among those praising him in speeches was his friend the new St. Louis County Executive Buzz Westfall, whom Margulis had supported in the election.

Sometimes late at night, when his wife is asleep, Margulis sits on the screened porch nursing a drink and wondering, "What would Julie say?"

Julie's brother Carter Miller, not understanding the adversarial system, blames Margulis for devastating his sister's reputation and his own. "The only reason I didn't kill myself after the trial and my wife left was that I was afraid my life would flash before my eyes and I would have to relive it. Sometimes, I think, is this my life? Is this really happening? It's so absurd.

"I owe it to my sister to keep going."

Carter finally inherited his sister's estate: their mother's jewelry, silver, china, furniture; Julie's life insurance, stocks, bonds and bank accounts. Not only was Dennis disqualified as an heir, any settlement of the fire insurance claim goes to Julie's estate.

Dennis could be charged under federal mail fraud statutes for any insurance claim for the fire he started.

Now a father himself, Carter feels sorry for Dennis's parents. "I've felt the loss of just about everything else, I can't imagine the loss of a child as they had to go through [the death of Cindy Bulloch] and then this with Dennis. It's like that old saying, a dead cross is easier to bear than a living one."

Carter is grateful for the moral support Lt. Denny Niere gave him. "Denny was a constant comfort. A hand on the shoulder. He kept me going one step to another."

Lt. Denny Niere still spends free time tracking down new leads in the case. "He thinks of nothing else," DePriest says. Niere remains convinced Bulloch is a serial killer.

Jas Kossuthski, fresh from the jungles of Brazil and a stint with the Peace Corps, took a job in the St. Louis office of D'Arcy Massius McManus, the international advertising firm. "Ohhhh, the things I could tell you about Dennis," Jas said, giggling as he flounced into a chair in a co-worker's office. "He's kinky, kinky, kinky."

What will Dennis do if he is paroled, around 1995–96? "He'll probably move to the Coast, take a job and marry," predicted his high school friend Ed Schollmeyer. "Children is [sic] not a priority. But Dennis will remarry. He's too much a people person to be a loner."

On June 18, 1990, the day Dennis was paroled from prison on the manslaughter charges pending the outcome of his second arson trial, Jane Muster and the vanpoolers and other Bell employees wore buttons in commeration of Julie. Small black buttons with white capital letters saying, "REMEMBER JULIE MILLER."

"That's all that's left of her as a person, her name," explained Jane. "These make you remember this was a real person. She had a real life and all she asked from life is what you and I would like—happiness—someone who cares for you, who truly cares whether you live or die. Dennis didn't care because he let her die.

"Sometimes, my husband and I get into it and I say, 'Who would really spit on you if you're on fire? Me. That's who you should care for.' "

The vanpoolers keep their buttons and wear them on various occasions.

In the basement of the county courthouse is a small room

called the evidence locker. Here records and exhibits from major murder trials are stored. On top of packing boxes rests the homely wooden chair in which Julie Bulloch died.

Alone in death as she was in life, Julia "Julie" Alicia Miller Bulloch lies in a county cemetery plot. Her brother bought it for her; their parents rest in a veterans' cemetery that does not allow grown children. Her headstone reads: "Beloved daughter and sister, 1954–1986."

There is no mention that Julie Miller was ever married to Dennis Bulloch.